REAL FOOD

·ANNE WILLAN·
REAL FOOD
—FIFTY YEARS OF GOOD EATING—

PAPERMAC

First published in 1988 by Macmillan London Limited

First published in paperback in 1989 by
PAPERMAC
A division of Macmillan Publishers Limited
4 Little Essex Street London WC2R 3LF
and Basingstoke

Associated companies in Auckland, Delhi, Dublin, Gaborone,
Hamburg, Harare, Hong Kong, Johannesburg, Kuala Lumpur,
Lagos, Manzini, Melbourne, Mexico City, Nairobi, New York,
Singapore and Tokyo

Designed by Robert Updegraff
Illustrations by Hannah Firmin
Picture research by Juliet Brightmore

ISBN 0-333-48282-4

A CIP catalogue record for this book is available
from the British Library

Typeset by Columns of Reading

Printed in Hong Kong

CONTENTS

Recipe Note

Amounts are given first in British imperial measures, then in metric equivalents. For successful results, follow one set of measures consistently. Teaspoons and tablespoons should be measured level, not heaped. Unless otherwise indicated in the recipe, 'flour' is plain flour, 'sugar' is caster sugar, and 'butter' may be salted or unsalted. Seasoning instructions, however, assume unsalted butter.

Asterisks refer to the Glossary (page 263) where basic cooking terms and methods are elaborated in more detail.

Introduction

Now that I can celebrate fifty years of good eating, I look back with delight on my life in the kitchen. More than ever, I believe that good food – real food – is without pretension. It is instantly recognisable by its elemental warmth. It delights by its surprise; it appeals to all the senses – the sight, the smell, the touch (nothing like the little finger for testing flavour), even the hearing, as well as the taste. Above all, real food has roots in our past.

Consider George Orwell's biting comment on our daily fare in *Coming Up for Air*: 'No real food at all. Just lists of stuff with American names, sort of phantom stuff that you can't taste and can hardly believe in the existence of. Everything comes out of a carton or a tin, or is hauled out of a refrigerator or squirted out of a tap or squeezed out of a tube'. Come to think of it, there is something rather 1984-ish about the excesses of *nouvelle cuisine*. Kitchen artistry turned on its head. Colours that fool, textures that delude, tastes that confound. Worst of all, food that does not nourish. What could be more perverse?

So often real food is associated with a personality. In this book you will meet cooks, teachers, writers, gastronomes and, of course, myself. Born in England, a naturalised American, and long-time resident of France, my style of living borrows from all three countries. When it comes to cooking, however, I must own to favouring the French. Without such a prejudice, how could I have had the cheek a dozen years ago to launch and direct La Varenne in Paris?

Personal as this book may be, it is not the work of one person. As with all my efforts, I rely enormously on the help – and patience – of colleagues, in this instance Henry Grossi, Suzanne McLees, Amanda Phillips Manheim, Margo Miller, Randall Price and Tina Ujlaki. They share the proscenium with me; and backstage there is, as ever, my husband Mark and our dear children, Simon and Emma. Without the real world and real life that they sustain around me, there would have been little to inspire *Real Food*.

Anne Willan
Paris, Burgundy and Washington
1987–8

Soups

First things first. Soup is the doyenne of the table, a true mother food. It comes thick or thin, hot or cold, meat or vegetable. No wonder then that through the ages the basis of the evening meal has been soup. We even get our word 'supper' from it. I am certain that *'Mange ta soupe, chéri!'* is the command on which the French empire was founded.

Curiously, although Italy has its *minestrone*, France its *pot au feu* and *garbure*, Russia its *borsch*, Spain its *puchero* and Holland its *erwtensoep*, England has no nourishing soup of its own. Watery and tasteless concoctions have been the rule. Sir Walter Scott relates that when, as a child, he said to his stern Presbyterian father 'Oh, how nice the soup is', the bowl set before him was promptly diluted with a pint of cold water!

Potage Germiny

SORREL SOUP

Just occasionally at La Varenne cooking school in Paris, Chef Chambrette will recreate one of the classic Escoffier-style soups that have totally disappeared from the current repertoire. His velvety Potage Argenteuil, using up the trimmings of white asparagus stems, is a miraculous concentration of flavour which I have never managed to emulate. Luckily, his Potage Germiny is within the reach of ordinary mortals. The acidity of sorrel is balanced by a rich egg-yolk-and-cream liaison.

SERVES 6

1oz *(30g)* butter
½lb *(250g)* sorrel, stemmed
   and chopped
1 medium potato, thinly sliced .
2 pints *(1.25 litres)* light
   chicken stock*
salt and pepper

To finish
2 egg yolks (optional)
8fl.oz *(250ml) crème fraîche** or
   double cream
1oz *(30g)* butter

1 In a large saucepan, melt the butter. Add the sorrel and potato, press a piece of foil on top and cover. Sweat over a very low heat for about 15 minutes, stirring occasionally, until the vegetables are tender. (*Note*: Do not allow them to brown.)

2 Add the stock with salt and pepper. Cover, bring the soup to a boil and simmer for 10–15 minutes. Purée the soup in batches in a food processor or blender, or work it by hand through a sieve. The slightly coarse texture given by a food processor can be pleasant here. The soup can be refrigerated for up to 3 days, or frozen.

3 *To finish.* Bring the soup back to a boil. If using egg yolks, whisk them with half the cream in a small bowl and stir in a few spoonfuls of the hot soup. Stir this mixture back into the remaining soup. (If you prefer a lighter soup, omit the egg yolks and simply whisk in half the cream.) Heat gently, stirring, until the soup thickens slightly. (*Note*: Do not allow it to boil or it will curdle.)

4 Take the soup from the heat, stir in the butter and taste for seasoning. Spoon into bowls, add a spoonful of the remaining cream to each bowl and swirl lightly to create a marbled effect.

Cook's Comment. Fresh sorrel is as easy to grow as spinach, but outside one's own garden it can be hard to find. I've often substituted a mixture of equal weights of spinach and watercress. The soup is good cold, but in this case the egg yolks should be omitted.

Potage d'Automne

AUTUMN SOUP

A master's hand is clear in this classic soup with its perfect balance of four green vegetables. Its creator was the legendary Antonin Carême, cook to Tsar Alexander, the Prince Regent and Prince Talleyrand. Until horrors were perpetrated in the early 1970s on the old Les Halles area of Paris, where the wholesale food markets used to be, Carême was honoured by a street in his memory, appropriately cheek by jowl with the kitchen supply shops (many of them, like Dehillerin, still there).

Why Carême calls this recipe 'Autumn Soup', I do not know, since the fresh vegetable flavours and vivid colours are the epitome of spring.

SERVES 6–8

2⅓ pints (1.5 litres) veal or chicken stock*
white part of 3 leeks, thinly sliced
3 stalks celery, thinly sliced
½lb (250g) cos lettuce, shredded
4oz (125g) fresh or frozen shelled green peas
pinch of sugar
salt and white pepper
croûtons* made with 6 slices white bread and 6 tablespoons vegetable oil (for serving)
6fl.oz (175ml) double cream
celery leaves (for garnish)

1 Bring the stock to a boil. Add leeks, celery, lettuce, fresh peas, sugar, and salt and pepper to taste. Simmer, uncovered, until the vegetables are tender: 15–20 minutes. Taste for seasoning. If using frozen peas, add them 5 minutes before the end of cooking.

2 Meanwhile make the croûtons. The soup can be refrigerated for up to 24 hours; keep the croûtons wrapped in foil.

3 To finish. Reheat the croûtons in foil in a low oven. Bring the soup just to a boil on the stove. Stir in the cream, spoon the soup into bowls and top each one with a celery leaf. Serve the croûtons separately.

Cook's Comment. A dynastic original for green vegetable soups, this recipe can be varied by adding diced green beans, diced courgette or shredded greens of any kind. Coarser vegetables like cabbage benefit from being served with a sprinkling of cheese.

Zha Cai Rou Si Tang

CANTONESE PORK AND KALE SOUP

My knowledge of native Chinese cooking is elementary, limited to a brief, vivid visit to Canton in 1984. How many parallels I found with France! There was the same emphasis on fresh ingredients, and the same care taken in raising them. Just like French chefs, the Chinese balanced mild and spicy, tender, chewy or crisp in a succession of courses ending with a grand finale. Sauces played a great part, as did the ceremonial presentation of a dish.

Near our hotel the street market selling produce from privately owned plots occupied at least six blocks. The only Westerners on the go at 5 a.m., we attracted much nudging and an encouraging number of warm smiles as we wandered around. I stood entranced watching fish being boned with a cleaver. Snakes, turtles, snails and even civet cat were offered for the table . . . later I discovered that the Cantonese are notorious for their kinky carnivorous tastes. Poultry was plentiful and there was a limited selection of vegetables, including great bunches of greens with a little yellow flower. This was *gai choy*, a type of kale.

SERVES 6–8

½lb *(250g)* pork fillet
2 tablespoons soy sauce, or more if necessary
2 tablespoons rice wine or dry sherry
1 teaspoon sesame oil
½ teaspoon ground Szechuan pepper, or black pepper to taste

1 tablespoon Chinese black vinegar (optional; see Cook's Comment below)
1 teaspoon cornflour
½lb *(250g)* kale
1 tablespoon vegetable oil
1 clove garlic, finely chopped
1 spring onion, sliced
3½ pints *(2 litres)* light chicken stock*

1 Slice the pork fillet very thinly, discarding any fat. Toss the pork with the soy sauce, wine or sherry, sesame oil, Szechuan or black pepper, black vinegar if using, and cornflour, and leave to marinate for 15 minutes. Finely shred the kale, discarding any thick stems but including tender ones.

2 Heat the oil in a large saucepan or wok. Fry the garlic and spring onion, stirring, for 1 minute. Add the kale and toss to coat it with oil. Pour in the stock and bring to a boil. Simmer until the kale is tender: 1–2 minutes. Stir in the pork and marinade and bring just to a boil, stirring constantly. Taste, adding more soy sauce if necessary. Spoon into bowls and serve.

Cook's Comment. From the little I've seen, how I do appreciate the speed of Chinese cooking methods!
Black vinegar is available in most Oriental supermarkets.

[12]

Iced Cucumber Soup with Chives or Mint

Travelling in the Hebrides in 1773, Samuel Johnson put cucumbers in their place in a laconic aside that seems very modern: 'A cucumber should be well sliced, and dressed with pepper and vinegar, and then thrown out, as good for nothing.' Cucumber may be bland, but I would not go so far as that. This celadon green soup, a version of Turkish Çacik, does perfect justice to the chilly crispness of this member of the gourd family.

SERVES 6–8

1 pint (600ml) natural yoghurt
2 cucumbers, unpeeled
salt and pepper
1oz (30g) walnut pieces
1 clove garlic, crushed
1 tablespoon white wine vinegar,
  or more to taste

2 tablespoons chopped fresh
  chives or mint
3 tablespoons olive oil
4fl.oz (125ml) iced water, or
  more if necessary
1 tablespoon chopped chives or
  6–8 sprigs mint (for garnish)

1 Put the yoghurt in a strainer lined with muslin or cheesecloth and leave to drain for 1–2 hours.

2 Halve the cucumbers lengthwise and scoop out the seeds with a teaspoon. Slice them crosswise, sprinkle with salt and leave for 30 minutes to draw out the juices. Drain them and rinse thoroughly.

3 In a blender or food processor, combine the cucumbers with the walnut pieces, garlic, vinegar and drained yoghurt. Purée briefly or more thoroughly, depending on whether you like a coarse or a fine-textured soup.

4 Stir in the chives or mint and the olive oil, and taste for seasoning. Cover and chill for at least 3 hours, or for up to 24 hours, before serving.

5 Thin the soup with iced water to the consistency you prefer. Serve very cold, garnishing each bowl with chopped chives or a sprig of mint.

Cook's Comment. Deep-green, shiny skin on a cucumber shows it has been waxed to prevent drying. Though edible, waxed skin gives this soup a rough texture and you may prefer to discard the peel.

Oxtail and Barley Soup

Shades of my youth! My mother is the first to confess that she hates to cook, so she has always looked for recipes that require minimum attention and can preferably be stashed away in a low oven so that she can escape into the garden and forget them. Braised oxtail fills the bill nicely, simmered for 4 or 5 hours until the meat falls from the bone and the gelatine dissolves to enrich the sauce. The longer it is cooked, and the more often it is reheated, the better. The only problem is the bones, which take up an inordinate amount of room in the pan and on the plate. So I've taken to this Oxtail and Barley Soup, which has all the intrinsic flavour of oxtail with none of the inconvenience. It is an ideal dish for large numbers, substantial enough to form a main dish if served with Irish Soda Bread (see page 224) or Wholewheat Walnut Bread (see page 225).

SERVES 12 AS A FIRST COURSE OR 6–8 AS A MAIN DISH

2 tablespoons vegetable oil
5lb (2.3kg) oxtails, cut between
  the vertebrae
1½lb (750g) onions, thinly sliced
¾lb (375g) carrots, coarsely
  chopped
3 stalks celery, sliced
1oz (30g) flour
4 pints (2.5 litres) beef stock*
1 pint (600ml) fruity red wine

4 pints (2.5 litres) water, or more
  if necessary
1lb (500g) fresh tomatoes,
  peeled, seeded and chopped,*
  or a 1lb (500g) tin chopped
  tomatoes
large *bouquet garni**
salt and pepper
½lb (250g) pearl barley

1 Heat the oven to Gas 2/150°C/300°F. In a large ovenproof casserole heat the oil. Add the oxtail pieces a few at a time and brown them on all sides. (*Note*: Thorough browning adds a good deal of flavour to the soup.) Take out the pieces and discard all but 3 tablespoons of fat from the casserole.

2 Add the onions, carrots and celery and cook gently until lightly browned. Add the flour and cook gently, stirring, until it and the vegetables are well browned. Stir in the beef stock, wine, water, tomatoes, *bouquet garni*, salt and pepper, and bring to a boil.

3 Return the oxtails to the soup, cover the casserole and cook in the oven for 4–5 hours or until the meat is falling from the bones. Stir from time to time during cooking and add more water if the liquid evaporates rapidly. At the end of cooking the soup should be rich and dark but not too thick.

4 Let the soup cool to tepid, then lift out the oxtails and remove the meat, discarding any bones and fat. Chop the meat and return it to the soup. Add the barley, cover and continue cooking in the oven until the barley is tender: 25–35 minutes.

5 Discard the *bouquet garni* and taste the soup for seasoning. Prepare the soup at least 12 hours ahead and chill it thoroughly so that the fat rendered from the meat during cooking solidifies on the surface of the soup and can be skimmed off. The soup can be refrigerated for up to 3 days, or frozen.

6 Skim off all fat and bring the soup to a boil before serving; it can be kept warm for several hours without harm.

Cook's Comment. Whole oxtails can be tricky to cut up at home. You will need a sharp knife and patience in finding the joints. Take your time and never use brute force. The next best cut for soup is shank or shin of beef, but neither has the mellow richness of oxtail.

Potage Palestine

JERUSALEM ARTICHOKE SOUP

The French have got their geography right but their botany wrong in associating Palestine with a soup made from Jerusalem, or root, artichokes. In fact they have nothing to do with the Holy Land, having originated in South America. Jerusalem is a corruption of the Italian *girasole*, or sunflower, the family to which root artichokes belong. Stubbornly prolific and not unlike the globe artichoke in flavour, *helianthus tuberosus* is the gardener's bane. A long row stands sentinel against the wall of our Burgundian garden, planted at my instigation for their tingling and slightly lemony taste. Each year Monsieur Milbert, who does the digging, mutters imprecations as he tries to control their relentless spread. Apparently Jerusalem artichokes have never gone down well with the locals. In the 1633 edition of his *Herball*, Gerard notes: 'the use of these roots was forbidden in Burgundy where they call them Indian artichokes for that they were persuaded the too frequent use of them cause the leprosie.'

SERVES 8

2lb *(1kg)* root artichokes
2oz *(60g)* butter
2 medium onions, sliced
2 medium potatoes, sliced
salt and pepper
2⅓ pints *(1.5 litres)* water

croûtons* made with 6 slices white bread and 6 tablespoons vegetable oil (for serving)
½ pint *(300ml) crème fraîche** or double cream

1 Peel and thinly slice the artichokes. (*Note*: They must be cooked at once as they discolour rapidly.) Melt half the butter in a large saucepan and add the artichokes, onions and potatoes. Sprinkle with salt and pepper and press a piece of foil on top. Cover with a lid and sweat over a very low heat, stirring occasionally, until the vegetables are very soft but not brown: 15–20 minutes. Stir in the water and bring to a boil. Cover and simmer, stirring occasionally, for 35–45 minutes. Make the *croûtons*.

2 Purée the soup. If possible, use a blender; with a food processor the texture will not be as smooth. Alternatively, work the soup through a sieve or food mill by hand. Taste for seasoning. Tightly covered, the soup can be refrigerated for up to 2 days. Wrap the *croûtons* in foil.

3 *To finish.* Reheat the *croûtons* in foil in a low oven. Bring the soup just to a boil on the stove, stir in the cream and boil again. Remove the soup from the heat and stir in the remaining butter. Season to taste and, if necessary, thin the soup with a little water: it should have body without being heavy. Serve very hot and pass the *croûtons* separately.

Cook's Comment. Nasty little things to peel, root artichokes are cheap so I don't hesitate to discard knobs and bumps with the skin. The same soup is good made with turnips, when it becomes *Potage Fréneuse*, named after a town west of Paris.

Scallop Soup

Originally intended for oysters, this recipe, indigenous to Maryland's eastern shore, also perfectly suits the sweetness of scallops. In the USA oyster crackers – little hexagonal *croûtons* – are added to the soup in large quantities. Next best is to crumble water biscuits or matzo crackers over your bowl at the table.

SERVES 8

8 thin slices streaky bacon, diced
1 tablespoon vegetable oil
2 onions, chopped
6 stalks celery, thinly sliced
2⅓ pints *(1.5 litres)* milk
16fl.oz *(500 ml)* double cream

salt and pepper
1lb *(500g)* shelled scallops
2 tablespoons chopped parsley
oyster crackers, water biscuits or
matzo crackers (for serving)

1 Fry the bacon in the oil in a large saucepan, stirring until the fat runs. Add the onions and celery and cook until soft but not brown. Stir in the milk and bring to a boil; simmer for 2 minutes. Add cream and pepper – salt may not be needed as the bacon is salty. Bring back to the boil and taste for seasoning. The soup base can be refrigerated for up to 24 hours.

2 Drain the scallops, adding any liquid to the soup. Discard the crescent-shaped muscle from the sides of the scallops. Cut large scallops into 2–3 slices, separating any coral and trimming the coral of skin. Bring the soup to a boil, add the scallops and poach for about 1 minute – they should still be slightly transparent in the centre. (*Note*: Do not overcook them or they will be tough.)

3 Remove the soup from the heat, stir in the parsley and taste for seasoning. Serve at once, passing water biscuits or oyster crackers separately.

Cook's Comment. All scallops should have the small crescent muscle discarded from the white meat, as it is inedibly tough. If the coral is included, detach it, leaving it whole. For oyster soup, sauté oysters in a little butter until the edges curl (about 2 minutes) before adding them to the hot cream and milk.

STARTERS

A soup is a soup, but a starter can be one of many things. 'Appetiser', 'entrée' and 'hors-d'œuvre' all have different shades of meaning in different countries, the most curious being the American appropriation of entrée to denote the main course in a meal. This solecism is now spreading via the international hotel chains with their pompous menus full of verbiage.

Words apart, only one attribute is essential to a good starter: it must be a happy beginning, a tantalising hint of grander things to come. Like a musical overture, a starter should define the score – country, classical or contemporary – of the menu that follows. There are endless possibilities, far more than this chapter, which concentrates on terrines and vegetable tarts, might suggest. Many ideas are hidden elsewhere, under eggs, fish and particularly vegetables. Stir-fried mixtures, *gratins*, pastas, even Corn Pudding or Bubble and Squeak (see pages 154 and 156) are opening notes unheard of a generation ago. As for salads, almost every recipe is a potential starter.

Potted Ham and Beef

Like the French *confit*, the British custom of potting meats transforms humble ingredients. This method of preserving, where meat or fish is cooked long and slowly to destroy the bacteria, then packed in a crock and sealed with lard or butter to exclude air, deserves to be better known. The following recipe, mixing beef and country ham, originated in Washington DC, where we found the famous Virginia hams far too salty for our taste. Any home-cured ham will do, raw or cooked – an excellent way to use scrag ends (Yorkshire for leftovers!).

SERVES 6–8

1½lb (*750g*) country ham, with
   plenty of fat
1½lb (*750g*) lean steak
1½ teaspoons ground allspice
1 teaspoon pepper

12fl. oz (*370ml*) water
salt (optional)
3oz (*90g*) clarified butter,*
   melted (to seal)

1 Heat the oven to Gas 2/150°C/300°F. Cut the ham and beef into 1in (*2.5cm*) cubes, discarding sinew but keeping the ham fat. Sprinkle allspice and pepper over the meat, mix until coated and put the meat into a small, heavy casserole with the water. (*Note*: The meat should fill the casserole completely.) Cover with a lid. Cook in the oven for 3 hours, then allow to cool without removing the lid so that the juices are retained.

2 Coarsely chop the meat mixture in a food processor or using the coarse blade of a mincer. (*Note*: If using a food processor, don't chop the meat too fine or it will become sticky.) Stir any leftover melted fat into the ground meat, but discard any meat juices as they will turn potted meat sour. Taste the mixture for seasoning. If the ham was salty, more salt may not be needed.

3 Tightly pack the potted meat into a crock, eliminating all air. Smooth the top and pour over a layer of melted clarified butter. (*Note*: Be sure the meat is completely sealed.) Potted meat will keep up to 3 weeks in a refrigerator if the seal is not broken.

Cook's Comment. Potting suits tough, well-aged meat and in the UK I'd suggest chuck or round steak, with round, rump or chuck steak in the USA. Game meats are good, too, with or without the addition of ham for flavour, so this recipe offers a happy end for elderly venison and mature game birds older than one year.

Potted Shrimps

Whenever I return to England, two dishes top my list of desiderata: sole meunière and a double order of potted shrimps. Sadly, both are ever more expensive and ever less frequently spanking fresh. At least I can reproduce potted shrimps at home, though the little pink shrimps which are commonly available do not have the same bite as the spicy grey ones, which usually have to be peeled by hand.

SERVES 6–8

2lb (*1kg*) cooked, peeled baby
  shrimps
½ teaspoon grated nutmeg
⅛ teaspoon cayenne
salt and pepper

½lb (*250g*) clarified butter,*
  melted
For serving
brown or wholewheat toast
1 lemon, cut into wedges

1 Heat the oven to Gas 2/150°C/300°F. In a bowl mix the shrimps with the nutmeg, cayenne and a little salt and pepper. Put the shrimps into a small casserole and pour over three-quarters of the clarified butter. (*Note*: The shrimps should completely fill the casserole.) Cover with a lid.

2 Bake the shrimps in the oven for 1 hour. Allow to cool before removing the lid. Taste the shrimp mixture for seasoning. (*Note*: The mixture should be quite spicy.)

3 Pack the shrimps and butter tightly into a crock so that all air is excluded. Smooth the top and pour over the remaining clarified butter to seal the shrimps completely. Potted shrimps can be kept for up to a week in the refrigerator provided the seal is not broken. Serve chilled with hot brown or wholewheat toast and lemon wedges.

Cook's Comment. Potted shrimps are also good hot: fry them quickly in a frying pan or wok, adding a tablespoon of sherry if you like. If using pink shrimps, you may need to add allspice and pepper along with the nutmeg and cayenne.

Terrine de Canard au Poivre Vert

TERRINE OF DUCK WITH GREEN PEPPERCORNS

This recipe evolved as a technical exercise when a colleague claimed that it was possible to bone a bird without slitting the skin. Possible indeed it is. The trick is to keep cutting meat from the main carcass until meat and skin are completely detached in one piece, forming the ideal container for a terrine mixture.

At the time, a dozen years ago, green peppercorns were the rage, a showy contrast to the richness of duck. This combination continues happily in my repertoire, though I am aware that finely chopped chilli peppers might now be considered more the thing. Yet another alternative is a classic studding of pistachios, blanched to accent their brilliant green.

SERVES 8–10

a 4–5lb (*about 2kg*); duck, with its liver
salt and pepper
For the stuffing
¾lb (*375g*) lean minced veal
¾lb (*375g*) lean minced pork
½lb (*250g*) minced pork fat
¾lb (*375g*) pork liver, finely chopped
2 cloves garlic, finely chopped

3 tablespoons brandy
2 eggs
½ teaspoon ground allspice
½ teaspoon ground nutmeg
½ teaspoon ground cloves
3 tablespoons green pepper-corns, rinsed and drained

3¼-pint (2-litre) oval terrine

1 *To bone the duck keeping the skin in one piece.* Pull back the neck skin of the bird to reveal its breast and cut out the wishbone. Using your fingers and short, sharp strokes of the knife, half cut, half ease the breast meat and skin away from one side of the bird, cutting down until you reach the wing joint. (*Note:* Keep the knife in contact with the carcass so that the skin is not severed.) Sever the wing joint, leaving the bone attached to the meat. Repeat this on the other side, working up to the point where the skin is attached to the breastbone.

2 Turn the bird over and go on to ease the skin away along the backbone. As you cut, fold the meat and skin back from the carcass, continuing to cut all the way to the tail. When you reach the leg joints, sever them, leaving the bones attached to the meat and skin. Finally the carcass will be separated from the meat, attached to the skin only at the breastbone. Lift the carcass so that the meat hangs down. Carefully sever the skin and meat, cutting along the breastbone.

3 *To remove the leg and wing bones.* Holding the end of a wing bone in one hand, cut through the tendons and scrape the meat from the bone. Pull out the bone, using the knife to free it. Holding the end of a leg bone, cut through the tendons attaching flesh to bone. Use the knife to scrape the meat from the bone, pushing the meat away from the end as if sharpening a pencil. Cut the bone free from the skin. Repeat with the remaining wing and leg bones.

4 Sprinkle the duck meat with salt and pepper, then turn it skin side outwards. Tie the vent end with string to form a pouch. Finely chop the duck liver.

5 *For the stuffing.* Mix the minced veal, pork and pork fat with pork and duck livers and garlic. Stir in brandy, eggs, allspice, nutmeg, cloves, green peppercorns, 1 tablespoon salt and 1 teaspoon pepper. Fry a piece of stuffing in a small pan and taste – it should be quite spicy. Adjust seasoning in the remaining stuffing if necessary. Beat the mixture with a wooden spoon or with your hand until it holds together – this gives the terrine body. Heat the oven to Gas 4/175°C/350°F.

6 Fill the duck with the stuffing. Tie the neck end together to seal and trim any excess skin. Put the duck in the terrine and cover with a lid. Set the mould in a *bain marie** and bring to a boil on top of the stove.

7 Cook the terrine in the oven for 1½–1¾ hours or until a skewer inserted in the centre of the terrine is hot to the touch when withdrawn after 30 seconds. Let the terrine cool to tepid, then remove the lid and set a board or plate with a 2lb (*1kg*) weight on top. Refrigerate the terrine until firm and keep it for at least 2 days, and up to a week, before serving.

8 Serve the terrine at room temperature, with the classic French accompaniment of black olives, cornichon pickles and French bread.

Cook's Comment. When serving just a few people, I like to leave the terrine in the mould so that everyone can help himself. With larger groups this is impractical and the terrine should be sliced and arranged on a serving dish or plates with a few lettuce leaves and pickles. However, don't do this more than a couple of hours ahead, as the terrine dries out surprisingly quickly. The slices should be quite thick.

Terrine de Poisson au Caviar

FISH TERRINE WITH CAVIAR

Why did mousses and purées sweep the menus of smart restaurants in the late 1970s? The answer is the food processor, which reduces half an hour's hard hand-labour of working fibres through a flat sieve to a minute's buzz with an electric blade. Equally manageable now are fish quenelles (see page 66) and terrines like this one, which is held together only with egg whites and cream (technically speaking, a *mousseline*).

Unless you want to run to the luxury of scallops, the fish for this recipe need not be expensive. Whiting, perch, flounder, and the New Zealand newcomer orange ruffie, which lives on underwater mountains in the Pacific, all make an excellent terrine.

SERVES 8

2lb (*1kg*) skinless white fish
  fillets, cut into strips
4 egg whites, lightly beaten
½ teaspoon ground nutmeg
salt and white pepper
½ pint (*300ml*) *crème fraîche** or
  double cream

2oz (*60g*) jar red salmon caviar
large head of lettuce, coarsely
  shredded (for garnish)
Green Olive Mayonnaise (see
  opposite) (for serving)

2-pint (1.25-litre) terrine or loaf tin

1 Butter the terrine or loaf tin, line the base with greaseproof paper and butter the paper. Heat the oven to Gas 4/175°C/350°F.

2 Purée the fish in a food processor. With the machine on, gradually add the egg whites. Season with nutmeg, salt and pepper and gradually work in the cream. Transfer the mixture to a bowl and chill in the freezer or over ice, stirring occasionally, until very cold. Taste for seasoning.

3 *For the filling*. Lightly fold together about 4–5 tablespoons of the mixture with the caviar. Pack half the fish mixture into the prepared mould and spread the filling down the centre, leaving a 1in (*2.5cm*) gap on each side. Fill the mould with the rest of the mixture and smooth the top. Press buttered greaseproof paper on top. Cover with a lid or, if using a loaf tin, cover with foil. Put the terrine in a *bain marie** and bring to a boil on top of the stove.

4 Cook the terrine in the oven for 1–1¼ hours or until a skewer inserted in the centre is hot to the touch when withdrawn after 30 seconds. Let the terrine cool to tepid, then remove the lid and set a board or plate with a 2lb (*1kg*) weight on top. Chill until cold. The terrine can be kept for up to 2 days in a refrigerator.

5 *To finish.* Not more than an hour before serving, unmould the terrine and cut it into ⅜in (*1cm*) slices. Spread shredded lettuce in a bed (a *chiffonade*) on individual plates or a large serving plate. Arrange the terrine slices overlapping on top. Serve the Green Olive Mayonnaise separately.

Cook's Comment. This fish terrine is also delicious served hot, with White and Red Butter Sauces (see page 55).

Mayonnaise aux Olives Vertes

GREEN OLIVE MAYONNAISE

Green Olive Mayonnaise is an excellent companion to hard-boiled eggs or cold roast chicken as well as Fish Terrine with Caviar (see opposite). Like many puréed sauces, you will need a blender or food processor to do the hard work. Without one, I'd opt for plain mayonnaise, flavoured with chopped herbs.

MAKES 12fl. oz (350ml) MAYONNAISE TO SERVE 8

4oz (*125g*) green olives, drained
  and stoned
1 clove garlic, crushed
2 egg yolks
salt and pepper

½ teaspoon Dijon mustard
8fl. oz (*250ml*) olive oil
juice of 1 lemon, or more to
  taste

1 If the olives are salty, blanch them by boiling in water for 3 minutes and draining. Purée them in a food processor. Add the garlic, egg yolks, salt, pepper and mustard, and purée for 1 minute. Puréeing constantly, add oil a teaspoon at a time until the mayonnaise is quite thick.

2 Add the remaining oil in a slow, steady stream, followed by the lemon juice. Taste, adding more lemon juice, salt and pepper if needed. The mayonnaise should just fall easily from a spoon. If necessary, thin it with 2–3 tablespoons hot water. The mayonnaise can be kept, tightly covered, for 2 days in the refrigerator. (*Note:* When making Green Olive Mayonnaise in a blender, the mixture gets too thick to churn. Purée only half the olives with the egg yolks, puréeing the rest after all the oil has been added.)

Three Flamiches

Long before the first pizza invaded the fast-food parlours of the world, Flanders had its *flamiche*, a bread-based tart usually filled with pungent Maroilles cheese. As the basic principle is the same for any flamiche, here I'm giving three versions, one with the traditional cheese filling, one with leeks, and one with a more avant-garde combination of Brie and tomato. Flamiche is an excellent picnic dish, or serve it with salad as a main course for lunch or supper.

MAKES 2 FLAMICHES TO SERVE 8

Brioche Dough (see opposite)
choice of fillings (see below)

two 10in (25cm) deep cake tins

1 Make brioche dough and chill for at least 4 hours, or overnight. Assemble ingredients for two chosen fillings.

2 *To shape the flamiche.* Generously butter the tins. Punch the dough to knock out the air and divide it in half. On a floured surface roll each piece to a 14in (35cm) round. Line tins with dough, letting the dough drape over the rims. Pour the fillings over the dough. Lift up the overhanging dough to half cover the fillings. Leave flamiches for 15–20 minutes to rise. Heat the oven to Gas 6/200°C/400°F.

3 Bake both flamiches in the oven until the crust is browned and the filling is set: about 45 minutes. If the top browns too quickly, cover loosely with foil. Flamiche is best eaten freshly baked, but it can be kept for a few hours. It can also be frozen. Serve it warm or at room temperature.

Cook's Comment. Flamiche is not like pizza, for the dough is thick. It needs 45 minutes' cooking, otherwise it will be soggy in the centre.

Fillings for Flamiche

Cheese Flamiche. Slice 8oz (250g) strong creamy cheese – such as Maroilles, French Munster or Vacherin – discard the rind, and lay the cheese on the dough. Pour over a custard made with 1 egg, 1 egg yolk and 4fl. oz (125ml) double cream and seasoned with salt, pepper and a little grated nutmeg.

Tomato and Brie Cheese Flamiche. Discard the rind from 10oz (300g) ripe Brie and slice the cheese. Lay the cheese on the dough. Top with 4 medium, sliced tomatoes. Whisk together 2 eggs, 4fl. oz (125ml) double cream, 1 tablespoon chopped chives, salt and pepper, and pour over the cheese and tomatoes.

Leek Flamiche. Trim 1½lb (*750g*) leeks, leaving some green top. Quarter them lengthwise, wash them thoroughly and slice. Melt 1oz (*30g*) butter in a large frying pan, add the leeks, season with salt and pepper, then cover with buttered foil and a lid. Cook over a low heat, stirring occasionally, until the leeks are very soft: about 20 minutes. Do not allow them to brown. Spread the leeks over the dough. Beat 2 egg yolks with 2½fl. oz (*75ml*) double cream, season with salt and pepper, and pour over the leeks.

Brioche Dough

Toasted brioche bread is my personal choice for breakfast, with homemade peach or raspberry jam.

MAKES DOUGH FOR 2 FLAMICHES TO SERVE 8–10

½oz (*15g*) fresh yeast or
  ¼oz (*7g*) dried yeast
4 tablespoons lukewarm water
1lb (*500g*) flour, or more if needed
6 large eggs, at room temperature

1½ teaspoons salt
2 tablespoons sugar
8oz (*250g*) unsalted butter,
  softened

1 In a small bowl, crumble the yeast over the water and leave until dissolved: about 5 minutes. Sift the flour into a large bowl and make a well in the centre. Break the eggs into the well and add salt, sugar and yeast mixture. With your fingertips blend the ingredients in the well, then gradually draw in flour to make a dough. The dough should be moist, but if it is very sticky work in more flour.

2 On a lightly floured surface knead the dough until it is smooth and very elastic: about 5 minutes. Add the softened butter and thoroughly knead it into the dough. (*Note*: The mixture will be very sticky at first.) Alternatively, use a mixer with a dough hook for kneading.

3 Transfer the dough to a lightly oiled bowl, turn it over to coat all sides with oil and cover it with a damp cloth. Leave it to rise in a warm place until doubled in bulk: about 2 hours. If preparing ahead, the dough can be left to rise in the refrigerator for up to 12 hours. Use as a bread base for *flamiches* (see opposite and above) or for traditional brioche loaves. Brioche dough can also be used to wrap a whole fish (see page 54) or a fillet of beef.

4 *To bake loaves.* Divide the dough in half, shape it and put it into two large loaf tins. Leave it to rise for an hour or until the dough fills the pans. Brush with egg glaze and bake in the oven at Gas 6/200°C/400°F for 35–45 minutes until the loaves are very brown and sound hollow when tapped on the bottom.

Quiche aux Légumes de Provence

PROVENÇAL VEGETABLE QUICHE

Quiche is nothing more than an open pie with a custard filling. I was brought up with just such a bacon and egg pie in the north of England, and recently I was amused to come across it in a farmhouse kitchen in the guise of bacon quiche. In the cafeteria of one American newspaper, the Thursday special is quiche, or 'quish', as the burly pressmen call it. Now, thirty years after quiche conquered the globe, fancier versions such as this Provençal vegetable tart have almost done away with the custard that was their original claim to the name.

SERVES 6–8

4–5 tablespoons olive oil
1 onion, chopped
1½lb (750g) tomatoes, peeled,
   seeded and chopped*
2 cloves garlic, crushed
2 sprigs fresh thyme or
   1 teaspoon dried thyme
salt and pepper
1 small aubergine
2 courgettes
3oz (90g) Gruyère cheese,
   thinly sliced

For the pâte brisée
6½oz (200g) flour
3¼oz (100g) unsalted butter
1 egg yolk
½ teaspoon salt
3 tablespoons cold water, or
   more if needed
For the custard
2 eggs
4fl. oz (125ml) double cream
pinch of grated nutmeg
salt and pepper

10in (25cm) tart tin with removable base

1 Make the *pâte brisée** and chill for 30 minutes. Butter the tart tin. Roll out the dough, line the tin, chill for 15 minutes and bake blind,* cooking the shell completely.

2 Leave the oven at Gas 5/190°C/375°F. In a frying pan heat 2 tablespoons of the olive oil and fry the onion until soft but not brown. Add the tomatoes, garlic, thyme, salt and pepper and cook, stirring occasionally, until the mixture is quite thick: 15–20 minutes.

3 Meanwhile peel the aubergine and cut it into ⅜ × 2in (1 × 5cm) strips. Wipe the courgettes and cut them into strips too. In a frying pan heat two more tablespoons of oil, add the aubergine strips and season with salt and pepper. Sauté, stirring, until tender and lightly browned. Take them out, add the courgettes with seasoning and more oil if needed, and fry until tender but still firm.

[28]

4 Put half the sliced cheese in a layer in the tart shell. Add half the tomato mixture and top with the aubergine. Cover with the remaining tomato mixture and top with courgettes.

5 *For the custard.* Whisk together the eggs, cream, nutmeg, salt and pepper and pour over the vegetables. Top with the remaining cheese. Bake the quiche in the oven until browned and the custard is set: 20–25 minutes. Serve hot or at room temperature. (The quiche can be made up to 2 days ahead and warmed before serving.)

Cook's Comment. Provençal mixtures like this are an invitation to invention. Peppers of all colours can be added, for example, and the herbs can be varied, depending on what is in season. Anchovy and olive would be good, too, and I see nothing wrong with including a can of drained flaked tuna to make a more substantial main-course dish.

Tourte aux Légumes du Feÿ

TORTE OF CABBAGE AND LEEKS

Our caretakers in Burgundy, Monsieur and Madame Milbert, come of peasant stock. To me they epitomise a lifestyle that has vanished, for without the smallest sense of deprivation they live almost entirely off the land. Monsieur cultivates nearly 2 acres of fruits and vegetables, including potatoes to lay down for winter. He brews cider and has one of the few remaining private licences to distil Calvados – a privilege that will die with him. Some years he makes ratafia, a mixture of apple juice and *eau de vie*, while *cassis* (blackcurrant liqueur) is the province of his wife. Madame Milbert raises rabbits by the dozen, as well as ducks and chickens, and has a plentiful supply of eggs. Until recently the Milberts also kept cows for milk, butter and cheese. Basically, food follows the seasons, though Madame also indulges in some canning and jam-making. Two vegetables which seem to be available all year are leeks and cabbage – hence this *tourte*.

SERVES 6

1 medium head Savoy cabbage	2 egg yolks
2lb (*1kg*) leeks	8fl. oz (*250ml*) milk
1 tablespoon butter	8fl. oz (*250ml*) *crème fraîche** or
salt and pepper	double cream
Tomato Coulis (see opposite) or	3 tablespoons grated Parmesan
White Butter Sauce (see	cheese
page 55) (for serving)	salt and pepper
For the custard	pinch of nutmeg
2 eggs	
	9in (23cm) deep round cake tin

1 Discard the tough outer leaves of the cabbage. Cook the whole cabbage in boiling salted water to cover until the outer leaves are tender: 7–8 minutes. During cooking, use two spoons to separate the leaves as they loosen from the head. Drain the cabbage and rinse under cold water. Separate the outer leaves, keeping them whole. Quarter the cabbage heart and shred it, discarding the core.

2 Halve the leeks lengthwise and wash them thoroughly. Slice them crosswise, including some of the green top. Melt the butter in a heavy pan, add the leeks, season with salt and pepper and press a piece of foil on top. Cover with a lid and cook over a very low heat, stirring occasionally, until the leeks are very tender: 15–20 minutes. (*Note*: Do not allow them to brown.) The vegetables can be refrigerated for up to 24 hours. If serving with Tomato Coulis (see opposite), it too can be made ahead.

3 Heat the oven to Gas 4/175°C/350°F.

4 *For the custard.* Beat the eggs, egg yolks, milk and cream until smooth. Stir in the Parmesan cheese and season highly with salt, pepper and nutmeg.

[30]

5 Generously butter the cake tin and line the bottom and sides with cabbage leaves, draping them over the rim. Chop any remaining leaves. Layer the shredded cabbage and the leeks in the tin, seasoning each layer with salt and pepper. Pour over the custard, adding enough to just cover the vegetables. Fold the draped leaves on top and cover the tin loosely with foil.

6 Bake the torte in the heated oven for 1½–2 hours or until firm. Remove it from the oven and allow to stand for 5–10 minutes in a warm place. Meanwhile, reheat the Tomato Coulis or make White Butter Sauce (see page 55). Unmould the torte on to a serving dish, spoon a little sauce around the edge and serve the rest separately.

Cook's Comment. All sorts of vegetables can be cooked in this custard mixture – for example, a combination of green vegetables such as broccoli, green beans, cauliflower and spinach. Another idea might be a Provençal mix of aubergine, courgettes and a variety of peppers, flavoured with garlic and chopped herbs.

Coulis de Tomates Fraîches

TOMATO COULIS

When tomatoes are in season it is well worth making Tomato Coulis to freeze. It is an excellent flavouring for soups and stews, as well as acting as a sauce.

MAKES ½ PINT (300ml)

1 shallot, finely chopped	*bouquet garni**
2 tablespoons vegetable oil	salt and pepper
2lb (*1kg*) tomatoes, peeled, seeded and chopped*	

1 In a shallow pan sauté the shallot in the oil until soft but not brown. Add the tomatoes, *bouquet garni* and seasoning and cook over a medium heat, stirring often, for 20–30 minutes until nearly all the moisture has evaporated. Work through a sieve and taste for seasoning.

2 Tomato Coulis can be refrigerated for 2–3 days, or frozen.

Aubergine Charlotte

Yoghurt and aubergine are very Middle Eastern ingredients, yet to treat them French-style is not inappropriate. Puff pastry, sorbets and sweetmeats like macaroons are just a few of the dishes which came to France from the Arab world via Spain or Italy. In fact, the Arab influence on French cooking continues apace, thanks to the considerable North African presence in France, with *merguez* sausages and dishes like couscous, now commonplace in backstreet cafés.

SERVES 6–8

2lb (*1kg*) aubergines
5–6 tablespoons olive oil, or more
1 onion, finely chopped
1lb (*500g*) fresh tomatoes,
    peeled, seeded and chopped,*
    or a 1lb (*500g*) tin tomatoes,
    drained and chopped

1 tablespoon tomato purée
2 cloves garlic, crushed
salt and pepper
*bouquet garni**
8fl. oz (*250ml*) natural yoghurt
3 tablespoons dry breadcrumbs

3-pint (1.5-litre) charlotte mould

1 Trim stems from aubergines and cut into ⅜in (*1cm*) rounds. Sprinkle with salt and leave for half an hour to draw out the juices. Rinse under cold water and dry.

2 Meanwhile, heat the oven to Gas 4/175°C/350°F. Oil the charlotte mould and two baking sheets. Heat 2 tablespoons of the oil in a frying pan and fry the onion until lightly browned. Stir in the tomatoes, tomato purée, garlic, salt, pepper and *bouquet garni* and cook, stirring occasionally, until the mixture is thick: 15–20 minutes. Discard the *bouquet garni* and taste for seasoning.

3 Place the aubergine slices on the oiled baking sheets and brush the slices generously with olive oil. Bake them in the oven for 15–20 minutes or until tender. Brush from time to time with more oil and turn them to brown evenly. Leave the oven on.

4 Line the bottom and sides of the charlotte mould with slices, overlapping them to form a pattern. Spread a layer of the tomato mixture in the bottom, top with 2–3 spoonfuls of yoghurt and sprinkle with breadcrumbs. Cover with another layer of aubergine slices. Continue the layers until all the ingredients are used and the mould is full, ending with a layer of aubergine. Cover the mould with foil.

5 Set the charlotte in a *bain marie** and bring to a boil on top of the stove. Cook in the oven for ¾–1 hour or until a skewer inserted in the centre of the charlotte is hot to the touch when withdrawn. Let the charlotte cool. It can be refrigerated for up to 3 days.

6 *To finish.* Let the charlotte come to room temperature, or warm it slightly in the oven. Unmould it and, for serving, cut it into wedges like a cake.

Cook's Comment. Pursuing the Middle Eastern theme, this dish is good with black olives, pitta bread and purées such as hummus and taramasalata.

Angels and Devils on Horseback

Anyone of a certain age in Britain knows that the angels in this recipe are oysters, the devils chicken livers or prunes, and both ride horses of buttered toast. Such savouries, which once rounded out even a modest English dinner, have more or less disappeared from view. But there is no reason why a savoury cannot take on a new life as a first course. If only for the romance of their names, I vote for a revival of devilled mushrooms, Welsh Rarebit (toasted cheese), Scotch Woodcock (anchovy scrambled eggs), and, of course, this cavalcade of angels and devils.

MAKES 32 ROLLS TO SERVE 8

4oz (125g) chicken livers, or
16 stoned prunes
16 slices (about ¾lb (375g))
streaky bacon

16 shelled oysters
16 slices white bread
butter for toast

4–5 skewers

1 Trim chicken livers of fat and membranes and cut them into two or three pieces to make 16. Cut each bacon slice in half. Wrap a bacon piece around each chicken liver or prune, and then around each oyster. String on skewers. The rolls can be refrigerated for up to 12 hours.

2 Heat the grill. Make toast, discarding crusts and cutting each slice into two strips. Grill the bacon rolls for 2–3 minutes on each side until the bacon is crisp; chicken livers should remain pink in the centre. Set the rolls on toast and serve two of each per person

Cook's Comment. Speared on toothpicks without their mounts of toast, angels and devils make good cocktail hors-d'œuvres.

Rillettes de Lapin

PATE OF RABBIT

Beatrix Potter's Mr McGregor was part of my real fantasy world, for when I was a child we waged war against the wild rabbits. In vain was the garden fortified with chicken wire; in vain did Old Metcalfe the mole-catcher set snares to catch them. The rabbits gambolled on the front lawn regardless. On fine mornings my mother would rise early to take a pot-shot with a rifle from the bedroom window, but the rabbits had a sixth sense and off they would scamper just as she was taking aim. Now, forty years later and five hundred miles to the south in Burgundy, we again have an abundance of rabbits. These ones are tame, raised by our caretaker Madame Milbert, so rabbit can be on the menu any day at an hour's notice.

SERVES 6–8

2 rabbits (weighing about 5lb (2.3kg) in total), cut into pieces	bouquet garni*
	2 whole cloves
	1 teaspoon black peppercorns
3 onions, sliced	16fl. oz (500ml) white wine
3 carrots, sliced	salt and pepper
2 cloves garlic, peeled	1 pint (600ml) veal stock*
4–5 sprigs fresh thyme or 2 teaspoons dried	2 shallots, finely chopped
	2fl. oz (60ml) vermouth

1 Layer the rabbit in a heavy casserole with the onions, carrots, garlic, thyme, *bouquet garni*, cloves and peppercorns. Pour over the wine, cover and marinate in the refrigerator for 12–24 hours.

2 Heat the oven to Gas 4/175°C/350°F. Mix a little salt and pepper with the stock and pour it over the rabbit, shaking the casserole to mix it with the wine. Cover the casserole, set it in a *bain marie** and bring to a boil on top of the stove. Cook in the oven for 1¾–2 hours or until the meat falls easily from the bones.

3 Allow to cool slightly, then lift out the meat and remove the bones. In a deep glass bowl shred the meat with two forks and stir in the shallots and vermouth. Skim any fat from the cooking liquid and boil it, if necessary, until reduced to 2 pints (1.25 litres). Taste it for seasoning and strain over the meat. Cover and chill until set. Rillettes can be refrigerated for up to 3 days; the flavour mellows on standing.

Cook's Comment. These rillettes are much less fatty than the traditional ones made with pork, but they share the characteristic coarse texture. The cooking liquid runs down into the meat and sets as aspic. For flavour and colour I sometimes add about 6 tablespoons of chopped fresh tarragon to the hot liquid before pouring it over the meat, giving an effect like Burgundy's famous Parsleyed Ham in Wine Aspic (see page 182), though the taste is quite different.

Escargots à l'Anise

SNAILS WITH ANISE

In the interests of culinary education, I once insisted we buy live snails for the students at La Varenne. Thirty dozen was the minimum order, so 360 snails were duly locked in the cellar to be purged by the traditional expedient of a fast. When Chef Claude arrived one morning, the snails had escaped and were racing up the walls. Not a pleasant sight! After that experience, I decided that the savvy cook turns to a tin or to the freezer and buys snails ready for the pan.

SERVES 8

4 dozen cooked, canned snails
1oz (*30g*) butter
3 cloves garlic, finely chopped
1 pint (*600ml*) *crème fraîche** or double cream
1 teaspoon anise seed
pinch of grated nutmeg

salt and pepper
2–3 teaspoons Pernod or other anise liquor
2 tablespoons chopped parsley
French bread (for serving)

8 heatproof ramekins

1 Drain and rinse tinned snails or defrost frozen ones.

2 In a sauté pan or shallow saucepan melt the butter and sauté the garlic for 1 minute without browning. Add the cream, anise seed, nutmeg, salt and pepper and simmer for 10–15 minutes until the sauce has reduced by half and is well flavoured. It can be kept for up to 3 days in the refrigerator.

3 *To finish.* Bring the sauce to a boil, add the snails and simmer for 5 minutes. Add the Pernod and parsley and taste for seasoning. Spoon into hot ramekins and serve at once, with plenty of French bread. Snails must be piping hot!

Cook's Comment. For a true gastronomic indulgence, fill puff pastry *feuilletés* or *bouchées* with these snails.

[35]

EGGS AND CHEESE

The indispensable egg! Without eggs we would lose soufflés and omelettes, mayonnaise, hollandaise, meringues and most cakes. We take their availability and freshness for granted but only twenty-five years ago, when I trained in the kitchen, we always broke eggs separately in case one should be rotten. During the Second World War it was worse, for the British egg ration was one per person per week. We kept eggs in a crock in the larder in a silicate solution called waterglass – the silicate seals the shell so, in theory, the egg does not spoil. In practice, however, one egg in five had a cracked shell – how well I remember the sulphur smell when they were rotten!

My mother had not heard of 'candling' – holding the egg up to a candle flame to see if the shell is intact. A New England friend adds that her mother candled eggs not just to detect cracks, but to sort out double yolkers, which were set aside for scrambled eggs or cakes in which the eggs were not separated. Pullet eggs, often small enough to throw off the proportions of a recipe, were hard boiled and marked with a pencil before being immersed in the waterglass. Such measures helped a household survive the winter, but a waterglass egg is very much second best. Now, when I taste Madame Milbert's duck and hen eggs, freshly laid that day, I am reminded all the more vividly of how good an egg can really be!

A Trio of Omelettes

Omelettes are ancient. The Romans reportedly cooked eggs in a frying pan, flavouring them with honey and calling them *ovamellita*. The three which follow illustrate three quite different cooking methods. First comes the classic, folded omelette, filled here with wild mushrooms, garlic and herbs. Then follows a flat version, often called a Spanish omelette, which is always cooked more firmly than folded ones. The recipe here is English, created at the Savoy grill in its halcyon days and named after the novelist Arnold Bennett, who enjoyed the good life. 'A man of 60', he once observed, 'has spent more than three years of his life in eating.' Finally comes the Italian version of omelette, *frittata*, cooked very slowly, without stirring, so that the egg forms a cake, flavoured of course with all sorts of delectable fillings.

Omelette Forestière

OMELETTE WITH WILD MUSHROOMS

SERVES 2

4oz (125g) fresh wild
   mushrooms or ½oz (15g)
   dried wild mushrooms
3 tablespoons butter
2 shallots, finely chopped

1 clove garlic, chopped
1 tablespoon chopped parsley
salt and pepper
6 eggs

10in (25cm) omelette pan

1 Trim the stems of fresh mushrooms and rinse them quickly in several changes of cold water. Soak dried mushrooms in warm water to cover for ½–1 hour; drain well and rinse thoroughly, trimming any tough stems. Cut fresh or dried mushrooms into slices.

2 In a frying pan, melt 1 tablespoon of butter and fry the shallots until soft. Add the mushrooms, garlic, salt and pepper and sauté, stirring, until tender and all the liquid has evaporated. Cooking time depends on the type of mushroom. Stir in the chopped parsley. The mixture can be cooked a day ahead and refrigerated.

3 *To cook the omelette.* Whisk the eggs with salt and pepper until frothy. Heat the remaining butter in the omelette pan until foaming and beginning to brown. Add the eggs and stir briskly with the flat of a fork for about 30 seconds or until they start to thicken. Add the mushroom mixture, reserving a tablespoonful for garnish. Continue stirring, pulling the cooked egg from the sides of the pan to the centre until the omelette is soft or firm, according to your taste: ½–1 minute.

4 Leave the omelette for 10–15 seconds to brown the bottom, then fold over one side. Tip it on to a warm plate so that the other side is folded too. Serve the omelette at once, topped with the reserved mushroom mixture as garnish.

Cook's Comment. Any kind of wild mushroom can be used here, and Chinese dried black mushrooms are a real bargain. Some fresh mushrooms, particularly the so-called wild kinds which are cultivated, will produce a lot of liquid in cooking and this should be boiled until it has evaporated completely.

Omelette Arnold Bennett

SERVES 2

2 tablespoons butter
6oz (175g) flaked cooked
   smoked haddock
4 tablespoons double cream
6 eggs

salt and pepper
2–3 tablespoons grated
   Parmesan cheese

10in (25cm) omelette pan

1 Heat the grill. Melt 1 tablespoon of the butter in a small saucepan, add the haddock with half the cream and stir over a high heat for 1–2 minutes. Allow to cool. Whisk the eggs with salt and pepper until they are frothy and well mixed.

2 Melt the remaining tablespoon of butter in the omelette pan, add the eggs and cook over a high heat for about 30 seconds, stirring constantly until they begin to thicken. Add the haddock mixture and continue stirring for about 1 minute, drawing the egg from the sides to the centre of the pan, until the omelette is firm but still soft on top.

3 Take the omelette from the heat, pour over the remaining cream and sprinkle with cheese. Place under the hot grill until browned, slide on to a hot dish and serve at once.

Cook's Comment. Any smoked fish can be substituted for the haddock. Salmon is a particular treat.

Frittata di Zucchine

COURGETTE FRITTATA WITH GARLIC

SERVES 4

3oz (*90g*) butter
2 onions, thinly sliced
salt and pepper
1lb (*500g*) courgettes, thinly
    sliced

2 cloves garlic, finely chopped,
    or more to taste
1 tablespoon chopped parsley
6 eggs

10in (25 cm) omelette pan

1 In a frying pan, melt half the butter. Add the onions, season with salt and pepper and cook gently, stirring occasionally, until golden brown: 10–15 minutes. Add the courgettes and garlic, cover and cook, stirring occasionally, until the courgettes are tender: 5–7 minutes. Stir in the parsley. This filling can be cooked up to 4 hours ahead.

2 *To cook the frittata.* Whisk the eggs in a bowl with salt and pepper until frothy and completely mixed. Stir in the courgette mixture. Heat the remaining butter in the omelette pan until foaming. Pour in the egg mixture, lower the heat, cover and cook as slowly as possible until the centre of the frittata is set: 12–15 minutes.

3 Turn the frittata on to a warm dish so that the browned side is upwards, cut it into wedges and serve.

Cook's Comment. Frittata is the effortless omelette – an invitation to sit back and enjoy a glass of wine while it cooks. To save even more work, the courgettes can be grated in a food processor instead of sliced. Cold frittata is excellent stuffed into pitta bread for a snack.

Stilton Cheese Ramekins

When I was a child, for Christmas my mother used to buy a whole Stilton cheese weighing at least 15 pounds. The cheese would arrive in October to finish maturing in the cold larder on the north side of the house. Twice a week she would turn it and from time to time a sample was cut from the centre with an apple corer, then replaced after inspection. Was it aging nicely to creamy, blue-veined perfection? Or was there a trace of the rancid acidity which can suddenly develop, causing the death of a good cheese? If we feared the worst, then to save its life we ate it long before the festive season, disguising its shortcomings in recipes like these cheese ramekins. Heavier than a classic soufflé, this mixture resembles an agreeably light fondue.

SERVES 8–10 AS A FIRST COURSE

4oz (*125g*) butter
4oz (*125g*) flour
1¼ pints (*750ml*) milk
6 eggs, separated
6oz (*175g*) Stilton cheese,
   crumbled

6oz (*175g*) grated Parmesan
   cheese
pinch of cayenne
salt and pepper

8–10 ramekins (8fl. oz (250ml)
   capacity each)

1 Melt the butter in a saucepan. Off the heat, work in the flour with a wooden spoon, then stir in the milk to make a thick paste. Heat the mixture, stirring constantly, until it thickens. Continue cooking until the mixture is very thick and holds the shape of the spoon when pressed: 5–8 minutes.

2 Take the pan from the heat, let the mixture cool slightly and beat in the egg yolks. Stir in the Stilton and Parmesan and season with cayenne, salt and pepper to taste. (Salt may not be needed as the cheese is salty.) The cheese mixture can be kept for 24 hours in the refrigerator.

3 Half an hour before serving, heat the oven to Gas 5/190°C/375°F. Butter the ramekins and set them on a baking sheet. Stiffly whip the egg whites. Warm the cheese mixture over a gentle heat to soften it. (*Note*: Do not boil, or the mixture will become stringy.) Fold the egg whites into the cheese mixture as lightly as possible. Spoon the mixture into the ramekins and bake in the oven until puffed and brown: 18–20 minutes. Serve at once.

Cook's Comment. Any blue cheese can be used for these ramekins, though Stilton has a piquancy all its own. The ramekins should be served at once, while still puffed, but they taste good deflated too. I once baked the mixture in a big shallow dish and took it on a most successful picnic to serve cold.

Soufflé au Fromage à la Françoise

FRANÇOISE'S CHEESE SOUFFLE

Françoise is that teacher's dream – a born cook. A Norman through and through, for twenty-five years, beginning at the age of fourteen, she faithfully reproduced the soggy cabbage and limp fruit salad preferred by my mother-in-law, but given her head she was brilliant. Her sole meunière was crisp, buttery and with that even-toasted sheen which professionals strive to achieve. It was she who taught me the key to roast chicken – 'I just baste it often with butter,' she said. One day there appeared on the table a perfect Tarte Tatin (see page 250), the caramelised apple tart which is the showpiece of at least a dozen starred restaurants. Cooks make a great fuss about Tarte Tatin, since caramelising apples so that they still hold their shape is not easy. Recipes call for special copper moulds and discuss varieties of apple at length. But Françoise had simply buttered and sugared the dish, added some windfalls from the garden, and baked them. I thought it was a fluke, but she repeated it on demand. Her cheese soufflé is also infallible – a rich fluffy tower of gold.

SERVES 6

2½oz (75g) butter	5 eggs, separated
1oz (30g) flour	2½ oz (75g) grated Gruyère
12fl. oz (375ml) milk	cheese
salt and pepper	3 egg whites
pinch of grated nutmeg	
	3½-pint (2-litre) soufflé dish

1 Melt the butter in a saucepan, whisk in the flour and cook until foaming. Whisk in the milk and bring to a boil, stirring constantly until the sauce thickens. Season with salt, pepper and nutmeg, and simmer for 2 minutes. Take from the heat and whisk the egg yolks into the hot sauce so that they cook and thicken slightly. Stir in the cheese, reserving 1 tablespoon, and taste for seasoning. (*Note*: The mixture should be highly seasoned to compensate for the bland egg whites.) Rub a piece of butter on top of the sauce to prevent a skin from forming. It can be kept at room temperature for up to 6 hours.

2 *To finish.* Heat the oven to Gas 7/220°C/425°F and thickly butter the soufflé dish. Stiffly whip all 8 egg whites, adding a pinch of salt to help them stiffen. Reheat the cheese mixture until hot to the touch. Add about a quarter of the egg whites and mix together thoroughly. Add this mixture to the remaining egg whites and fold together as lightly as possible. Spoon the mixture into the prepared dish – it should fill to within ¾in (2cm) of the rim. Sprinkle the reserved cheese over the top. The soufflé can be refrigerated at this point for up to 1 hour.

3 Bake the soufflé low down in the heated oven until puffed and brown: 15–18 minutes. If you prefer the centre to be soft, remove the soufflé when it still wobbles slightly if gently shaken. Serve at once.

Cook's Comment. Smaller soufflés are always less risky than one big one and, in ramekins, this soufflé mixture will take only 10–12 minutes to bake. For a surprise, add a spoonful of cooked shrimps marinated in brandy to the bottom of each ramekin.

La Gougère

CHEESE GALETTE

No pick-me-up can beat a good *gougère* – a fact appreciated by Paris's three-star Taillevent restaurant, which serves these little cheese puffs with apéritifs. In Burgundy, their birthplace, the best cafés set out a basket of *gougères* as big as your fist to accompany a glass of Beaujolais. I found the following version in our local village, baked as a first-course Sunday treat.

When the dough is spread flat and sprinkled with cheese, *gougère* bakes to be half quiche, half pastry, and is deliciously crisp.

SERVES 6

4oz (125g) finely diced Gruyère cheese
1oz (30g) grated Gruyère cheese
1 egg, beaten, to mix with
½ teaspoon salt (for glaze)
For the milk choux pastry
6fl. oz (175ml) milk

½ teaspoon salt
2½oz (75g) unsalted butter
4oz (125g) flour
3–4 eggs

10in (25cm) tart tin with removable base

1 Heat the oven to Gas 5/190°C/375°F. Generously butter the tart tin. Make choux pastry* substituting milk for water. Beat in half the diced Gruyère.

2 Spread the dough evenly in the tart tin and brush with the egg glaze. Sprinkle with the grated cheese and the remaining diced cheese. Bake in the oven until the *gougère* is puffed and brown but still soft inside: 30–40 minutes. (*Note*: It will shrink as it cools.)

3 *Gougère* is best eaten while still warm, but it can be baked up to 8 hours ahead. Keep it in an air-tight container and warm it in a low oven. Cut it into wedges for serving.

Cook's Comment. Unlike choux pastry, *gougère* should be slightly underbaked so that it remains soft in the centre. Using milk instead of water also enriches the dough and gives it a deep golden colour.

Gnocchi Romana

SEMOLINA OR CORNMEAL DUMPLINGS WITH CHEESE

This dish dates from my catering days in Paris in the early 1960s, when I cooked for an Anglo-American clientele, all of whom seemed to live in spacious, high-ceilinged apartments on the *'grands boulevards'*. The back quarters were usually as ample as the front, with butler's pantry, a side entrance for deliveries and a massive cast-iron range for the cook. I soon became familiar with the protocol. It was up to the cook to wash the pots and pans but not the tableware. The cook must present *'plats cuisinés'* ready for the table, but the *maître d'hôtel* was responsible for carving roasts, for the cheese tray, for coffee and drinks. Etiquette required that, once dinner was over, all of us in the kitchen be offered champagne. Even in those Gaullist days life on the wrong side of the baize door was a polyglot world of Spanish, Portuguese and North Africans, into which I was accepted without question.

SERVES 4–6 AS A FIRST COURSE

1⅔ pints (*1 litre*) milk, or more
  if needed
1 medium onion, stuck with a
  clove
1 bay leaf
1 teaspoon whole peppercorns
pinch of grated nutmeg
salt and pepper
6 oz (*175g*) coarse semolina or
  white cornmeal

3 egg yolks
4oz (*125g*) grated Parmesan
  cheese
1 tablespoon Dijon mustard
4oz (*125g*) butter, melted

*2in (5cm) biscuit-cutter or glass;
10 × 15in (25 × 37cm) Swiss-roll tin*

1 Scald the milk in a pan with the onion, bay leaf, peppercorns, nutmeg, salt and pepper. Cover, leave to infuse for 10–15 minutes, then strain.

2 Return the milk to the pan and bring back to a boil. Gradually whisk in the semolina or cornmeal. Bring to a boil and simmer, stirring constantly, until the mixture is thick but still falls fairly easily from the spoon: 5–8 minutes. It should not be sticky. If necessary, add more milk. (*Note:* The cooking time and amount of milk needed will vary with the type of grain used.)

3 Remove the mixture from the heat and beat in the egg yolks, one by one. Stir in half the cheese and all the mustard and taste for seasoning. Thickly butter the Swiss-roll tin and spread the *gnocchi* mixture to form a ½in (*1.25cm*) layer. Brush with melted butter and chill for 2 hours or until set.

4 Warm the tin lightly over the heat to melt the butter and cut out 2in (*5cm*) rounds or squares of *gnocchi*. Arrange them overlapping in a deep heatproof dish. Pour over the remaining melted butter and sprinkle with the remaining cheese. The *gnocchi* can be refrigerated for 2 days, or frozen.

5 *To finish.* Heat the oven to Gas 8/230°C/450°F or heat the grill. Bake or grill the *gnocchi* until browned and very hot: 5–8 minutes.

Cook's Comment. A caterer's delight, *gnocchi* keep well, can be frozen, and take only a few minutes to reheat. What is more, they make a good accompaniment for a main course of flesh, fish or fowl.

Quiche aux Oignons et Roquefort

ROQUEFORT AND ONION QUICHE

Paul Levy, author, columnist for the *Observer* newspaper and the original foodie, puts my usually abundant energy to shame. A trifle portly, but none the worse for it, Paul's pursuit of the very best, and inevitably the not-so-good, in fine wining and dining is indefatigable, and his capacity to talk about it is a match even for mine. I well remember his sweep through our part of Burgundy, when between noon one day and sundown the next, and in a heatwave to boot, he visited one two-star and two three-star restaurants. Such a marathon would puncture most gastronomes, but the following morning I found Paul seated at the typewriter in the blazing sun, with coffee mug and ritual breakfast of wholewheat bread generously topped with cheese to hand, writing up our experiences with the gusto of the born epicure. How he does it, I don't know, but here is just one of the treats we enjoyed together.

SERVES 6–8 AS A FIRST COURSE, 4–6 AS A MAIN DISH

For the filling
1oz (30g) butter
3 large onions, thinly sliced
salt and pepper
½ teaspoon chopped fresh
    thyme or a pinch of dried
    thyme
6½oz (200g) crumbled
    Roquefort cheese
For the pâte brisée
6½oz (200g) flour
3¼oz (100g) unsalted butter
1 egg yolk

½ teaspoon salt
3 tablespoons cold water, or
    more if needed
For the custard
1 egg
2 egg yolks
4fl. oz (125ml) milk
4fl. oz (125ml) *crème fraîche** or
    double cream
salt and pepper
pinch of grated nutmeg

*10in (25cm) tart tin with
    removable base*

1 Make the *pâte brisée** and chill for 30 minutes. Butter the tart tin. Roll out the dough, line the tin, chill for 15 minutes and bake blind,* cooking the shell for 15 minutes. Leave the oven heat at Gas 5/190°C/375°F.

2 *For the filling.* Melt the butter in a heavy pan, add the onions, salt, pepper and thyme and press a piece of foil on top. Add the lid and sweat the onions over a very low heat, stirring occasionally, until they are very soft: 15–20 minutes. Do not allow them to brown. Add the Roquefort and stir until melted and smooth. Spread the mixture in the tart shell.

3 *For the custard.* Whisk the egg and egg yolks with the milk and cream until mixed. Season to taste with salt, pepper and nutmeg and pour over the onion mixture. Bake in the heated oven until the custard is set and browned: 40–45 minutes. Let the quiche cool slightly before unmoulding. Quiche is best eaten the day of baking but it can be refrigerated for a day or two. Warm it lightly before serving.

Cook's Comment. Roquefort is an over-rated cheese, I think, but here its saltiness is balanced by a rich custard and sweet onions.

Aunt Louie's Cheese Balls

I was blessed with but one aunt, plump and generous, a *grande dame* with bouffant white hair and an English-rose complexion. Her progress as she drove down the village street, bowing right and left to acquaintances, was positively regal. Auntie Louie was famous for her luck at the tombola and for her cocktail parties, powered by vicious gin martinis and sharp little cheese balls which exploded into crumbs if you tried to bite them.

MAKES 25–30 CHEESE BALLS

4oz (125g) flour	½ teaspoon pepper
4oz (125g) grated Parmesan cheese	½ teaspoon dry mustard
½ teaspoon salt	3½oz (110g) melted unsalted butter, or more if needed

1 Grease a baking sheet. In a bowl, mix the flour, cheese, salt, pepper and mustard. Stir in the melted butter so that the mixture forms crumbs. Press the mixture into balls the size of a walnut. (*Note:* The mixture should be dry, but if it is too crumbly to shape, add more butter.) Set the balls on the baking sheet and chill for 30 minutes. Heat the oven to Gas 5/190°C/375°F.

2 Bake the cheese balls in the oven until lightly browned: 15–20 minutes. Transfer them to a rack to cool. They can be stored for up to 2 weeks in an air-tight container, or frozen.

Cook's Comment. Only Parmesan gives the right taste in this recipe, though in wartime we were reduced to using dry 'mousetrap' Cheddar.

FISH

Like many cooks, I enjoy messing around with fish. Boning and skinning the more complex varieties, like herring, requires some dexterity. Keeping a fish moist during cooking, developing the delicate flavour, and achieving just the right degree of cooking, tax all my skill. But at the end of it I find I'm reluctant to face the creature, eye to eye on the plate, within the hour. So over the years I've built up the following repertoire of fish dishes almost all of which can be prepared hours ahead and cooked at the last moment.

I must have stayed in a dozen marine catchment areas, each associated with quite different kinds of fish, and I've been reminded so many times of the obvious lesson that the nearer to its home, the better the fish. Freshness is indeed all. When we lived outside Dieppe, the fish were so lively that I once had to stun sole with a mallet before I could proceed. In Washington, flounder from the Chesapeake Bay is a better buy than imported Dover sole or Florida pompano, both for quality and price. So, while the following recipes may indicate a particular fish, I've tried also to suggest as many alternatives as possible. The supply of fresh fish in the market should dictate the menu, never the other way around. My best advice would always be to try whatever smells sweet and has a shiny skin and a bright eye.

Hot Poached Salmon with Whisky Sauce

Not being an outdoor type, I was less than overwhelmed when in 1984 I was invited to visit the Alaskan wilderness on a food journalists' junket. A little seaplane bore a dozen of us over mountainous inlets reminiscent of the Norwegian fjords to a lodge 600 miles from the nearest road network, the Alaska highway. For 48 hours we were destined to do nothing but fish. Pink salmon was running – not the best of fighting fish, but quite wily enough for a beginner like myself. I learned to cast and reel in the line and soon it was I, not the fish, that was hooked. The competition between us amateurs to land the biggest catch was intense. Back home in the lodge, picturesquely named Yes Bay, supper of the freshest of fresh crab and salmon was unforgettable.

SERVES 10

one 8lb (*3.6kg*) salmon, or two
   4lb (*1.8kg*) salmon, scaled and
   cleaned
4 pints (*2.5 litres*) fish stock*
Whisky Sauce (see opposite)

For the garnish
10 large cooked peeled prawns
2 bunches parsley or watercress
5 lemons, halved

*large fish poacher or large roasting
tin, and some string*

1 If the salmon has been slit along the belly, fold the flaps under the fish and set the fish, belly down, on the poacher rack. Tie the fish in place and lower the rack into the poacher. Pour over the fish stock, adding more water if necessary to cover the salmon completely. Set the tin over two burners and heat over a medium flame until the liquid begins to simmer. Cover with the lid.

2 To calculate cooking time, measure the fish at its thickest part and allow 7 minutes per inch (nearly 3 minutes per centimetre) from the time the poaching liquid simmers. A quick-reading thermometer inserted at the thickest part should read 55°C/130°F.

3 Leave the salmon to cool in the liquid for 10 minutes. Lift up the rack and prop it on the poaching tin. Discard the string and peel the skin from the fish, leaving the head and tail intact. Remove small bones from along the backbone. The salmon can be prepared up to 30 minutes ahead.

4 *To finish.* Make the Whisky Sauce. To reheat the fish, bring the poaching liquid to a boil. Immerse the salmon for 5 minutes, then drain it well.

5 Transfer the salmon to a serving dish and keep it warm. Immerse the prawns in the hot poaching liquid for 1 minute. Drain and arrange them along the back of the fish. Arrange a border of parsley or watercress around the fish and decorate it with lemon halves. Serve the sauce separately.

Cook's Comment. The above method for timing the cooking of poached fish is strictly accurate. However, taking a less scientific approach, I have developed the following rule of thumb which I find works for any fish over 6lb (2.7kg). Bring the fish slowly to a boil, taking about 20 minutes. Let it simmer for 10 minutes, then leave it to cool for at least 15 minutes in the liquid. I leave you to make the choice.

Whisky Sauce

With a professional's nonchalance, La Varenne's Chef Chambrette invented this sauce to please the American clientele of his two-star Parisian restaurant, La Boule d'Or. Throwing the ingredients together as described is quite against the rules, but to my surprise it seems to work every time. Lemon juice can be substituted for the whisky.

MAKES 12fl. oz (375ml) SAUCE TO SERVE 8–10

6 egg yolks	2 tablespoons whisky or
3fl. oz (90ml) *crème fraîche** or	bourbon
double cream	4fl. oz (125ml) fish stock*
½lb (250g) cold butter, cut into	salt
cubes	pinch of cayenne

1 In a heavy saucepan, whisk the egg yolks with the *crème fraîche*, butter, whisky or bourbon and fish stock over a low heat until the sauce is thick enough to coat a spoon: about 5 minutes. (*Note:* The sauce will curdle if it gets too hot.) Take it from the heat and season with salt and cayenne.

2 The sauce can be kept warm in a tepid *bain marie** for up to 15 minutes.

Baked Fish Delaware

This recipe evolved in a beach house on the Atlantic coast of Delaware. Grand cooking was an impossibility after a sun-drunk day on the sand. Back home, I would slice any vegetables available, set one of the local fish on top with a shower of oil and seasoning, then sit back and leave everything to bake happily together. The fish we preferred was sea bass, caught that day and astonishingly cheap. Since then I have found that almost any big fish can be cooked this way, be it hake, cod, snapper, sea trout or salmon. In winter the vegetables can be varied with mushrooms, and in summer I often add aubergine or courgettes to the mix.

SERVES 6–8

6–8 tablespoons olive oil
2 onions, sliced
3 red peppers, cored, seeded
  and sliced
3 green peppers, cored, seeded
  and sliced
1lb (*500g*) tomatoes, peeled,
  seeded and chopped

8–10 sprigs fresh or 4–5
  teaspoons dried thyme
2 cloves garlic, crushed
salt and pepper
one 6–7lb (*3kg*) whole fish, or
  two 4lb (*1.8kg*) fish, scaled
  and cleaned
2 lemons

1 Heat the oven to Gas 5/190°C/375°F. In a large flameproof baking dish or roasting tin heat 2 tablespoons of oil and fry the onions until browned. Stir in the peppers, tomatoes, a sprig of fresh or ½ teaspoon of dried thyme, garlic, salt and pepper, and remove from the heat.

2 Wash the fish, trimming off the tail and fins but leaving the head intact. Pat it dry with paper towels. Score the flesh deeply with three or four slashes on each side so that it cooks evenly. Set the fish on top of the vegetables and tuck a sprig of fresh or a sprinkle of dried thyme into each slash. Spoon over the remaining oil and sprinkle with salt, pepper and the juice of 1 lemon. The fish can be prepared up to 3 hours ahead and kept in the refrigerator.

3 *To finish.* Heat oven to Gas 5/190°C/375°F. Bake the fish uncovered, basting occasionally, until it just flakes easily. Allow 35–45 minutes for a large fish, or 20–25 minutes for the smaller ones. Transfer the fish to a serving dish and keep it warm.

4 Cook the vegetables on top of the stove for 1–2 minutes, until they are very tender and all the liquid has evaporated. Spoon them around the fish and decorate it with the remaining lemon, cut into wedges.

Cook's Comment. To fit a big fish in the oven, don't be tempted to ruin its beauty by cutting off its head, but curve it instead in a semi-circle, tying head to tail with string if necessary.

Pickled Fish with Herb Butter

Just recently I returned to Japan, where I was baffled yet again by the complexities of such an alien cuisine. In the market at least half the dried and pickled fish were unrecognisable, while on the vegetable stand jars of pickles bemused my eye with the pink, acid-yellow and jade-green colours of a child's toy.

At the table, however, I began to observe parallels with French *nouvelle cuisine* – not just the much-touted emphasis on presentation, but also the penchant for a series of small 'tasting' portions. There is, too, the same close interface between chef and diner, with the chef cooking and chatting as his clients sit at a bar. As for cooking methods, marinating and steaming have become a Western as well as an Eastern passion, while this fish, lightly pickled with salt in Japanese style, is now also found on Western tables. I've added an occidental accompaniment of herb butter.

One oriental custom I wish the West would adopt is the use of chopsticks. Soft wood or bone chopsticks are much kinder to the tongue than our crude metallic implements.

SERVES 4

4 whole fish, weighing about 1lb (*500g*) each
1½oz (*45g*) coarse salt
For the herb butter
2½oz (*75g*) butter
2 tablespoons lemon juice
salt and pepper

1 tablespoon chopped fresh chives
1 tablespoon chopped fresh tarragon or basil
1 tablespoon chopped fresh parsley

1 Clean and scale the fish if necessary, removing the gills. Trim the fins and cut the tail to a 'V'. Wash them and dry on paper towels. Slash each side of the fish diagonally, almost to the bone, three or four times. Set the fish on a tray and sprinkle them on both sides with the coarse salt. Leave them in the refrigerator for 2–3 hours, turning occasionally.

2 *To make the herb butter.* Cream the butter and beat in the lemon juice, herbs, and salt and pepper to taste. Roll the mixture into a cylinder, wrap in foil and chill.

3 *To finish.* Heat the grill. Rinse the fish with cold water to remove all salt and dry them on paper towels. Grill them, without turning, just until the fish flakes easily: 16–20 minutes. Cut rounds of herb butter, set them on the fish and serve at once.

Cook's Comment. Salting adds an interesting flavour to all manner of fish. Bream or mullet are my top choice for this recipe, with red snapper, perch and pompano as runners-up. Half an hour suffices to pickle thin fillets and escalopes, and after the salt is rinsed away they can be grilled and served with herb butter or with a sprinkling of olive oil and fresh herbs.

Loup en Brioche

SEA BASS IN BRIOCHE

A gastronomic spectacular, this speciality of Paul Bocuse, the 'Emperor' and founder of the *nouvelle cuisine* movement, is much easier to prepare than it appears. A whole fish – sea bass or salmon for preference – is wrapped in brioche dough and decorated with eyes, a mouth, scales and a tail, as your fancy suggests. The brioche face takes on a distinctive personality: I've noticed that mine seem to acquire a somewhat raffish glint in the eye, with a sardonic smile.

SERVES 6–8

Brioche Dough (see page 27)
a 4–5lb (*about 2kg*) sea bass,
   scaled and cleaned
1–2 tablespoons vegetable oil
large *bouquet garni*

1 egg, beaten, to mix with
   ½ teaspoon salt (for glaze)
Red and White Butter Sauces
   (see opposite) (for serving)

1 Make the brioche dough and chill for at least 4 hours or overnight. Wash the fish inside and out, and dry thoroughly. Cut off the fins and trim the tail to a 'V'. Cut a paper pattern the same shape and a little larger than the bass. Butter a baking sheet.

2 Divide the dough in half. Roll out one half a little longer than the length of the fish and set this dough on the baking sheet. Brush the dough down the centre with oil and set the fish on top, lying on its side. Brush the top of the fish with more oil (this prevents the skin from sticking) and place the *bouquet garni* in the stomach. Trim dough, leaving a 1in (*2.5cm*) border. Brush border with glaze.

3 Add any dough trimmings to the rest of the dough and roll it out to the length of the fish. Cut a fish shape, using the paper pattern, and set the dough on top of the fish. Press the edges together to seal.

4 Brush the dough with egg glaze and decorate the fish with a mouth, eye and fins made from dough trimmings. Mark scales on the body by snipping with scissors or indenting with one side of a plain piping tube. Score the tail in lines. The fish can be kept overnight in the refrigerator, tightly covered with cling film, or frozen.

5 *To finish.* Let the dough rise at room temperature until slightly puffed: 30–40 minutes. Heat the oven to Gas 7/220°C/425°F. Bake in the oven for 10 minutes, reduce the heat to Gas 5/190°C/375°F and continue baking for 30–35 minutes longer or until a skewer inserted in the centre for 30 seconds is hot to the touch when withdrawn.

6 Transfer the fish to a large flat serving dish. At the table, cut around the edge of the brioche to loosen the crust and lift it off to disclose the fish. Serve a piece of brioche with each portion of fish, with Red and White Butter Sauces.

Cook's Comment. Tightly wrapping an ingredient for cooking, whether in pastry, bread dough or clay, retains its flavour to such a degree that this fish in brioche requires no seasoning other than a bunch of herbs. Far be it from me ever to advocate freezing raw fish, but this is one instance where it survives very well, protected by the brioche dough.

Sauces Beurre Blanc et Beurre Rouge

WHITE AND RED BUTTER SAUCES

During my cooking career, White Butter Sauce has risen from obscure origins in the Loire Valley to become a cornerstone of *nouvelle cuisine*. When I studied at the Cordon Bleu school in Paris nearly thirty years ago, it was not even in our curriculum. Friends asked me how to make it and took me to try it at Mère Michel near the Arc de Triomphe. (The restaurant is still there, and still specialises in *beurre blanc*.) At the time I would never have believed such a modest little recipe with so few ingredients could have so many possibilities. It is the milk solids (i.e. the whey in butter) which stabilise the sauce, taking the place of the egg yolk in hollandaise. In effect, the old chef's trick of adding a tablespoon of cream (more milk solids) to the wine-and-shallot reduction ensures that the mixture will not separate. Even so, the sauce can be kept warm – never hot! – for no more than half an hour. Serve White Butter Sauce, and its twin, Red Butter Sauce, with poached, baked and grilled fish and vegetables, as well as with terrines and fish in brioche (see opposite).

MAKES 8fl. oz (250ml) SAUCE TO SERVE 6–8

3 tablespoons white wine vinegar	1 tablespoon double cream
3 tablespoons dry white wine	8oz (*250g*) cold unsalted butter, cut into small pieces
2 shallots, very finely chopped	salt and white pepper

1 In a small heavy saucepan (not aluminium), boil the vinegar, wine and shallots until the liquid is reduced to 1 tablespoon. Add the cream and boil until reduced to 1 tablespoon. Gradually whisk in the butter, working on and off the heat so that the butter melts creamily and emulsifies to form a lightly thickened sauce. (*Note*: Do not let it melt to oil.)

2 Season the sauce with salt and pepper. It can be kept warm on a rack over a pan of warm water for up to 30 minutes.

Cook's Comment. For Red Butter Sauce, substitute 4fl. oz (*125ml*) red wine for the white wine vinegar and white wine. If the colour of the finished sauce is grey, whisk in a little tomato purée.

[55]

Sole en Goujons

DEEP FRIED STRIPS OF SOLE

This classic recipe is an interesting contrast to the previous recipe for *goujonettes*. Here *goujons* (a French term for 'little fish') are made of strips of sole, deep fried and served with piquant mayonnaise. I've eaten real *goujons* several times, but none are as good as my initiation to sole *en goujons* at the age of eleven, when on a birthday visit to London's Connaught Hotel. At least it seemed wonderful in 1949.

SERVES 6 AS A MAIN DISH, 10 AS A FIRST COURSE

2lb (*1kg*) sole fillets	Remoulade Sauce (see
fat or vegetable oil (for deep	opposite) (for serving)
frying)	*For the garnish*
6–8 tablespoons flour	bunch of parsley
salt and pepper	3 lemons, halved crosswise

1 Wash and dry the sole fillets and cut them into ½in (*1.5cm*) strips. Wash the parsley for the garnish, dry very thoroughly and tie with a long string.

2 Heat the deep fat to 180°C/350°F. Mix the flour with salt and pepper. Toss the fish strips in the seasoned flour until thoroughly coated. Fry the strips, a handful at a time, in the hot fat until they turn golden brown: 2–3 minutes. Lift them out and drain them on paper towels. Keep the fish warm in a low oven with the door open while frying the remaining strips.

3 Let the fat cool slightly, then add the parsley. (*Note*: Stand back as it will spit.) Fry for 10–15 seconds until it stops spluttering, then remove it. Detach the crisp sprigs, discarding the stems.

4 Pile the sole in a dish and sprinkle lightly with salt. Scatter fried parsley sprigs on top, decorate the edges with lemon halves and serve at once, passing the Remoulade Sauce separately.

Cook's Comment. Flounder or lemon sole are acceptable, if humdrum, alternatives to the real Dover sole.

Remoulade Sauce

MAYONNAISE WITH CAPERS, GHERKINS AND HERBS

The name 'remoulade' may come from the *remola* of Picardy – a piquant black radish. Serve remoulade with cold roast beef or chicken as well as with deep fried fish.

MAKES 16fl. oz (500ml) SAUCE TO SERVE 10

½ pint (*300ml*) mayonnaise
2 teaspoons Dijon mustard
3 tablespoons chopped gherkin
  pickles
2 tablespoons chopped capers
1 tablespoon chopped parsley

2 teaspoons chopped fresh
  chervil
2 teaspoons chopped fresh
  tarragon
salt and pepper

Mix all the ingredients and taste for seasoning. The sauce can be refrigerated for up to 2 days.

Seafood à La Minute

New-style cooking may have its faults, but its strengths are exemplified in the following two recipes. Both combine vegetables with fish and rely on fresh herbs for flavour. Each dish is quick to make, with a lively sauce cooked in the pan, and both recipes make an expensive fish go a long way.

Escalopes de Saumon à la Moutarde et à l'Estragon

SALMON ESCALOPES WITH MUSTARD AND TARRAGON

SERVES 6

1 large salmon fillet, weighing
   1½lb (750g)
1 carrot, cut into julienne strips
green of 1 leek, cut into
   julienne strips
salt and pepper
1 tablespoon butter

8fl. oz (250ml) double cream
2 teaspoons Dijon mustard, or
   to taste
2 tablespoons chopped fresh
   tarragon
tarragon sprigs (for decoration)

large non-stick frying pan

1 *To cut the escalopes.* With a long sharp knife, cut the salmon fillet into the largest possible diagonal slices, about ¼in (6mm) thick, working towards the tail and discarding skin.

2 *To cook the julienne.* Bring a pan of salted water to a boil, add the carrot and leek juliennes and boil until tender but still firm: 3–5 minutes. Drain, rinse with cold water and drain again thoroughly. The salmon and vegetables can be refrigerated for up to 4 hours.

3 Sprinkle the escalopes with salt and pepper. Heat a frying pan until hot, then brush it with the butter. Add as many escalopes as will fit in a single layer and cook until lightly browned: about 1 minute. Turn them and brown the other side. Remove from the pan and keep them hot while cooking the remaining escalopes in the same way.

4 Add the cream to the pan and bring it to a boil. Whisk in the mustard, salt and pepper. Add the julienned vegetables and heat gently for 2 minutes. Stir in the tarragon and taste the sauce for seasoning.

5 Arrange the escalopes on individual heated plates, allowing 2–3 per person. Spoon over enough sauce to cover the salmon partly and decorate with tarragon sprigs.

Cook's Comment. Any firm fish such as sea bass or swordfish can be cooked this way, though nothing quite replaces the colour of salmon.

Goujonettes de Sole au Fenouil et Basilic

STRIPS OF SOLE WITH FENNEL AND BASIL

SERVES 6 AS A MAIN DISH, 10 AS A FIRST COURSE

1oz (*30g*) butter
3 bulbs fennel, thinly sliced
salt and pepper
2lb (*1kg*) skinless sole fillets
fresh or dried noodles (see
 page 162)
8fl. oz (*250ml*) white wine

8fl. oz (*250ml*) *crème fraîche** or
 double cream
2oz (*60g*) bunch fresh basil,
 coarsely chopped
1oz (*30g*) bunch fresh chives, chopped
3 tomatoes, peeled, seeded and
 chopped*

1 Melt half the butter in a saucepan, add the fennel and season with salt and pepper. Press a piece of foil on top, cover with the lid and sweat until very tender: 20–25 minutes. (*Note*: Do not let the fennel brown.) Wash and dry the sole and cut it into ⅜in (*1cm*) strips. The fennel and sole can be refrigerated for up to 4 hours.

2 Cook the noodles. Reheat the fennel over a low heat. Melt the remaining butter in a frying pan. Sprinkle the sole with salt and pepper, add to the pan, cover and cook gently, stirring occasionally, until the fish stiffens and turns white without browning: 3–4 minutes. Lift it out with a draining spoon and keep it warm. Add the wine to the pan and boil until it has reduced to 2 tablespoons. Add the cream and boil for 2 minutes.

3 Stir the basil and chives into the sauce and taste for seasoning. Spoon a bed of noodles on to individual plates. Place the fennel on top and add the fish. Spoon over the sauce, sprinkle with the chopped tomatoes and serve at once.

Cook's Comment. I would suggest *goujonettes* of monkfish as a variation if I did not have a rooted dislike of its gristly texture. Excellent, if expensive, alternatives to sole are scallops or raw peeled prawns.

Kulebiak

SALMON WITH MUSHROOM DUXELLES AND RICE, IN PASTRY

'Kulebiak should be appetising, shameless in its nakedness, a temptation to sin,' wrote Anton Chekhov in *The Siren*. With its pastry made with sour cream, its salmon-and-mushroom filling and its traditional binding of rice pilaf, crêpes and dried sturgeon marrow, that seems a minimum requirement. Even this scaled-down version kulebiak would have lived up to Chekhov's expectations.

SERVES 10

2lb (*1kg*) skinless salmon fillets, cut into 8–10 pieces
1 egg, beaten, to mix with
 ½ teaspoon salt (for glaze)
4 hardboiled eggs, sliced
For the sour-cream pastry
1lb (*500g*) flour
6oz (*175g*) unsalted butter
2 teaspoons salt
2 eggs
5 tablespoons sour cream, or more if needed
For the rice pilaf
1oz (*30g*) butter
1 onion, chopped

6½oz (*200g*) long-grain rice
16fl. oz (*500ml*) fish stock*
salt and pepper
For the duxelles
1oz (*30g*) butter
1 onion, finely chopped
1lb (*500g*) mushrooms, finely chopped
salt and pepper
1 tablespoon chopped parsley
For serving
8fl. oz (*250ml*) White Butter Sauce (see page 55)
8fl. oz (*250ml*) butter, melted
8fl. oz (*250ml*) sour cream

1 Make sour-cream pastry dough as for *pâte brisée*,* substituting sour cream for water. Chill the dough for ½–1 hour. Heat the oven to Gas 4/175°C/350°F.

2 *For the rice pilaf.* Heat the butter in a casserole and fry the onion until soft but not brown. Stir in the rice and cook for 2–3 minutes, stirring constantly, until transparent. Add the stock, season with salt and pepper, cover and bring to a boil. Cook in the oven for 18 minutes or until all the stock has been absorbed. The rice should be tender but still firm. If it is still hard, continue cooking for a few minutes longer. Let it cool without stirring, then chill.

3 *For the duxelles.* Melt the butter in a frying pan and fry the onion until soft but not brown. Add the mushrooms and salt and pepper and cook, stirring occasionally, until all the liquid has evaporated and the mushroom purée is stiff: 10–15 minutes. Stir in the parsley and taste for seasoning. Let the *duxelles* mixture cool, then chill.

4 *To assemble the kulebiak.* Roll out the pastry dough to a 10 × 16in (*25 × 40cm*) rectangle. Arrange half the rice in a 3½ × 12in (*9 × 30cm*) strip in the centre. Set slices of hardboiled egg overlapping on the rice and top with the *duxelles* mixture. Set the salmon pieces neatly on the *duxelles* and top with the remaining rice. (*Note*: Do not allow the filling to spread at the sides.)

5 Cut a 2in (*5cm*) square from each corner of the dough and brush the edges with some of the egg glaze. Lift one long edge of dough over the filling and fold over the opposite side to enclose the filling completely. Fold up the ends to make a neat package. Roll the package on to a baking sheet so that the seams are underneath. Brush the kulebiak with egg glaze and chill it.

6 Roll out the pastry trimmings and cut long strips, using a fluted cutter if you like. Decorate the top of the kulebiak with crosswise strips of dough and press a long strip around the base to neaten it. Brush again with glaze. Make a hole in the centre of the kulebiak for steam to escape and add a 'chimney' of rolled foil. Chill the kulebiak for at least 30 minutes. Provided the pilaf and *duxelles* were completely cold when the kulebiak was assembled, it can be kept for 24 hours. It can also be frozen.

7 *To finish.* Heat the oven to Gas 6/200°C/400°F. Brush the kulebiak again with glaze and bake until the pastry is lightly browned: about 15 minutes. Reduce the heat to Gas 4/175°C/350°F and continue baking for 30–40 minutes, until a skewer inserted in the centre of the kulebiak is hot to the touch when withdrawn after 30 seconds. If the pastry dough begins to brown too much, cover it loosely with foil.

8 To serve, transfer the kulebiak to a flat serving dish. Let it stand for 5–10 minutes before cutting into 1in (*2.5cm*) slices for serving. Serve White Butter Sauce, melted butter and sour cream separately.

Cook's Comment. Combining fish and vegetables in one spectacular slice, kulebiak is the perfect party dish – a fact appreciated by the *nouvelle* maestros who produce bastardised 'light' versions. I've even had one filled entirely with vegetables. Ugh!

Creamed Cod
with Mushrooms and Oysters

Baby cod (weighing up to 2½lb (1.1kg)) is known in the USA as 'scrod' and is the subject of raunchy humour. No American food journalist writes with such stylistic flair – and thorough knowledge – as Craig Claiborne, king of New York food critics, so I'll pass on this story in his own words:

'A man arrives in Boston on a first visit. All his life he has hungered for Boston scrod. He goes to a restaurant, glances at the menu, and tells the waitress "I'd like an order of Boston scrod, please."

' "Sorry, sir, I just sold the last order."

'He leaves the restaurant and goes to a fish house across the street, looks at the menu there and tells the waitress, "I'd like an order of Boston scrod, please."

' "Sorry, sir, we're out of Boston scrod."

'He departs, goes to the curb and hails a cab. "Is there any place in Boston," he asks the driver, "where a man can get scrod?"

'The driver stares at him a moment and says, "Mister, I been driving a hack in this town 30 years, but you're the first person I ever heard ask for it in the pluperfect past tense." '

SERVES 6

2lb (1kg) cod, haddock, hake or
  other white fish steaks
2 shallots, finely chopped
3–4 tablespoons white wine
salt and pepper
1oz (30g) butter
¾lb (375g) mushrooms, thinly
  sliced
juice of ½ lemon
12 shelled oysters, with their
  liquor

For the béchamel sauce
1 pint (600ml) milk
1 slice onion
*bouquet garni**
5 peppercorns
3oz (90g) butter
1½oz (45g) flour
4–5 tablespoons double cream
To finish
3–4 tablespoons browned
  breadcrumbs
1 tablespoon melted butter

1 Heat the oven to Gas 4/175°C/350°F. Set the fish steaks in a buttered baking dish and sprinkle with the shallots, wine, salt and pepper, and dot with half the butter. Cover loosely with buttered foil and bake in the oven until the fish just flakes easily: 15–20 minutes. Allow to cool, then flake the fish, discarding skin and bones. Strain the cooking liquid and reserve it.

2 Put the mushrooms in a pan with the remaining butter, the lemon juice and the liquid from cooking the fish. Cover and cook until the mushrooms are just tender: 3–4 minutes. Drain, and reserve the liquid, adding the mushrooms to the fish.

3 Put the oysters and their liquor in a saucepan and heat gently just until their edges curl: 1–2 minutes. Drain, reserving the liquor, and add the oysters to the fish.

4 *For the béchamel sauce.* Scald the milk with the onion, *bouquet garni* and peppercorns, cover and leave to infuse for 10–15 minutes. In a large saucepan melt the butter, stir in the flour and cook until foaming. Remove from the heat and strain in the milk. Whisk until mixed, then bring to a boil, whisking constantly until the sauce thickens. Simmer for 2 minutes.

5 Stir the fish liquid and oyster liquor into the sauce and taste for seasoning. Add the cream and continue simmering, stirring occasionally, until the sauce coats a spoon quite thickly: 5–10 minutes. Taste the sauce for seasoning.

6 Add the sauce to the fish mixture and stir gently to mix. (*Note*: Sauce for coating fish should always be quite thick to compensate for liquid in the fish.) Pour into a shallow buttered baking dish and sprinkle with the breadcrumbs and melted butter. The fish can be kept for a day in the refrigerator, or frozen.

7 *To finish.* Heat the oven to Gas 4/175°C/350°F and bake the fish until hot and browned: 25–35 minutes.

Cook's Comment. With a border of piped Pommes Duchesse (see page 135), this dish achieves dinner-party status. Covered with a layer of sliced tomatoes and topped with mashed potatoes, it becomes plain fish pie. Mussels can be substituted for oysters in the recipe; steam them open in the usual way.*

Turbot en Meurette

TURBOT IN RED WINE SAUCE WITH MUSHROOMS, ONIONS AND BACON

'They say Fish should swim thrice . . . first it should swim in the Sea . . . then it should swim in Butter; and at last, Sirrah, it should swim in good Claret' (Jonathan Swift, *Polite Conversation*). Burgundians heartily agree that a swim in red wine is an honourable end for a fine fish, though they would favour a local vintage rather than a claret from Bordeaux. Burgundian *meurette* sauce, served with both fish and poached eggs, is a rich reduction of red wine, onions, mushrooms and bacon, needing a robust fish such as brill, halibut, or salmon.

SERVES 8 AS A FIRST COURSE, 4–6 AS A MAIN DISH

3lb (*1.4kg*) skinless turbot fillets
2 cloves garlic, peeled
3 shallots, thinly sliced
1 bottle red Burgundy wine
1 pint (*600ml*) fish stock*
*bouquet garni**
2oz (*60g*) kneaded butter*
salt and pepper
pinch of sugar (optional)

For the garnish
½lb (*250g*) piece streaky bacon,
  cut into lardons*
1oz (*30g*) butter
20–25 baby onions, peeled
½lb (*250g*) mushrooms, quartered
triangular *croûtes** made with
  8 slices white bread
1 tablespoon chopped parsley

1 Wash the fish, pat dry with paper towels and cut into 8–12 even-sized pieces. Butter a flameproof baking dish, sprinkle with garlic and shallots and lay the fish on top. Add the wine, stock and *bouquet garni*. Cover with foil and poach on top of the stove until the fish just flakes easily: 6–8 minutes. Lift out the fish and reserve it.

2 Meanwhile cook the garnish. Fry the bacon in half the butter until browned, then drain on paper towels. Add the onions, sprinkle with salt and pepper and cook until tender and browned: 10–15 minutes. Remove them, add the remaining butter with the mushrooms, more salt and pepper, and sauté them until tender. Add to the bacon and onions. Fry the *croûtes*, let them cool and wrap them in foil.

3 Boil the fish cooking liquid until reduced to about 1¼ pints (*750ml*), then strain it into a pan. Whisk in the kneaded butter. Add the mushrooms, onions and bacon, simmer the sauce for 5–6 minutes, season with salt and pepper, and taste, adding a little sugar if the sauce seems sharp. The sauce should be highly seasoned. The fish and sauce can be kept for up to 8 hours in the refrigerator.

4 *To finish.* Bring the sauce to a boil on top of the stove. Cover the fish and heat it in a very low oven for 10–15 minutes. Warm the *croûtes* in the foil. Arrange the fish on individual warm plates or on a large dish, and spoon over the sauce. Dip a point of each *croûte* in sauce, then parsley and add to side of dish.

Cook's Comment. To give an idea of the power packed by *meurette* sauce, chefs often pep it up even further with a teaspoon of meat glaze.

Soufflé de Saumon Ali-Bab

SALMON SOUFFLE ALI-BAB

When I'm looking for new ideas, I often turn to Henri Babinski (alias Ali-Bab), a mining engineer who as early as 1912 wrote his own brilliant *Livre de Cuisine*. Sandwiched between stodgy classics, Ali-Bab inserts new-style ideas like flourless sauces and fruit garnishes for meat at least fifty years before their time. He flavours lamb with fresh pineapple (try it!) and potato salad with Château Yquem.

This salmon soufflé, using only three ingredients, could hardly be simpler. When I first read the recipe I was sure it wouldn't work. The base is a classic *mousseline* purée, which I've never heard of used in a soufflé. But iconoclast Ali-Bab delivers yet again, and the soufflé is consistently delicious, firm but delicate.

SERVES 8

1lb (*500g*) skinless salmon
   fillets, cut into pieces
6 egg whites
½ pint (*300ml*) double cream
salt and pepper

White Butter Sauce (see
   page 55) or Sauce Nantua
   (see page 67)

eight 4fl. oz (125ml) ramekins

1 Purée the salmon in a food processor for 2 minutes. Whisk two of the egg whites until frothy and work them gradually into the salmon. With the machine on, add the cream a spoonful at a time. Scrape the mixture into a bowl, set it over ice, and beat in salt and pepper to taste. The mixture of salmon and egg white can also be prepared, a little at a time, in a blender; the cream should be beaten in over ice with the seasonings.

2 Heat the oven to Gas 4/175°C/350°F and butter the ramekins. Bring a *bain marie** to a boil on top of the stove. Stiffly whip the remaining egg whites.

3 Thoroughly mix about a quarter of the egg whites into the soufflé mixture. Add this mixture to the remaining egg whites and fold together as lightly as possible. Spoon into the prepared ramekins and set them in the *bain marie*. Bring to a boil again, then bake in the oven until firm, 12–15 minutes. The soufflés can be refrigerated for up to 24 hours. Make Nantua Sauce, if serving this.

4 *To finish.* Reheat the soufflés in a *bain marie* on top of the stove. Make the White Butter Sauce or reheat the Nantua Sauce. Unmould the soufflés on to individual plates, spoon over the sauce and serve at once.

Cook's Comment. This recipe is also excellent with white fish such as sole or turbot, when it is best served with Red Butter Sauce (see page 55).

Quenelles Nantua

FISH DUMPLINGS WITH CRAYFISH SAUCE

Pike is the traditional fish for *quenelles*, mainly because it contains so many bones that puréeing is a good way to deal with it. However it also has to be sieved to remove the bones, so I prefer to use any fine-textured white fish with plenty of flavour, such as whiting, hake, lemon sole or flounder. If you suspect that the fillets have been frozen, add an extra egg white to hold the *quenelles* together. Although a couple of preparations – fish stock and choux pastry – are involved, don't be discouraged by the length of the recipe. The actual making of the *quenelles* and sauce is shorter than you would think, provided you possess a food processor.

SERVES 6–8 AS A MAIN DISH, 12 AS A FIRST COURSE

4lb (*1.8kg*) whole white fish
6–7 egg whites
pinch of grated nutmeg
salt and pepper
16fl. oz (*500ml*) *crème fraîche** or
   double cream
Nantua Sauce (see opposite)

crayfish or prawns from Sauce Nantua
For the choux pastry
4fl. oz (*125ml*) water
½ teaspoon salt
1½oz (*45g*) unsalted butter
2½oz (*75g*) flour
2 eggs

1 Clean the fish if necessary, then fillet it and remove the skin from the fillets. Wash the fillets, dry and reserve them; there should be 2lb (*1kg*). Use the fish heads and bones to make fish stock for the Nantua Sauce (see opposite). Make the choux pastry.*

2 *To make the quenelles.* Purée the fish in a food processor. Puréeing constantly, gradually add the egg whites and season with nutmeg, salt and pepper. Work in the choux pastry, a little at a time. Finally work in the cream, a spoonful at a time. Transfer the mixture to a bowl and chill for at least 15 minutes in the freezer or over ice, stirring occasionally. Taste the mixture for seasoning. If it seems soft, continue chilling until it stiffens.

3 *To poach the quenelles.* Bring a large shallow pan of salted water to a simmer. Using two tablespoons dipped in the water, shape an oval of *quenelle* mixture and drop it in the water. If the *quenelles* start to break up, beat another egg white into the mixture and continue chilling for 15 minutes longer. Shape the remaining mixture into ovals, drop them into simmering water and poach until they are firm: 10–15 minutes, depending on size. Drain them on paper towels. *Quenelles* can be tightly covered and refrigerated for up to 2 days, or frozen. Make the Nantua Sauce.

4 *To finish.* Arrange the *quenelles* in individual buttered heatproof dishes or on one large dish. Add crayfish or prawn tails and coat completely with sauce. Heat oven to Gas 5/190°C/375°F. Bake *quenelles* until browned and slightly puffed: 10–15 minutes. Serve them very hot.

[66]

Cook's Comment. Surely it is indicative of British cooking that there is no word for *quenelle* other than the prosaic 'fish dumpling'. And it is equally typical of French perfectionism that there is only one correct way to cook *quenelles* – with crayfish from Nantua or, at a scholastic pinch, with prawns of lesser pedigree. Certainly no other sauce packs the necessary richness and intensity of flavour.

Sauce Nantua

CRAYFISH SAUCE

MAKES 1⅔ PINTS (1 LITRE) SAUCE TO SERVE 8

6oz (*175g*) butter
1 onion, finely chopped
1 carrot, finely chopped
2lb (*1kg*) raw crayfish or large
   prawns, preferably with heads
2 tablespoons brandy, or more
   if needed
4fl. oz (*125ml*) white wine

1⅔ pints (*1 litre*) fish stock*
*bouquet garni**
1½oz (*45g*) flour
16fl. oz (*500ml*) *crème fraîche** or
   double cream
1 teaspoon tomato purée (optional)
pinch of cayenne
salt and pepper

1 Melt a quarter of the butter in a large shallow pan and sauté the onion and carrot until soft. Add the crayfish or prawns and sauté, tossing, over a high heat until they turn red: about 2 minutes. Add the brandy and flame. Add the white wine, fish stock, *bouquet garni*, salt and pepper. Simmer for 8–10 minutes. Remove the shellfish and shell them, discarding the intestinal vein and reserving the tail meat.

2 Work the shells in a food processor, with a little liquid from the pan, until finely chopped. Return them to the pan and simmer for 10 minutes longer. Strain, pressing hard on the shells and vegetables to extract all the liquid.

3 Melt all but 3 tablespoons of the remaining butter in a saucepan, whisk in the flour and cook until foaming but not browned. Whisk in the shellfish liquid and bring the sauce to a boil, whisking constantly until the sauce thickens. Simmer for 10–15 minutes or until the sauce just coats a spoon. Add the cream and bring just back to a boil. If the sauce is pale, stir in a little tomato purée.

4 Nantua Sauce can be refrigerated for up to 2 days. Reheat it on top of the stove. Stir in the remaining butter in small pieces, add cayenne and season the sauce to taste, adding a little more brandy if you like.

SHELLFISH

Memory is an odd thing. We lived for seven years near Dieppe, home of the little salty 'moules de bouchot' (bouchots are the poles on which they are grown), the very best mussels in the world. Yet the mussel dish I remember most clearly – giant stuffed mussels – is Belgian. To me Dieppe means mounds of nutty little grey shrimps, some still wiggling their tails, and scallops, sold by the dozen in the shell by weather-beaten market women clad in ancient greatcoats and outsize rubber boots. I had to clean the molluscs myself, but at the price I couldn't complain.

So many shellfish experiences are hard to repeat – yabbies (crayfish) and Balmain Bay bugs (a relative of lobster) in Australia; tiny Olympia oysters in Portland, Oregon; giant crabs swimming in nets off the bows of a Hong Kong junk. Crabs take me back to my childhood and summer visits to Scarborough on the Yorkshire coast. On the sea front, booths were set up like a Punch and Judy show where you could buy shrimps, winkles and giant boiled crabs which would be dressed to order before your eyes. Are they still there, I wonder?

As for lobster, all the three-star delicacies I have enjoyed cannot erase the memory of a torrid August day in Boston when the price of New England lobster was so low we splurged on monsters weighing 2lb apiece, eating them on the back porch with melted butter and a bottle of Meursault. Every country has a royal food which is better and cheaper than anywhere else: for my tastes it is lobster in the United States, raspberries in Scotland and cheese in France.

Moules Farcies Bruxelloise

STUFFED MUSSELS WITH TOMATOES, GARLIC AND CHEESE

Just off the Grande Place in Brussels lies a cobbled street with a group of the best eating houses in Belgium. I say 'eating houses', for the style is rough, the windows steamy and the fare limited to crêpes and mussels, cooked in a dozen styles. But what mussels! Order them *à la marinière* and they come in a huge casserole, just for one person. When stuffed, as in the recipe that follows, a whole tray arrives carpeted with two dozen big fat Spanish mussels ('Spanish' refers to the variety, perhaps a throwback to the days of the Spanish Netherlands). Even the crêpes are memorable, with thin rings of apple trapped in batter and coated with caramel, of a succulence I've never quite managed to copy.

SERVES 6–8 AS A FIRST COURSE

3lb (*1.4kg*) large mussels,
  cleaned*
4fl. oz (*125ml*) white wine
1½oz (*45g*) butter
1 onion, finely chopped
3 cloves garlic, finely chopped
1lb (*500g*) tomatoes, peeled,
  seeded and chopped*

sprig of fresh thyme or
  ½ teaspoon dried thyme
salt and pepper
For the topping
2oz (*60g*) grated Gruyère cheese
2 tablespoons melted butter

*4 heatproof dishes or trays, filled
with rock salt*

1 Put the mussels in a large pan with the wine. Cover and cook over a high heat for 4–5 minutes or until the mussels open, stirring them once. Drain the mussels. Discard the top shell from each mussel and remove the rubbery ring around each. Discard any mussels which have not opened.

2 Melt the butter in a sauté pan or deep frying pan and fry the onion until soft but not brown. Add the garlic, tomatoes, thyme, salt and pepper, and simmer, stirring often, until the mixture is thick: 10–15 minutes. Discard the thyme sprig, if using, and season the mixture.

3 Spoon a little of the tomato mixture over each mussel and set them flat in the rock salt, packing them as close as possible. Sprinkle them with the grated cheese and melted butter. The mussels can be refrigerated for up to 6 hours.

4 *To finish.* Heat the grill. Grill the mussels as close to the heat as possible for 2–3 minutes or until browned.

Cook's Comment. Serve the mussels piping hot with plenty of French bread.

Baked Oysters in Herb Butter

When we have a special dinner in Washington, we enlist the services of a butler of the old school. Portly, smiling Clay Wilson sets the atmosphere just as much as my husband and I do. In his black or cream tuxedo (depending on the season) and crêpe-soled shoes, Clay recalls a more leisured era of servants and stately southern charm. He freelances at the 'Moonie' paper, the *Washington Times*, and at the White House, regaling us with anecdotes about the nobs. Best of all, Clay delights in cooking. He and I exchange recipes and I find myself challenged to try a new dish each time he is serving dinner. He tarts up fish with turnip roses and roast meat with forests of lettuce; once he carved us a whale from an aubergine. This recipe is a combined effort, with Clay enlivening my baked oysters with just the right touch of pepper and vinegar.

SERVES 4–6 AS A FIRST COURSE

20–24 medium shelled oysters, drained
3oz (90g) butter
4 shallots, finely chopped
2 cloves garlic, finely chopped
2 tablespoons chopped parsley
1 tablespoon chopped fresh chives

1 tablespoon chopped fresh tarragon
salt and pepper
French bread, pepper and vinegar (for serving)

4–6 ramekins (8fl. oz (250ml) capacity each)

1 Divide the oysters among the ramekins. In a small pan, melt the butter, add the shallots and cook until soft: 2 minutes. Allow to cool, then add the garlic, parsley, chives, tarragon and a little salt and pepper. Spoon the herbed butter over the oysters and cover tightly with foil. They can be refrigerated for up to 6 hours.

2 *To finish.* Heat the oven to Gas 7/220°C/425°F. Bake the oysters just until the edges curl: 12–14 minutes. Serve at once, leaving guests to remove the foil at table. Serve with pepper and vinegar as seasonings, and French bread to sop up the juices.

Cook's Comment. Quick to cook and even quicker to prepare, I only wish more fish could be cooked this way. Clams are pleasantly salty, while scallops produce a sweet juice which is just asking to be mopped up with lots of crusty French bread.

Coquilles Saint-Jacques à la Parisienne

SCALLOPS WITH MUSHROOMS, WHITE WINE AND CREAM

I'm often asked whether La Varenne in Paris is like the London Cordon Bleu. Led by its founder, Rosemary Hume, the Cordon Bleu did wonders for the standard of French cooking in England – in homes, directors' dining rooms and restaurants. However, the British idea of French cooking is still, I think, a shadow of the real thing. My first exam at the London Cordon Bleu in 1961 included Scallops Parisienne – such a handy classic, calling for the fish to be delicately cooked in a nicely thickened sauce with a neat border of piped potato. But not until I reached Paris and an everyday café near Les Halles market did I learn what Scallops Parisienne could really taste like – great chunks of sweet meat, brilliant coral, a few shrimps thrown in with the mushrooms for good measure, all in a perfumed creamy sauce. Unhappily, soon after my arrival in France, Scallops Parisienne dropped out of sight, submerged in a wave of scallops with lime, ginger, green peppercorns or fruit vinegar, sometimes all at once. So how glad I am now to see signs of its revival, complete with the traditional border of Pommes Duchesse (see page 135).

SERVES 6 AS A MAIN DISH, 10 AS A FIRST COURSE

2lb (*1kg*) shelled scallops
1 pint (*600ml*) fish stock*
8fl. oz (*250ml*) white wine
¾lb (*375g*) mushrooms, quartered
juice of ½ lemon, or more to taste
salt and pepper
For the sauce
2oz (*60g*) butter
1 shallot, finely chopped
1oz (*30g*) flour

6fl. oz (*175ml*) *crème fraîche** or double cream
For the garnish
Pommes Duchesse (see page 135)
2 tablespoons browned breadcrumbs
2 tablespoons melted butter

10–12 scallop shells or individual baking dishes; pastry bag and large star tube

1 *To cook the scallops.* Discard the crescent-shaped muscle from each scallop and cut large scallops horizontally in half. Put them into a pan with the fish stock and wine, cover and poach for 2–3 minutes, just until the scallops whiten. (*Note:* Do not overcook scallops or they will be tough.) Let them cool slightly, then remove them with a slotted spoon. Boil the stock until it is reduced to about 1 pint (*600ml*) and reserve.

2 *To cook the mushrooms.* Put the mushrooms into a pan with the juice of half the lemon, salt, pepper and ¼in (*6mm*) of water. Cover and cook over a high heat until tender: 4–5 minutes. Drain them and add them to the scallops, reserving the liquid.

3 Butter the scallop shells or baking dishes. Make the Pommes Duchesse and pipe them in a border around the shells.

4 *For the sauce.* Melt the butter in a saucepan and cook the shallot until soft but not brown. Stir in the flour and cook until foaming. Whisk in the reserved fish stock and mushroom liquid and bring to a boil, whisking constantly until the sauce thickens. Taste for seasoning and continue simmering, stirring occasionally, until the sauce lightly coats a spoon: 5–10 minutes. Add the cream and simmer again until the sauce reaches coating consistency. Season to taste with more lemon juice, salt and pepper.

5 Stir the mushrooms and scallops into the sauce and spoon the mixture inside the potato bordering each individual shell. Sprinkle with breadcrumbs and melted butter. The scallops can be refrigerated for up to a day, or frozen.

6 *To finish.* Heat the oven to Gas 6/200°C/400°F. Set the shells or dishes on a baking sheet and bake until the scallops are very hot and browned: 10–15 minutes.

Cook's Comment. Some recipes suggest slicing both scallops and mushrooms, but I prefer to leave them in juicy chunks.

Fricassée de Coquilles Saint-Jacques au Safran

FRICASSEE OF SCALLOPS WITH SAFFRON

The main ingredients for this recipe are essentially the same as for Coquilles Saint-Jacques Parisienne, but the approach is by no means the same. Here the sauce is an archetypal *nouvelle* reduction of cooking juices mounted with cream and butter, quite different from the traditional flour-based sauce, though no less rich. As well as flavouring the scallops, the saffron dyes them a vivid buttercup yellow.

SERVES 4–6 AS A MAIN DISH, 8 AS A FIRST COURSE

6oz (*175g*) mushrooms, cut into
   julienne strips
juice of ½ lemon
salt and pepper
1 tablespoon butter
2lb (*1kg*) shelled scallops
large pinch of saffron threads,
   soaked in 2–3 tablespoons
   boiling water

For the sauce
1 shallot, finely chopped
2 tablespoons dry vermouth
2 tablespoons white wine
½ pint (*300ml*) *crème fraîche** or
   double cream
small pinch saffron threads (if
   necessary)
3oz (*90g*) cold butter

1 *To cook the mushrooms.* Put the mushrooms in a buttered pan with the lemon juice, salt and pepper, and press a piece of buttered foil on top. Cover with the lid and cook gently until the mushrooms are tender: 4–5 minutes.

2 *To cook the scallops.* Melt the butter in a frying pan, add the scallops and pour over the saffron and liquid. Cover and cook very gently just until the scallops whiten: 3–5 minutes. (*Note*: Do not overcook the scallops or they will be tough.) Lift them out with a draining spoon.

3 *For the sauce.* Add any cooking juices from the mushrooms to the scallop liquid with the shallot, vermouth and wine. Boil until reduced to a glaze.* Whisk in the cream, add any liquid produced by the scallops and boil for 5–7 minutes or until reduced by about a third. Taste, adding more saffron if necessary.

4 Take the pan from the heat and gradually whisk in the cold butter, working on and off the heat so that it melts and thickens the sauce creamily. When all the butter is added, bring the sauce just to a boil. (*Note*: The high proportion of cream prevents the sauce from separating.) Add the scallops and mushrooms to the sauce, heat gently for 1–2 minutes and spoon the mixture on to individual warm plates.

Cook's Comment. The scallops can be kept warm in a *bain marie** for 15 minutes or so, but as they stand they tend to toughen and the saffron will lose the force of its perfume.

In the late 1970s, at the height of the *nouvelle cuisine* movement, this dish would undoubtedly have been served with a garnish of little vegetables – turned carrots, green beans, mangetouts. Lately, however, pasta has become the popular companion for a rich sauce like this.

Crab and Corn Fritters

In these Indonesian fritters, crab and ground coriander form a background seasoning to fresh corn, cut from the cob. The fritters make an unusual cocktail hors-d'œuvre or first course, and can accompany grilled fish and poultry dishes.

MAKES ABOUT FORTY-EIGHT 2in (5cm) FRITTERS

6 ears fresh corn	3 eggs, beaten to mix
1 medium onion, grated	2oz (60g) crab meat
2 tablespoons chopped fresh coriander leaves	1½oz (45g) flour
1 teaspoon ground coriander	salt and pepper
2 cloves garlic, crushed	4–5 tablespoons peanut oil (for frying)

1 Cut the kernels from the corn with a sharp knife, and scrape out any additional milk from the cob with the back of the knife. Mix the kernels with the onion, fresh and ground coriander, garlic, eggs, crab meat, flour, and salt and pepper to taste. Cover the batter and refrigerate for at least an hour, and up to 12 hours.

2 *To fry the fritters.* Heat a tablespoon of oil in a frying pan and drop in tablespoonfuls of batter to form 2in (5cm) rounds. Fry briskly until brown – about 2 minutes – then turn and brown the other side. (*Note:* Stand back, as the kernels may burst during frying.)

3 Keep the fritters warm in a low oven with the door open while frying the rest in the remaining batter, and serve as soon as possible.

Cook's Comment. It is interesting how the addition of a single exotic seasoning like coriander gives such character to this dish.

Seafood Gumbo

SHELLFISH STEW WITH OKRA AND TOMATOES

A good Trivia question for cooks is, 'Where is Acadia and why is it important?' The answer is it is the home of Cajun (rhymes with the Emperor Trajan) cooking – the cooking of the Mississippi delta around New Orleans. The region was settled in the time of George III by French speakers expelled from Nova Scotia, then known as Acadia in loose imitation of a native Indian place-name.

Famous for its spice, Cajun cooking has recently been in the forefront of the regional cuisine movement in the USA. One reason may be Chef Paul Prudhomme, a colourful figure as famous for his massive girth as for his food. A good introduction to Cajun cooking is provided by 'gumbo', local dialect for the okra which gives this stew a special gelatinous texture. It is thickened with Cajun 'roux' – a deep-brown mixture of fat and flour roasted for 20–30 minutes until it bears but little resemblance to the classic French preparation of the same name.

SERVES 10

For the dark roux
5fl. oz (*150ml*) vegetable oil
4oz (*125g*) flour
1 large onion, chopped
2–3 cloves garlic, chopped
1lb (*500g*) tomatoes, peeled, seeded and chopped*
1½lb (*750g*) fresh or tinned okra, sliced
3¼ pints (*2 litres*) hot water
1 tablespoon salt, or more to taste
large bay leaf
pinch of dried thyme

1 teaspoon whole allspice
½ teaspoon dried chillis or ground hot red pepper, or more to taste
2lb (*1kg*) raw prawns, peeled
1lb (*500g*) crab meat, from the claws
20 medium shelled oysters, with liquid
6 spring onions, sliced
7–8 tablespoons chopped parsley
long-grain rice (for serving)

1 *For the dark Cajun roux.* Heat the oil in a heavy casserole, stir in the flour and cook very gently, stirring occasionally, over a medium heat until the flour toasts very brown: 20–30 minutes. Alternatively, the roux can be toasted in a hot oven: Gas 8/230°C/450°F. (*Note*: Do not allow it to scorch.)

2 Add the onion and garlic and cook slowly until soft but not brown. Add the tomatoes and cook over a low heat, stirring occasionally, until the liquid has evaporated and the oil begins to separate: 20–25 minutes.

3 Add the okra, water and salt. Tie the bay leaf, thyme, allspice and chilli or hot red pepper in a piece of muslin or cheesecloth and add to the mixture. Partly cover with a lid and simmer, stirring occasionally, for 45 minutes. (*Note*: The okra will give the mixture a characteristic slightly glutinous consistency.) Discard the muslin bag of spices and taste the gumbo mixture for seasoning. The gumbo can be refrigerated for up to 3 days, and the flavour will mellow with keeping.

4 *To finish*. Boil the rice and keep it warm. Bring the gumbo to a boil. Add the prawns and simmer for 15 minutes. Add the crab meat and simmer for 15 minutes more. Finally, add the oysters and simmer for a further 5 minutes. Taste for seasoning, adding more salt, pepper or spice as needed.

5 Remove from the heat and stir in the spring onions and parsley. Serve in shallow soup bowls, spooned over the boiled rice.

Cook's Comment. This gumbo can also be made with chicken and spiced with hot sausages.

Julia Child's Lobster Stew

Julia Child first came to dinner at our house twenty years ago. Already her reputation as America's television chef was formidable, but her action in putting us at our ease was typical. Sighting a pâté on the table, she declared, 'My that looks good,' and cut herself a slice. Since then we have shared kitchens as far afield as Boston, Santa Barbara, Provence and Venice, and occasionally cooked together on the screen. Julia has been a decisive influence, part expert consultant, part friend, in the development of La Varenne in Paris. Last time we had dinner with Julia she was testing lobster stew while I whisked up a Yorkshire pudding for the roast beef. As always, we sat around the table in the kitchen, sipping Lillet or sparkling wine cocktails composed by her husband Paul. A pile of the latest cookbooks was stacked on the sideboard. Was the current crop up to last year's standards? Who was likely to win a *Tastemaker* award? Was it really true that Paul Bocuse had smuggled five kilos of fresh *foie gras* into the USA by the simple expedient of declaring half a pound to distract the customs? The cast-iron stove shed an encouraging warmth and from time to time one of us would baste the meat to a tantalising sizzle and waft of steam. Julia has a talent for combining the very best of good things, and not just on the plate.

SERVES 6 AS A FIRST COURSE OR A LIGHT MAIN COURSE

two 1¼lb (*625g*) boiled female
  lobsters (see opposite)
4oz (*125g*) butter
salt and pepper
2⅓ pints (*1.5 litres*) single cream

six ⅜in (*1cm*) thick slices chilled
  unsalted butter (for garnish)
white or wholewheat toast (for
  serving)

1 *To extract lobster meat.* Twist off the lobster claws. Twist off the legs and discard them (or eat them!). With kitchen scissors, cut open the claws and joints, extracting the meat with a pick. (If necessary, crack large claws with a mallet.) Set the lobster body on a board, hard shell downwards, and split it in half lengthwise with a large knife. Scoop out body meat, greenish liver (tomalley) and red coral, and reserve. Discard the membrane sac from the head. Pull the tail meat from the lobsters. Cut six thin crosswise slices and reserve for garnish. Cut the rest into small chunks.

2 Melt half the butter in a large sauté pan or shallow saucepan and sauté the tomalley and coral over a moderate heat for several minutes until it turns reddish brown. Add the remaining butter and the lobster chunks and cook, stirring gently, for 7–8 minutes. The meat will take on a salmon-pink blush. Season lightly with salt and pepper.

3 Meanwhile, warm the cream. Over a low heat gradually stir the warm cream into the lobster mixture a tablespoonful at a time so that it absorbs the butter and juices and thickens slightly to a smooth mixture. When all the cream has been added, remove from the heat and season the stew to taste. Let it cool, then refrigerate it for at least 24 hours, or up to 3 days, so that the flavours mellow.

4 *To finish.* Heat the stew slowly, almost to a boil. (*Note*: If it boils it will separate.) Take from the heat and divide the lobster meat among six warm bowls. Spoon the soup on top. Float a slice of chilled butter topped by a slice of lobster on each bowl and serve at once, with toast served separately.

Cook's Comment. Restaurateurs, a wily lot, tend to corner the hen lobster market to get hold of the coral which gives such colour to sauces and soups like this one. Do not be outwitted, but look underneath the lobster: at the joint between tail and body are two inch-long 'swimmerets'. In a female lobster they are feathery; in a male they are stiff.

To Cook Lobsters

Says Julia Child: 'Find a heavy kettle with a close-fitting lid, set a rack or colander in it and add 1–2in water. When it's boiling furiously, add the lobsters; weigh down the cover to keep in the steam; just as it starts to escape, lower heat slightly and set your time (12 minutes for a 1¼lb (625g) lobster). Is it done? Pull off a little side leg and eat it – if it's done, the lobster's done. *Bon appetit*!'

Maryland Crab Cakes

Crab cakes are one of the few instances where I approve of the American habit of adding a seemingly random selection of herbs and spices to a dish. Maryland Crab Cakes are not authentic without them. In contrast to British fish cakes, held together with potato, these crab cakes are light textured provided by bread soaked in milk.

European visitors to the East Coast have often admired American seafood – not only Maryland Crab Cakes, but also Maine lobsters, softshell crabs and terrapin from the Chesapeake Bay, and pompano from New Orleans. The great nineteenth-century restaurant emporium for all these delights was Delmonico's in New York. According to Oscar Wilde, 'the two most remarkable bits of scenery in the States are undoubtedly Delmonico's and the Yosemite Valley, and the former has done more to promote a good feeling between England and America than anything else has in this century.'

MAKES 16 CAKES TO SERVE 8 AS A MAIN COURSE

4 slices white bread, crusts removed
8fl. oz (250ml) milk
2lb (1kg) crab meat
2 tablespoons mayonnaise
½ teaspoon dry mustard
½ teaspoon celery salt
½ teaspoon paprika
2 teaspoons baking powder
2 tablespoons chopped parsley
½ teaspoon Worcestershire sauce
juice of ½ lemon
salt and pepper
2 eggs, beaten to mix
3–4 tablespoons lard or butter (for frying)
mayonnaise or Remoulade Sauce (see page 57) (for serving)

1 Put the bread in a bowl, pour the milk over and leave to soak for 15 minutes. Squeeze the bread fairly dry, transfer it to a large bowl and break it into crumbs with two forks.

2 Add the crab meat, mayonnaise, mustard, celery salt, paprika, baking powder and parsley, and stir until well mixed. Blend in the Worcestershire sauce, lemon juice, salt and pepper, and taste for seasoning. Stir in the beaten eggs. The mixture can be refrigerated for up to 6 hours.

3 *To finish.* Divide the mixture into sixteen parts and lightly pat it into cakes about 1in (2.5cm) thick. (*Note:* Work gently so that the cakes are light.) In a large frying pan heat half the lard or butter and fry half the cakes over a brisk heat until golden: about 2 minutes. Turn and brown the other side. Fry the remaining cakes in the rest of the lard and serve as soon as possible, with mayonnaise or Remoulade Sauce.

Cook's Comment. Crab cakes are often accompanied by hot vegetables, though I prefer them with a salad. Best of all, perhaps, is a crab cake sandwiched in a bun.

Paëlla

Paëlla takes me back to early married life in the late 1960s in Washington DC, with motley weekend gatherings where we drank Bloody Marys or sangria made with a hearty Burgundy from California. Paëlla was a dish of the decade. It had just enough of the exotic – saffron, chorizo, squid, mussels – to offer a challenge, with a familiar background of chicken and rice to reassure. What is more, it called for a special but inexpensive pan and could be cooked on the backyard barbecue. Real food of the most rewarding kind, paëlla is more than due for a revival.

SERVES 10

2½fl. oz (75ml) olive oil
3lb (1.4kg) chicken thighs or legs
salt and pepper
3 onions, chopped
1 green and 1 red pepper, cored,
 seeded and cut into strips
1½lb (750g) long-grain rice
2⅓ pints (1.5 litres) chicken
 stock or water, or more if
 needed
large pinch of saffron threads,
 soaked in a cup of boiling water

1lb (500g) cleaned squid, sliced
1lb (500g) strips raw smoked ham
1lb (500g) chorizo sausage, sliced
1½lb (750g) tomatoes, peeled,
 seeded and chopped*
1lb (500g) cod or haddock
 fillets, cut into strips
1½lb (750g) raw unpeeled prawns
3lb (1.4kg) mussels or clams, cleaned*

*20in (45cm) paëlla pan or shallow
 flameproof casserole*

1 Heat half the oil in the pan, season the chicken pieces with salt and pepper and brown them on all sides over a medium heat, taking 10–12 minutes, so that they are half cooked. Set the chicken aside, add the remaining oil and cook the onions and peppers until soft but not brown. Add the rice and cook, stirring, until the grains are transparent and the oil is absorbed. Add the stock or water, saffron, salt and pepper. Add the remaining ingredients (except the mussels or clams) in layers, in the following order: browned chicken, squid, smoked ham, chorizo, tomatoes, fish and prawns. Paëlla can be refrigerated for up to 2 hours provided that the stock or water was cool when the other ingredients were added.

2 *To finish.* Bring the liquid to a boil and boil fairly rapidly on top of the stove or on an outdoor barbecue for 25–30 minutes, until all the liquid has been absorbed and the rice is tender. Stir from time to time, especially when the paëlla starts cooking, and add more stock or water if the liquid evaporates before the rice is cooked. After 10 minutes' cooking, set the mussels or clams on top of the paëlla. Keep the paëlla warm over a very low heat for 5–10 minutes so that the flavours mellow before serving.

Cook's Comment. Like an omelette pan, a paëlla pan needs thorough seasoning if the rice is not to stick. Well-proved paëlla pans are treasures, no matter how grubby and dented. Good paëlla should include a broad range of ingredients, but this recipe can be simplified by reducing the range of fish. Be sure to serve with Spanish wine.

POULTRY

In my lifetime chicken must have changed more than any other ingredient. I can just remember when live birds were rural currency, bartered on market day in my home town of Northallerton. They were carried upside down in pairs, tied by the feet and squawking wildly, their beady eyes on the swivel. The raising of poultry was always a woman's domaine. Great was the wonder when a local entrepreneur gutted a stately mansion and turned it into one of the first battery chicken farms.

Within ten years chicken had become commonplace. Reading the first post-war cookbooks, it is important to remember that chicken was still a luxury and a Sunday treat; plump, white and expensive, the breast was truly the 'suprême'. Perhaps the first major British publication to exploit the potential of the battery bird, with its bland, tender, cheap meat was *The Cordon Bleu Cookery Course*, first published in 1969. In the USA the revolution took place earlier – and subsequently went to the extremes of Colonel Sanders and chicken McNuggets. There, alas, it has stayed.

In France, consumers showed some resistance to the mass-produced hen – and still do. There you can still routinely find three grades of chicken: battery, farm-raised, and expensive, red-labelled aristocrats raised and fed under strictly controlled conditions. Poulterers still sell the full range, from infant chicks of six weeks to tough old cocks who have seen it all. In shop windows by late autumn, geese jostle turkeys and game birds in full plumage, with perhaps a deer or a wild boar (curiously, game is the preserve of the poulterer in France).

But all is not lost in the USA. The magic words 'free range' guarantee a 50 per cent increase in price, whether or not it is justified by the bird's lifestyle. In fact, the bounty of offerings is growing, thanks to mail-order food companies. Mail-order, I surmise, is the gourmet trend of the future – your butcher, poulterer, game purveyor, all on the doorstep via catalogue, courtesy of overnight delivery.

Three Chicken Sautés

To use an American expression, a sauté is neat, so neat that I'm giving three recipes for it. The first advantage is that almost any flavouring ingredient – vegetables, wine, herbs, spices – can go into a sauté. This is the place to use up the tomato languishing on the window sill and the wine left over from last night. If you like garlic, go ahead and double the stated amount – experiment is the name of the game.

Another plus is that even with a supermarket chicken, the dish will have plenty of taste. Neutered young things of 2½–3½lb (1.1–1.6kg) are bound to be bland, but they appear at their best in a sauté where the cooking juices are deliberately concentrated to make a small quantity of highly flavoured sauce.

Finally, this method uses my very favourite kitchen utensil: a sauté pan. With its wide base and shallow sides, a sauté pan can double as a frying pan or casserole. It goes on top of the stove or in the oven. There are cheap aluminium models and Rolls-Royce copper ones with shiny brass handles to grace the table as well as the stove. And it appeals to my sense of order that they commonly come in a one-chicken – 10in (25cm) – and two-chicken – 12in (30cm) – size, allowing room for all the pieces of chicken to sit on the bottom of the pan in direct contact with the heat.

This Chicken Angevine recipe should be made with Muscadet wine from Anjou. You can use a different wine, of course, but in that case 'Angevine' is no longer the correct nomenclature.

Sauté de Poulet Angevine

SAUTE OF CHICKEN WITH MUSHROOMS, ONIONS AND MUSCADET WINE

SERVES 4

a 3–3½lb (about 1.5kg) chicken,
  cut into 4 pieces*
salt and pepper
1oz (30g) butter
1 tablespoon vegetable oil
18–20 baby onions, peeled
½lb (250g) mushrooms,
  quartered
2 shallots, chopped

4fl. oz (125ml) white Muscadet
Pommes Darfin (see page 160)
  (for serving)
4fl. oz (125ml) crème fraîche* or
  double cream
1 tablespoon chopped parsley
  (for sprinkling)

10in (25cm) sauté pan or deep
  frying pan

1 Sprinkle the chicken pieces with salt and pepper. Heat the butter and oil in the sauté pan and add the chicken, skin side down, starting with the legs because they need the longest cooking. When they are beginning to brown, add the two breast pieces. Sauté until very brown – 5–10 minutes – then turn and brown the other side.

[84]

2 Take out the chicken, add the onions and cook over a high heat until browned, shaking the pan so that they colour evenly. Remove them from the pan and reserve. Add the mushrooms to the pan, brown them, then remove and set them aside with the onions.

3 Add the shallots to the pan and cook for 1 minute. Replace all the chicken and pour over the wine. Cover and cook over a low heat until the chicken is very tender when pierced with a two-pronged fork: 20–30 minutes. If some pieces cook before others, remove them. Make the Pommes Darfin.

4 Take out the chicken pieces. If necessary, boil the pan juices until reduced to a glaze.* Skim the fat from the pan, add the cream and bring to a boil, stirring to dissolve the juices. Stir in the onions and mushrooms, heat gently for 2–3 minutes and taste the sauce for seasoning. Return the chicken pieces to the pan. The chicken can be refrigerated for up to 2 days; undercook it slightly to allow for reheating.

5 *To finish*. Reheat the chicken and Pommes Darfin over a low heat on top of the stove. Unmould the potatoes on to a round serving dish and arrange the chicken around the edge. Spoon the sauce and garnish over the chicken and sprinkle with parsley, leaving the golden potatoes uncovered.

Cook's Comment. I'm particularly fond of the French habit of serving fried potatoes with any dish which has a light sauce. Here the potatoes are cut into julienne strips and crisply fried in butter.

Sauté de Poulet à l'Hongroise

SAUTE OF CHICKEN WITH PAPRIKA AND SOUR CREAM

SERVES 4

2 red peppers, quartered and
  cored, or 3 bottled pimentos,
  drained
a 3–3½lb (about 1.5kg) chicken,
  cut into 4 pieces*
2 tablespoons sweet paprika
2 tablespoons lard or vegetable oil
1 onion, chopped
salt and pepper

8fl. oz (250ml) chicken stock,*
  or more if needed
1 tablespoon flour
4fl. oz (125ml) sour cream
Fresh Noodles (see page 162)
  (for serving)

*10in (25cm) sauté pan or deep
frying pan*

1 If using fresh peppers, light the grill. Brush the grill with oil and add the peppers, skin side up, and grill them for 8–12 minutes until the skin is charred and blistered. Cover the peppers with a wet cloth and leave them to cool. Peel them and cut them into thin strips. Cut the bottled pimentos into thin strips too. Roll the chicken pieces in the paprika until thoroughly coated.

2 Heat the lard or oil in the sauté pan. Add the chicken legs, skin side down, and sauté until beginning to brown. Add the breast pieces, and continue cooking until very brown: 10–15 minutes. Turn and brown the other side. (*Note*: Cook the chicken gently so that it browns without scorching the paprika.)

3 Remove the chicken, add the onion and sauté until soft but not brown. Return the chicken to the pan, sprinkle with salt and pepper and pour over half the stock. Cover and simmer for 10–15 minutes. Add the fresh roasted peppers (bottled pimentos, if substituted, are added later). Continue simmering, covered, until the chicken is tender when pierced with a two-pronged fork: 10–15 minutes more. Add more stock during cooking if the pan seems dry. If some pieces cook before others, remove them.

4 Remove the chicken and peppers from the pan. Boil the pan juices to a glaze* and skim off all but a tablespoon of fat. Stir in the flour and cook for 1 minute. Add the remaining stock and bring to a boil, stirring until the sauce thickens. Return the chicken and peppers to the pan; if using bottled pimentos, add them now. Heat for 2–3 minutes and taste the sauce for seasoning. The chicken can be refrigerated for up to 2 days; undercook it slightly to allow for reheating.

5 *To finish.* Reheat the chicken gently on top of the stove. Add the sour cream, and shake the pan so that the cream mixes and marbles the sauce. (*Note*: Do not boil or the sour cream will curdle.) Serve in the pan or on a serving dish with plain noodles.

Cook's Comment. The classic sauté of veal paprika is cooked just like chicken, substituting about 2lb (1kg) veal, cut into 2in (5cm) cubes. The veal will take about 1¼–1½ hours, and you should keep the pan moistened with stock during cooking.

Sauté de Poulet à la Marinière

SAUTE OF CHICKEN WITH CLAMS AND SAMPHIRE

Before you turn the page because clams and samphire don't come from round the corner, be assured that mussels can be substituted for clams, while green beans are a look-alike for the seaweed called samphire.

SERVES 4

a 3–3½lb (about 1.5kg) chicken, cut into 4 pieces*
3–4 tablespoons flour, seasoned with salt and pepper
1oz (30g) butter
1 tablespoon vegetable oil
12oz (375g) samphire
2 tablespoons white wine
2 tablespoons dry vermouth
12 hardshell clams, cleaned*

4fl. oz (125ml) chicken stock, or more if needed
1 tablespoon arrowroot mixed to a paste with 3 tablespoons water*
1 tablespoon chopped fresh chives
salt and pepper
boiled rice (for serving)

10in (25cm) sauté pan

1 Sprinkle the chicken pieces with seasoned flour, patting them until thoroughly coated. Heat the butter and oil in the sauté pan and add the chicken legs, skin side down. When they begin to brown, add the breast pieces and continue cooking for 10–15 minutes until very well browned. Turn and brown the other side. Cook the samphire in boiling salted water until just tender: 3–4 minutes. Drain and rinse.

2 Add the wine and vermouth to the chicken. Cover and cook until the chicken is almost tender when pierced with a two-pronged fork: 20–25 minutes. If some pieces cook before others, remove them. The chicken and samphire can be refrigerated for up to 2 days; undercook the chicken slightly to allow for reheating.

3 To finish. Set the clams on top of the chicken, cover and cook until the clams open: about 5 minutes. Remove the chicken and clams from the pan and keep them warm. Discard any fat from the pan, add the chicken stock and bring to a boil, stirring to dissolve the juices. Whisk in enough of the arrowroot paste to thicken the sauce so that it lightly coats a spoon. Stir in the chives, then add the chicken, clams and samphire, and heat very gently for 2–3 minutes. Season with salt and pepper. Serve on individual warm plates or in a serving dish, on a bed of boiled rice.

Cook's Comment. We first came across pleasantly salty samphire in Normandy, where a late summer crop grows wild and is sold for a song in fish shops. If you go for the mussel–green bean option, cook the mussels just like clams, and boil the green beans in salted water until just tender.

Poularde en Cocotte Jurassienne

CHICKEN EN COCOTTE WITH MORELS AND WHITE WINE

This dish reaches perfection in the Jura, which borders the town of Bresse from where the aristocrats of French chickens come. A boiling fowl is best for this recipe. Aged nine months or more, a fowl needs long simmering rather than roasting, and yields a superior sauce. The Jura is also the home of fresh morels and *vin jaune* (yellow wine), a potent dry white wine which is aged at least six years in the barrel, acquiring a taste of sherry, quite unlike any other. For cooking, the flavour can be reproduced by adding a little sherry to dry white wine.

SERVES 6

a 5lb (*2.3kg*) boiling fowl or
    roasting chicken, with the
    giblets
salt and pepper
2 pints (*1.25 litres*) chicken
    stock*
16fl. oz (*500ml*) white Jura
    wine, or dry white wine with
    2 tablespoons dry sherry
1 onion, sliced
1 carrot, sliced

*bouquet garni**
rice pilaf (for serving)
For the sauce
8oz (*250g*) fresh morels or
    1oz (*30g*) dried morel
    mushrooms
16fl. oz (*500ml*) *crème fraîche** or
    double cream
salt and pepper
2oz (*60g*) butter
1oz (*30g*) flour

trussing needle and string

1 Trim the stems of fresh morels, rinse them thoroughly in several changes of water, then drain them. Pour hot water over the dried morels and leave them to soak for 30 minutes. Drain them and strain the soaking liquid through muslin or cheesecloth to remove sand. Reserve the soaking liquid. Rinse the dried morels thoroughly to wash sand from the cracks.

2 Sprinkle the chicken inside with salt and pepper and truss it.* Put the bird into a large pan or casserole with its liver and giblets, the stock, liquid from the dried morels, wine, onion, carrot, and *bouquet garni*. If needed, add enough water to cover the bird. Cover the pan and simmer until the chicken juices run clear when the thigh is pierced with a skewer: about 1½–2 hours for a boiling fowl or 1–1¼ hours for a roasting chicken.

3 When the chicken is cooked, lift it out and cover it with foil to keep it warm. Skim any fat from the cooking liquid and boil, skimming occasionally, until the liquid is reduced to 1 pint (*600ml*) – this may take up to 45 minutes.

[88]

4 *For the sauce.* Simmer the morels in the cream with a little salt and pepper for 5–10 minutes. Melt the butter in a saucepan, stir in the flour and cook until foaming. Strain in the reduced stock and bring to a boil, whisking until the sauce thickens. Add the morels and cream and continue simmering the sauce until it lightly coats a spoon: 5–10 minutes. Taste for seasoning.

5 Discard the trussing strings from the chicken, place it in a clean pan and pour over the sauce. It can be kept for up to 2 days in the refrigerator, or frozen. Reheat it very gently on top of the stove and serve it in the pan. Rice pilaf is the best accompaniment.

Cook's Comment. Dried morels are expensive, but even a small quantity gives an intense flavour that many people prefer to canned truffles.

Dejaj Macfool Ma Matisha

MOROCCAN CHICKEN BAKED WITH VEGETABLES, CINNAMON AND SAFFRON

I spent New Year's Day of 1963 tossing on the Mediterranean, travelling fourth class in a cargo boat from Marseilles to Oran. Supine on the top bunk, I watched the cockroaches run races within inches of my face. For once in my life, I could not think of food. When finally we reached the Algerian shore and made our way to Tlemcen, a mecca for mosque mavens, we found ourselves in a lost land struggling with its independence. Traffic islands guided non-existent cars, shop-window displays gathered the dust, and the hotels were almost deserted. Once in Morocco, however, life looked up, including the cooking. We ate incomparable oranges, tried a rather greasy *mechoui* (baked lamb), and regaled ourselves on *bistaela* (leafy pastry with pigeon and cinnamon), all washed down with pints of sweet mint tea.

Finding recipes for these treats back in France proved difficult, for in those days the Western romance with exotic cuisines was barely underway. However, in due course my husband – who has a great nose for rare books, particularly cookbooks – tracked down a little book of *Moorish Recipes* written in 1954 by the Marquis of Bute, which is full of perceptive comments on recipe origins and styles of dining. Dishes 'usually one at a time, but not always so', are set in the centre of the table, he says. Food is picked up with fingers and sauce sopped up with bread. 'No utensils are used for eating, with the exception that spoons are sometimes provided for kuskus or some sweet dish, but individual plates are never used.' He closes with a recipe for locust bread, baked from the eggs of the female. 'Those who wish to enjoy this dish should be careful not to let an opportunity pass, as these little beasts make their visitation to the North of Morocco, at least, every nine years only. The last swarm occurred in Tangier in A.D. 1947 (the year of the Hegira 1367).' The ingredients for his other recipes are more commonly obtainable!

SERVES 3–4

a 3–3½lb (*about 1.5kg*) chicken,
   cut into 4 pieces*
2 long pieces cinnamon stick
6 onions (4 sliced, 2 chopped)
1lb (*500g*) tomatoes, peeled,
   seeded and cut into large
   pieces*

large pinch saffron soaked in
   3–4 tablespoons boiling water
8fl. oz (*250ml*) olive oil
1 teaspoon salt
½ teaspoon ground pepper
½ teaspoon ground ginger
3 tablespoons chopped parsley

tajine or other earthenware pot

1 Heat the oven to Gas 4/175°C/350°F. Set the chicken in the pot with the cinnamon stick, cover with the sliced onions and top with the tomatoes. Mix the chopped onion, saffron and liquid, olive oil, salt, pepper, ginger and parsley and spoon over the chicken. Cover and bake until the chicken is very tender: about 1½ hours.

2 Discard the cinnamon sticks and taste the sauce for seasoning. The chicken can be refrigerated for up to 3 days, or frozen. Reheat it in a Gas 4/175°C/350°F oven for 20–30 minutes and serve in the tajine with Green Bean, Black Bean and Chick Pea Salad.

Cook's Comment. How spoiled we are! Bute warns that the average Moroccan chicken weighs under 1lb, yet must be cooked for 1½ hours or more.

Salade aux Haricots et Pois Chiches

GREEN BEAN, BLACK BEAN AND CHICK PEA SALAD

SERVES 8–10

6oz (175g) black beans or red
   kidney beans, soaked
   overnight and drained
6oz (175g) chick peas, soaked
   overnight and drained
2 onions, each stuck with a clove
6fl. oz (175ml) vinaigrette
   dressing* made with red
   wine vinegar, olive oil and
   strong, grainy mustard

2 bouquets garnis*
½lb (250g) green beans, cut into
   1in (2.5cm) lengths
salt and pepper
1 red onion, chopped
2 cloves garlic, chopped
small bunch of radishes,
   trimmed and diced
3 tablespoons chopped parsley

1 Put the black or red beans and chick peas into separate saucepans, each with an onion, *bouquet garni*, and water to cover generously. Cover and simmer until very tender, adding more water as it is absorbed. Allow 1–2 hours for the beans, depending on type, and 1–2 hours for the chick peas. When cooked, drain them and, while still hot, mix each with 4–5 tablespoons of the vinaigrette.

2 Cook the green beans in boiling salted water until just tender: 2–3 minutes. Drain them, rinse with cold water and drain thoroughly. The vegetables can be prepared ahead and refrigerated for up to 24 hours.

3 Not more than 2 hours before serving, mix the black beans, chick peas, green beans, red onion, garlic, radishes and parsley with the remaining dressing. Season with salt and pepper to taste. Serve the salad at room temperature.

Cook's Comment. Any dried beans can be used for this salad, though black or red ones make a good colour contrast.

Ayam Panggang Besengek

INDONESIAN GRILLED CHICKEN IN COCONUT SAUCE

Indonesia is not only a land of temples, tea plantations and rice, I discovered on a trip to the Far East, but also an archipelago of extraordinarily good food. The tropical climate, tempered by high mountains, leads to an abundance of ingredients, and the ethnic mix of Malay, Melanesian, Chinese, Japanese, Arab and Indian, overlaid with colonial Dutch, produces spicy, exuberant dishes of great originality, all served with rice as the famous *rijstafel*: 'rice table', an Indonesian speciality that includes a big bowl of rice and a large variety of small dishes to accompany it. *Rijstafel* is more of a Dutch invention than a native of the East Indies, but is none the worse for that.

Sometimes it is fun to play tourist, as at the Oasis Restaurant in Djakarta, an old colonial mansion where you are served by 'twelve lovely Indonesian maidens', watched over by a robed madame with the most splendid long dark hair I have ever seen. Dish follows dish in dizzy succession, but I managed to extract the few which are scattered through this book. They are enough to assemble a modest *rijstafel*, including Crab and Corn Fritters (see page 75), Lamb Saté with Peanut Sauce (see pages 126–27), and Indonesian Vegetable Salad (see page 186). You might like to add fried banana, chutney, perhaps a cooling mixture of grated cucumber with yoghurt and mint, and *krupuk* (shrimp crisps).

SERVES 8

4 shallots, cut into 2–3 pieces	two 2½–3lb (*about 1.3kg*)
3 cloves garlic, cut into 2–3 pieces	chickens, each cut into 8 pieces*
8 macadamia nuts or 16	Toasted Coconut with Peanuts
blanched almonds	(see opposite)
2 teaspoons chilli powder	boiled rice (for serving)
2 teaspoons turmeric	*For the coconut milk*
1 teaspoon ground coriander	1⅔ pints (*1 litre*) boiling water
2 blades fresh lemon grass, or	1lb (*500g*) grated fresh coconut
the pared rind of 1 lemon	or unsweetened shredded
4 tablespoons peanut oil	coconut (see Cook's Comment)

1 *For the coconut milk.* Pour the boiling water over the grated or shredded coconut and leave until cool. Purée in a blender or food processor and then strain, pressing to extract all the liquid from the pulp. Discard the pulp.

2 In a food processor or blender, purée the shallots, garlic, macadamia nuts or almonds, chilli powder, turmeric, coriander and lemon grass or lemon rind.

3 Heat the peanut oil in a frying pan and fry the shallot mixture over a low heat for 1–2 minutes, stirring constantly. Add half the chicken pieces and cook gently until a deep yellow on all sides. Remove the chicken and cook the remaining pieces in the same way.

[92]

4 Stir the coconut milk into the pan, return all the chicken, cover and simmer, stirring occasionally, until the chicken is tender when pierced with a two-pronged fork: 15–20 minutes. Remove the chicken and reserve the sauce. The chicken and sauce can be refrigerated for up to 2 days.

5 *To finish.* Heat the grill or light a barbecue. Grill the chicken pieces close to the heat until well browned: about 5 minutes on each side. Bring the sauce to a rolling boil and cook until it thickens slightly: 3–5 minutes. Serve the chicken on a large dish, with the sauce, Toasted Coconut with Peanuts, and boiled rice served separately.

Cook's Comment. All sorts of outlandish ideas are offered for opening a coconut, from baking it in the oven to dropping it from a lofty balcony. The following method, however, works like a charm. When choosing the coconut, shake it to be sure it contains liquid. With an ice pick or awl, pierce two of the 'eyes' and drain off the liquid (this tastes quite different from 'milk' made from the coconut flesh). With the dull edge of a cleaver or heavy knife, tap the coconut about a third of the way down from the eyes, turning the nut slowly. Eventually you should hear a faint cracking sound, an indication that you've found the nut's fault-line. Continue tapping until the nut falls into two pieces. Pull out the coconut meat and pare off the brown skin. Grate the meat in a food processor or on a coarse grater.

Serundeng

TOASTED COCONUT WITH PEANUTS

Indonesian this may be, but it is also excellent with Indian curries.

MAKES 2 CUPS OF COCONUT MIXTURE TO SERVE 8

1 tablespoon peanut oil	1 tablespoon brown sugar
1 onion, finely chopped	1 tablespoon ground coriander
2 cloves garlic, finely chopped	1 tablespoon lemon juice
6oz (*175g*) grated fresh coconut or	1 tablespoon Indonesian soy
shredded unsweetened coconut	sauce or dark soy sauce
(see Cook's Comment above)	6oz (*175g*) unsalted peanuts, toasted

1 Heat the oven to Gas 4/175°C/350°F. Heat the peanut oil in a frying pan and fry the onion and garlic until lightly browned. In a bowl stir together the coconut, brown sugar, coriander, lemon juice, soy sauce and the fried onions and garlic.

2 Spread the mixture on a baking tray and toast in the oven until brown, stirring occasionally: 15–20 minutes. On a separate tray, bake the peanuts for 5 minutes to freshen them. Mix the coconut and peanuts, and leave to cool.

3 The mixture can be stored in an air-tight container for up to 2 weeks. If it has been prepared more than 3 days ahead, dry for 5–10 minutes in a low oven before serving.

Poussins en Cocotte au Citron

BABY CHICKENS EN COCOTTE BAKED WITH LEMON

Have you ever tried the New York custom of twisting lemon peel over a cup of expresso coffee and watching the oil spread over the surface? The zest is so strong it perfumes coffee, with none of the acidity of lemon juice. In the same way, lemon oil flavours this dish quite differently from lemon juice. A variant is suggested by an Italian friend who is accustomed to regarding Parmesan cheese as a seasoning. Cut the lemon down to a strip or two and, when the chickens are cooked, leave a tablespoon of fat in the pan with the glaze. Stir in a couple of tablespoons of grated Parmesan before adding the cream.

SERVES 4

four baby chickens or two
   2½–3lb (*about 1.3kg*) chickens
salt and pepper
1oz (*30g*) butter
1 tablespoon vegetable oil

pared rind of 2 lemons
½ pint (*300ml*) *crème fraîche** or
   double cream

trussing needle and string

1 Heat the oven to Gas 7/220°C/425°F. Sprinkle the chickens inside with salt and pepper and truss them.* Heat the butter and oil in a casserole, add the chickens and brown them thoroughly on all sides: 10–15 minutes. Add the lemon rind, cover and cook in the oven until the juice poured from the centre of the chickens runs clear, not pink. Allow 15–20 minutes for small birds and 20–25 minutes for large ones. The chickens can be refrigerated for up to 3 days; undercook them slightly to allow for reheating. Warm them in a Gas 4/175°C/350°F oven.

2 *To finish.* Remove the chickens from the casserole and keep them warm. Boil the cooking juices until reduced to a glaze* and discard all fat. Add the cream and boil, stirring to dissolve the pan juices. Strain the sauce into a small pan, bring just back to a boil and taste for seasoning.

3 Discard the trussing strings from chickens and leave the birds whole if they are small. If large, cut them in half.* Set the chickens on individual warm plates, spoon over the sauce and serve with boiled pasta.

Cook's Comment. Fattened baby chickens or poussins of about 1lb, small enough to be an individual serving, are a rare treat in any country. In the USA, a rather clammy crossbreed called a Cornish hen can be substituted, while in France little '*coquelets*' come in a size to serve one person.

Canard Rôti Normande

ROAST DUCK WITH SAUTEED APPLES

When our Norman friend Françoise, famous for her Cheese Soufflé (see page 42), comes on her yearly visit to Burgundy, she always brings with her a home-grown duck. In her honour I like to serve it with apples flamed in Calvados, the ubiquitous Normandy pick-me-up. The earthy kick in a glass of even the roughest Calvados mellows when it is flamed with veal chops, chicken, kidneys, or these caramelised apples.

SERVES 4

two 3½lb (1.5kg) ducks, with
   the giblets
salt and pepper
2 tablespoons Calvados
8fl. oz (250ml) chicken stock*
4fl. oz (125ml) crème fraîche,* or
   more chicken stock

2oz (60g) butter
6 tart apples, peeled, cored and sliced
3–4 tablespoons sugar
3–4 tablespoons Calvados

trussing needle and string

1 Sprinkle the inside of the ducks with salt and pepper and truss them,* trimming excess fat and skin. They can be refrigerated for up to 24 hours.

2 *To roast the ducks.* Heat the oven to Gas 10/260°C/500°F. Sprinkle the ducks with salt and pepper and set them on their backs in a roasting pan. Roast until starting to brown: about 25 minutes. Turn them on to their breasts and add the giblets, reserving the liver. Lower the oven heat to Gas 4/175°C/350°F and continue roasting for 20 minutes longer. Discard the fat from the pan, turn the ducks on to their backs and continue roasting until they are very tender and the skin is crisp: 15–25 minutes longer. The juices from inside the bird should run clear, not pink. Keep ducks warm.

3 Meanwhile, cook the apples. Melt half the butter in a frying pan, add half the apples and sprinkle with a tablespoon of sugar. Turn them, sprinkle with more sugar and fry briskly until caramelised and tender, turning them so that they brown evenly: 3–5 minutes. Remove them and repeat with the remaining butter, apples and sugar.

4 *For the gravy.* If necessary, boil the pan juices until reduced to a glaze.* Discard the fat from the pan. Chop the duck livers, add to the pan and cook for 1 minute. Add the 2 tablespoons of Calvados and flame. Add the stock and boil for 2–3 minutes, stirring to dissolve the juices. Strain the gravy into a small pan, add the cream or more stock and bring just to a boil. Taste the gravy for seasoning. Meanwhile, warm the apples over a low heat. Add the 3–4 tablespoons of Calvados to the apples and flame. Discard the trussing strings and cut the ducks in half.* Arrange the pieces on individual warm plates, or overlap them on a serving dish. Arrange the apples beside the duck and spoon over a little gravy, serving the rest separately.

Cook's Comment. For frying, you will need an apple which holds its shape.

Roast Duck with Prune Stuffing

In the world of grand French restaurants, duck means the three-star Tour d'Argent in Paris and evokes the memory of *maître d'hôtel* Frédéric, who made a legend of his massive silver duck press. Even today the rich and famous who flock to the fifth floor of 15 Quai Tournelle, splendidly situated across the river from Notre Dame, tend to go for this piece of gastronomic theatre and order *'canard pressé'*. At the top of the culinary tree, performance and presentation count as much as the cuisine.

As with all theatres, what goes on backstage can be very different. It was with much amusement that I was regaled with this backstage vignette from another three-star food temple in the French provinces. Monsieur and Madame, the proprietors, were standing side by side in proud review of their dining room on a Sunday afternoon. With even more satisfaction, Monsieur was surreptitiously gazing down the ample *décolletage* of a well-endowed female client. An inspiration for a new recipe, perhaps . . . would tomorrow's escalope be best *sautée, grillée* or *au vapeur*? A sharp elbow in his ribs recalled him: *'T'a fini, cochon?'* As the French say, you may desert rural life, but you never desert its habits.

I don't believe in trying to recreate three-star cuisine at home – this duck stuffed with prunes is more my style.

SERVES 8

two 5lb (*2.3kg*) ducks, with the
  giblets
salt and pepper
8fl. oz (*250ml*) white wine
8fl. oz (*250ml*) chicken stock*
bunch of watercress (for
  garnish)
For the prune stuffing
1lb (*500g*) stoned prunes

1 onion, chopped
1 tablespoon butter
1lb (*500g*) ground pork, half fat,
  half lean
salt and pepper
liver from the duck, chopped
3–4 tablespoons chopped
  parsley

trussing needle and string

1 *For the prune stuffing.* Soak the prunes in hot water until soft: about 1 hour. Drain and coarsely chop them. In a frying pan, fry the onion in the butter until soft but not brown. Add the ground pork, season with salt and pepper and cook, stirring, until the meat is no longer pink: about 5 minutes. Add the chopped duck liver and continue cooking for 1 minute. Remove from the heat, stir in the chopped prunes and the parsley, and taste for seasoning. Let the stuffing cool thoroughly. It can be refrigerated for up to 24 hours.

2 Trim fat and excess skin from the neck opening of the ducks. Stuff the ducks with the prune mixture and truss them.* Provided the stuffing was cold when added, the ducks can be refrigerated for up to 6 hours.

Continued overleaf

Continued from previous page

3 *To roast the ducks*. Heat the oven to Gas 10/260°C/500°F. Sprinkle the ducks with salt and pepper and set them, breast side up, in a roasting pan. Roast until starting to brown: about 30 minutes. Turn them on to the breast and add the giblets. Lower the oven heat to Gas 4/175°C/350°F and continue roasting for 30 minutes longer. Discard all fat from the pan, return the ducks to their backs and continue roasting until they are very tender and the skin is crisp: about 30 minutes longer. When the thigh is pierced with a skewer, the juices should run clear, not pink. Remove the ducks from the oven and keep warm.

4 *To make the gravy*. If necessary, boil pan juices until reduced to a glaze.* Discard all the fat, add the wine to the pan and boil until reduced by half, stirring to dissolve the juices. Add the stock and reduce also by half. Strain the gravy into a small pan, bring to a boil and taste for seasoning.

5 Discard the trussing strings from the ducks, set them on a serving dish and decorate them with watercress. Carve the ducks at the table, serving the gravy separately.

Cook's Comment. I'm a devotee of the dark, rich meat of duck, but regrettably it is not an economical bird. A duck of around 3½lb (*1.5kg*) serves only two, with a 4–5lb (*2kg*) bird needed for four. Roasting duck is one of the few occasions when I disagree with the French about food – I think their rare roast duck cannot be compared to one that is so well done it is almost falling off the bone.

Confit de Canard

PRESERVED DUCK

Most recipes for *confit* of duck resemble each other. It is what you do with the preserved duck when you have it in the crock that counts. A few slivers of *confit* make a world of difference when added to vegetable soup, to omelettes, and to baked bean dishes like cassoulet. Quite the best salad I've had recently was made of blanched, shredded red cabbage, mixed with vinaigrette dressing and shreds of a rich duck *confit*. But every winter I return with gratitude to the classic *confit* baked on its own in the oven until crisp and brown. The fat is used to fry wafer-thin potatoes with a touch of garlic until deep golden and crisp. Sorrel Purée is a classic accompaniment.

SERVES 3–4

a 4–5lb (*about 2kg*) duck, cut
  into 8 pieces*
3 tablespoons coarse salt
1 teaspoon black pepper
2–3 sprigs fresh or dried thyme
2–3 bay leaves, crumbled
3lb (*1.4kg*) lard, or more if
  needed

For serving
4 large potatoes, very thinly
  sliced
2 cloves garlic, chopped
2 tablespoons chopped parsley
salt and pepper
Sorrel Purée (see opposite)

1 Rub each piece of duck with some of the salt and put the pieces in a bowl. Sprinkle with the remaining salt and pepper, and add the thyme and bay leaves. Cover and refrigerate, turning the pieces occasionally, for 6–12 hours, depending on how strong a flavour you want.

2 Rinse the salt from the duck and dry the pieces on paper towels. Heat the oven to Gas 2/150°C/300°F. Lay the duck pieces, skin side down, in a frying pan and fry gently for 15–20 minutes so that the fat runs and they brown evenly.

3 Transfer the duck pieces to a small casserole and add enough melted lard to cover. Cover with a lid and cook in the oven until the duck is very tender and has rendered all its fat: about 2 hours. The meat should be almost falling from the bone.

4 *To preserve the duck.* Pour a layer of the rendered fat into the base of a preserving jar or small terrine. Pack the pieces of duck on top and pour over enough fat to cover them completely, adding more melted lard if necessary. Cover and refrigerate for at least a week to allow the flavour to mellow. If sealed with a cloth sprinkled with salt, and tightly covered, *confit* will keep for several months.

5 *To serve the confit.* Heat the oven to Gas 6/200°C/400°F. Extract the pieces of duck, wiping off excess fat, and put them in a shallow baking dish. Bake them in the oven for 5 minutes, then pour off any melted fat. Continue baking until they are very hot and the skin is crisp: 10–15 minutes.

6 Meanwhile, fry the potatoes. Heat 4–5 tablespoons fat from the *confit* in a large frying pan. Add the potatoes and fry briskly, turning often, until they are brown and crisp. (*Note*: One secret of good fried potatoes is to keep cooking them until they are very brown.) Add the garlic 2–3 minutes before the end of cooking. Sprinkle the potatoes with parsley, salt and pepper. Serve them with the *confit* on individual warm plates.

Cook's Comment. The length of time that the duck should be left to pickle in salt depends on whether you want a strong flavour for seasoning soups or other dishes, or a mild flavour for serving alone.

Sorrel Purée

Sorrel is an oddity, for it can be treated as a vegetable or as a herb. An acquired taste, it is acid enough to crimp your mouth like rhubarb, making butter and cream to blunt the bite almost mandatory. In fact, the flavour of sorrel is so strong that it can act in soup or salad as a herb. When heated, its leaves wilt to a purée which becomes softer and smoother the longer it is cooked, forming a somewhat tart vegetable. In the garden it offers yet another snare, looking deceptively like spinach. Beware!

SERVES 4

1½oz (45g) butter	4fl. oz (125ml) double cream
½lb (250g) fresh sorrel, rinsed and stemmed	pepper

1 Melt half the butter in a shallow saucepan, add the sorrel and cook over a low heat, stirring often until the sorrel forms a smooth purée and most of the moisture has evaporated: 8–10 minutes. Add the cream and continue cooking until fairly thick: about 5 minutes. Season to taste with pepper.

2 The purée can be refrigerated for 24 hours. Reheat it on top of the stove and stir in the remaining butter in small pieces.

Cook's Comment. A wonderful accompaniment to fish, the tang of Sorrel Purée can be softened by adding an equal quantity of spinach. The spinach should be cooked* separately, puréed in a food processor or blender and added to the sorrel with the cream.

Thanksgiving Goose with Oyster Stuffing

Please don't expect many suggestions from me for the big birds, goose and turkey. We like them roasted quite plain, with no stuffing, plenty of gravy and half a dozen accompaniments so everyone can choose their personal favourites. This recipe is an exception. One Thanksgiving, we were offered a wild goose from the Maryland shore and I jumped at the chance. A kind neighbour stuffed it for us with oysters, a local tradition I had heard about but never tried. So good were the results that I now use the stuffing in domestic goose.

SERVES 6–8

a 10lb (*4.5kg*) goose, with giblets
1oz (*30g*) softened butter
salt and pepper
1 onion, sliced
1 carrot, sliced
2 pints (*1.25 litres*) water
1½oz (*45g*) flour
For the stuffing
1lb (*500g*) loaf white bread, diced, crusts discarded
4 tablespoons chopped parsley

1 teaspoon paprika
½ teaspoon ground nutmeg
6oz (*175g*) butter
1 onion, chopped
6 stalks celery, chopped
salt and pepper
18 medium shelled oysters, liquor reserved
4fl. oz (*125ml*) milk, or more if needed

trussing needle and string

1 *For the stuffing.* In a large bowl, toss the diced bread with the parsley, paprika and nutmeg. Melt the butter in a frying pan. Fry the onion and celery with salt and pepper until soft but not brown: about 10 minutes. Add the drained oysters and fry just until the edges curl: 1–2 minutes. Remove from the heat and stir into the diced-bread mixture. Stir in the milk and the oyster liquid. Add more milk if the stuffing seems dry, and season it to taste. Leave to cool.

2 Remove the fat from the neck end of the goose. Fill it with stuffing – it should be loosely packed – and truss it.* The goose can be refrigerated for up to 12 hours, provided the stuffing was cold when added.

3 *To roast the goose.* Heat the oven to Gas 8/230°C/450°F. Spread the softened butter on the goose, sprinkle with salt and pepper and set the bird on its back on a rack in a roasting pan. Roast it in the oven, basting occasionally, until brown: about 40 minutes. Lower the oven heat to Gas 4/175°C/350°F and continue roasting, basting and pouring off excess fat, allowing 15 minutes' cooking time per pound. When the bird is done, the juices will run clear when the thigh is pricked with a skewer.

4 Meanwhile, make stock with the giblets. In a heavy saucepan, fry the giblets in a tablespoon of fat from the goose until very brown. Add the onion and carrot and brown them also. Pour in the water, season with salt and pepper and simmer for 1–1½ hours until the stock has reduced by about half and is concentrated.

5 When the goose is cooked, remove it from the oven and keep it warm. Cook the pan juices to a dark-brown glaze.* (*Note*: This gives flavour and colour to the gravy.) Pour off all but 3 tablespoons of fat and stir in the flour. Cook, stirring, for 1–2 minutes until brown. Strain in the goose stock and bring to a boil, stirring until the gravy thickens. Simmer for 2–3 minutes, strain into a saucepan, bring back to a boil and taste.

6 Discard the trussing strings from the goose and transfer it to a serving dish. Carve the bird at the table and serve the gravy separately.

Cook's Comment. Fat from a goose keeps us going in fried potatoes for months to follow – wonderful stuff, which crisps the potatoes at a high temperature without burning. I hesitate to stipulate other accompaniments to such a ritual bird as goose, though we enjoy the crunchiness of Corn Bread and the acidity of Confit of Cranberries (see below).

Confit of Cranberries

Two foods I had trouble with when I arrived in America were clams and cranberries. Clams cooked to rubber and cranberries to mush. The clam problem was simply a result of overcooking. As for cranberries, it was some time before I found this recipe in *Gourmet* magazine, in which the berries are cooked until tender but remain whole and shiny with glaze.

SERVES 6–8

1oz (*30g*) butter
6½oz (*200g*) sugar

1lb (*500g*) fresh or frozen
cranberries

1 Heat the oven to Gas 4/175°C/350°F. Spread half the butter in a shallow baking dish and add the cranberries. Sprinkle them with the sugar and dot with the remaining butter. Cover and bake in the oven until the cranberries are tender and all the liquid has evaporated so that the cranberries are very shiny: about 1 hour. If they produce too much juice, uncover for the last 15 minutes of cooking.

2 Cranberry *confit* can be refrigerated for up to 3 days, or packed in jars and sealed as a preserve. Serve it at room temperature, or reheat it in a low oven.

Cook's Comment. Breathtakingly acid, cranberries are a law unto themselves and need great quantities of sugar. (If you like things sweet you can add even more to this recipe.) Cranberries are classic with turkey, of course, but I like them with goose too.

Mrs Glasse's
Yorkshire Christmas Pie

Pies we had in abundance in Yorkshire when I was a child, but never one as elaborate as this! The recipe echoes the legendary medieval '*rôti sans pareil*' in which a dozen or more birds were boned and stuffed one inside the other, starting with a thrush stuffed with an olive and ending with a peacock in full plumage. Hannah ·Glasse, the first woman cook to achieve renown in England, gives a recipe in *The Art of Cookery Made Plain and Easy* (1747), which calls for five different domestic birds, a hare, a woodcock and 'what sort of wild fowl you can get.' All were encased in a double-crust raised pie. Hannah Glasse adds, 'These pies are often sent to London in a box as presents; therefore the walls must be well built.' The stagecoach journey from Yorkshire lasted about three days and, given winter temperatures, the pies would have arrived at their destination in prime condition.

SERVES 12

a 6–7lb (*3.2kg*) turkey
a 4–5lb (*2.3kg*) duck
2 pigeons
4oz (*125g*) melted butter
2 teaspoons dried thyme
2 teaspoons crushed bay leaf
grated rind of 3 lemons
1 tablespoon salt
2 teaspoons pepper
1 egg beaten with ½ teaspoon
    salt (for glaze)

For the shortcrust pastry dough
1lb (*500g*) flour
2 teaspoons salt
4oz (*125g*) unsalted butter
4oz (*125g*) lard
2 eggs, beaten to mix
4fl. oz (*125ml*) water, or more if
    needed

*5-pint (3.5-litre) pie dish or deep
baking dish*

1 Make the shortcrust pastry* and chill for 30 minutes. Bone all the birds,* cutting along the backbones so that skin and meat can be spread flat, and trimming away excess fat and skin.

2 Spread the turkey, skin side down, on a work surface and brush generously with melted butter. Mix the thyme, bay leaf, lemon rind, salt and pepper. Sprinkle half over the turkey. Spread the duck, skin side down, on top, brush generously with melted butter and sprinkle with half of the remaining seasonings. Lay the pigeons on top, skin side down and end to end. Brush with butter and sprinkle with the remaining seasonings. Starting at a long edge, roll up the turkey to form a cylinder with the other birds inside. Transfer the cylinder to the pie dish, seam side down, and pour over any remaining melted butter.

3 Brush the edge of the pie dish with water. Roll out the pastry 2in (*5cm*) larger than the pie dish and cut a 1in (*2.5cm*) strip from the edge. Set the strip on the edge of the pie dish and brush it with water. Lift the pastry on top, trim the edges and press them to seal it to the pastry strip. Scallop or flute the border and brush the pastry with egg glaze. Roll out pastry trimmings, shape leaves or flowers, decorate the top of the pie and brush again with glaze. Make two holes in the pie to allow steam to escape and insert a 'chimney' of rolled foil. Chill the pie for 30 minutes.

4 Heat the oven to Gas 5/190°C/375°F. Bake the pie in the oven for 35–45 minutes until the pastry is firm and browned. Lower the oven temperature to Gas 4/175°C/350°F. Cover the pie with foil, wrapping the foil edges under, and continue baking for 2¼–2¾ hours, until a skewer inserted in the centre of the pie is hot to the touch when withdrawn after 30 seconds.

5 The pie can be refrigerated for up to 3 days, or frozen. Serve it cold, or reheat it in the oven at Gas 4/175°C/350°F for 1–1¼ hours, until hot when tested with a skewer.

Cook's Comment. The bigger the goose, the better, but with a turkey, small and female is beautiful, despite the American obsession with monsters of up to 40lb (*18kg*). When serving Christmas Pie hot, it should have festive accompaniments like a Confit of Cranberries (see page 101) and Fried Onions and Apples with Bacon (see page 157). The pie is also good cold with salad.

Barbecued Quail
with Pepper Marinade

Picture the Cadillac Bar on a main street of Houston, Texas, on a Saturday night. The crowd is polyglot, half Mexican, half larger-than-life giants in jeans and high-heeled boots, straight out of Central Casting. The drinks, passed from hand to hand by the group four deep at the counter, are limited to beer or goblets of neon-green margueritas. At the table a great basket of barbecued wild quail awaits us and we tuck in greedily, using our hands. As fast as we empty one basket, another appears, until finally we lean back, look each other in the eye and smile. I made some long-lasting friends that evening ten years ago. This was long before the mesquite barbecue craze hit the headlines, and we were tasting it at the source. Unforgettable!

SERVES 8 AS A FIRST COURSE, 4 AS A MAIN DISH

8 quail, giblets removed
4fl. oz (125ml) olive oil
3 tablespoons lemon juice
1 teaspoon crushed
   peppercorns

½–1 teaspoon crushed dried
   red pepper (optional)
salt
green salad (for serving)

8 long skewers

1 *To prepare the quail.* Put the birds on a work surface, breast down. Cut along each side of the backbones with poultry shears and discard the bones. Turn the birds breast side up and, with a sharp downward movement of the heel of your hand, flatten them, breaking the breastbones. Thread the quail crosswise on two skewers, inserting them through the wings and again through the legs to hold the birds flat.

2 Whisk together the olive oil, lemon juice, peppercorns, and red pepper, if using. Put the quail on a baking tray, pour over the marinade and brush the birds to coat them thoroughly. Cover and leave to marinate at room temperature for up to 3 hours, turning the birds occasionally.

3 Light the barbecue or grill. Sprinkle the quail with a little salt and grill them 2–3in (5–7cm) from the heat for 5–6 minutes until brown and slightly charred. Turn and brown the other side. The quail should remain pink and juicy in the centre. Remove the skewers and, if serving as a first course, cut the quail in half. Serve them very hot on a bed of green salad.

Cook's Comment. Baby pigeon are excellent barbecued, while plain chicken wings become positively gourmet. The degree of heat added by hot red pepper is up to you.

Pigeon with Juniper

Strictly speaking, only baby pigeons (squab) are good to eat, as mature birds are almost incurably tough. However, I was brought up to consider pigeons of any age untouchable – dirty birds that gobbled up the grain of hard-working farmers. The prejudice extended to the table, where pigeon never alighted, even in a pie. It took a visit to northern Florida and a home-cooked dinner of squab and dove to hint at their charm. Back in France, I realised the culinary possibilities of these tasty little birds.

SERVES 8

2oz (60g) butter
2 tablespoons crushed juniper
    berries
4 cloves garlic, finely chopped
salt and pepper
8 baby pigeons, giblets removed
1 teaspoon dried thyme
16fl. oz (500ml) chicken or veal stock*

5–6 tablespoons Madeira
bunch of watercress (for garnish)
8 large rectangular croûtes*
    made with 8 slices white
    bread (for serving)
Wild Mushrooms with Garlic
    (see page 149) (for serving)

trussing needle and string

1 Cream the butter. Beat in half of the juniper berries and all the garlic. Season with salt and pepper. Loosen the skin from the breasts of the pigeons by gently inserting your fingers between the skin and meat. Spread the flavoured butter over the breasts, under the skin. Truss the birds* and refrigerate them for at least 1 hour and up to 12 hours for the flavours to permeate the meat.

2 Heat the oven to Gas 8/230°C/450°F. Set the birds on their backs in a roasting pan, sprinkle with the thyme and roast until starting to brown: 12 minutes. Add half the stock, baste the birds and continue roasting for a further 10–15 minutes. The juices from the centre of the birds should run pink but not red, showing the meat is still medium rare. Make the Wild Mushrooms with Garlic and Parsley and fry the croûtes.

3 When the birds are cooked, remove them from the oven and keep them warm. Boil the cooking juices until reduced to a glaze.* Add the remaining stock, half the Madeira and the remaining juniper berries. Bring to a boil, stirring to dissolve the glaze; boil until reduced and concentrated: 5–7 minutes. Add the remaining Madeira, strain the sauce, and taste for seasoning.

4 Remove the trussing strings from the birds, set them on croûtes on individual warm plates or on a serving dish, and spoon the sauce on top. Garnish with watercress and serve, accompanied by the Wild Mushrooms with Garlic and Parsley.

Cook's Comment. It must be my English ancestry, but I've always loved anything to do with juniper, including gin. If you feel the same way, substitute a couple of tablespoons of gin for Madeira in this recipe.

Braised Pheasant with Mushrooms and Bacon

I was brought up with pheasant cooked only one way – roasted until very well done with bacon to keep it moist, then served with bread sauce, fried breadcrumbs, thickened gravy and homemade potato chips. Young birds were incomparable, but old ones resisted the knife as fiercely as they had resisted predators in the wild. Hanging to mature the meat heightened taste, but hardly benefited the tenderness.

When I was a student at Cambridge we had two gas rings on a corridor for thirty students, and roasting anything was impossible. However, each autumn I was spurred to action by the arrival of a brace of pheasants in full plumage, sent from home in the mail in special cartons supplied by the Country Gentleman's Association. After a bit of experiment, I developed the following casserole, which suits tough and tender birds alike. To complete the undergraduate feast, I would happily steam a caramel custard on the companion gas ring over a galvanised tin laundry bucket. It was all excellent training for the adventures in cooking ahead.

SERVES 6–8

1 tablespoon vegetable oil
2 tablespoons butter
3 pheasants, weighing about
   2lb (1kg) each, cut into 6 pieces*
¾lb (375g) mushrooms,
   quartered
20–24 baby onions, peeled
½lb (250g) piece streaky bacon,
   cut into lardons*

1oz (30g) flour
1 pint (600ml) red wine
1 pint (600ml) veal or chicken
   stock,* or more if needed
2 cloves garlic, crushed
bouquet garni*
salt and pepper
Kasha (see opposite) (for
   serving)

1 Heat the oil and butter in a casserole and brown the pheasant pieces on all sides, a few at a time. Take them out, add the mushrooms and cook until tender: about 5 minutes. Remove them, add the onions and cook until brown, shaking the casserole so that they colour evenly. Remove the onions, add the bacon and brown it too.

2 Discard all but 2 tablespoons of fat, stir the flour into the bacon and cook gently, stirring, until brown. Stir in the wine, bring to a boil and simmer for 5 minutes. Add the stock, garlic, bouquet garni, salt and pepper, and replace the pheasant pieces. Cover the casserole and simmer on top of the stove, or cook in a Gas 4/175°C/350°F oven until the pheasant is very tender when pierced with a two-pronged fork. Cooking time varies from 1–2 hours, depending on the age of the pheasants. Stir from time to time, especially if cooking on top of the stove, and add more stock if the meat begins to stick. ·Wing and breast pieces may cook before the legs; if so, remove them.

3 Discard the *bouquet garni* and taste the sauce for seasoning. The pheasant can be refrigerated for up to 3 days, or frozen. Reheat it on top of the stove and serve with Kasha (see below) or boiled rice.

Cook's Comment. This multi-purpose recipe is like a starter kit for the novice cook. Chicken or guinea fowl can be used instead of pheasant, and white wine can be used instead of red.

Kasha

Kasha is whole buckwheat, a popular Central European grain, and I first came across it on the table of my father-in-law who was born nearly ninety-five years ago in the Pale of Russia. A musician who never went to school nor had much formal training on his instrument, the cello, it was natural talent that elevated him and his brothers to the stage in the 1900s as a youthful trio. Mischel Cherniavsky seems to have been born a foreigner, having no native language, nor any habitat other than where he happened to be living at the time. Fortunately he married a Canadian of more practical stock, and the romance that began in Fiji in 1917 lasted until they died in their mid-eighties. However, my mother-in-law could never cure her husband of his Jewish peasant habit of stuffing suitcases with kasha as if it were bubble paper. By the time the luggage reached the next port of call, kasha was into the undies, the sheets of music and the volumes of Boswell's *Dr. Johnson*, which was Mischel's favourite reading. To please him I tried kasha, but it came out as a disagreeable gluey porridge until I read in Edouard de Pomiane's *La Cuisine Juive* that the grains should be toasted with a whole egg.

SERVES 4–6

6oz (*175g*) kasha	16fl. oz (*500ml*) water
1 egg, beaten to mix	salt and pepper

1 Put the kasha in a heavy pan and stir in the egg. Heat the kasha, stirring constantly with a metal spoon, until the grains are dry and separate: 4–5 minutes. (*Note*: The mixture will form coarse crumbs at first before it dries.)

2 Add the water, salt and pepper, cover with a lid and bring almost to a boil. Cook the kasha very gently for 8–12 minutes or until the water is absorbed and the kasha is almost tender. (*Note*: Do not allow the kasha to boil or the grains will burst.) Turn off the heat and leave for 10–15 minutes to allow the grains to firm up. Stir with a fork, then taste for seasoning. Kasha can be refrigerated for 3 days. Reheat it on the stove.

Cook's Comment. Bulghur, or cracked wheat, is a different grain from kasha, which botanically speaking is a grass, but they are cooked the same way. Both are best when plump and coarse, and they share a nutty flavour, ideal with game or dark-fleshed birds. I call them the poor man's wild rice.

MEAT

Etymology can nicely illuminate eating habits. Take the case of meat. Why should mutton, beef, veal, bacon and pork be Norman-French words, but sheep, ox, calf and horse Saxon words? Is it because the Saxons were mere herdsmen while the Normans were the lords who ate the meat? Can we even infer that only the Normans appreciated the culinary potential of their livestock?

Such a hypothesis would help explain why the modern French have a keener nose for meats than their Saxon brothers in more northerly climes (and, I would add, across the Atlantic). The British and American taste is essentially for the cow, the sheep and the pig, in that order of merit, and with little enthusiasm for the nooks and crannies of the quadruped, like brains and sweetbreads. Pork has a particularly poor repute in North America, yet with their *charcuterie* the French prove the versatility of the pig again and again. What other animal is edible from its snout to the tip of its curly tail?

Rabbit is another example. Throughout France a plump domestic rabbit is regarded as a treat, but in Britain or the USA it seems to me it reaches the table only because its taste is indistinguishable from chicken and the same recipes can be used for cooking it. The same could be said of goat, a ringer for veal, although even in France the delicate meat has made few inroads beyond the Mediterranean. As for horse meat, its very mention raises an outcry in the Anglo-Saxon world, yet in France it is valued for its low cholesterol, and regularly commands higher prices than beef.

Wild game is another story, with French *gourmandise* overreaching itself. In the USA, the commercial sale of indigenous species is strictly forbidden, with the result that the animal kingdom is thick on the ground from coast to coast. Britain has a built-in set of controls in its class system – the prohibition against shooting on Sunday leaves the working man with only a few hours a week to make a sortie. But if you visit rural France on the Sabbath in the open season, it's best to stay well out of sight. Outside a few noble estates, the shooting or netting of wildlife is largely a free-for-all. There is scarcely anything left to put in the pot!

Fillet of Beef Cherniavsky

Coming from Yorkshire, I should regard roast beef as a solace, but instead it evokes one of my most harrowing cooking memories. In the early 1960s I lived in the Château de Versailles, supervising the kitchen of Florence van der Kemp, the American-born wife of the curator. They were a great celebrity couple – in two decades they did more to restore Versailles than anyone had done in two centuries – and their guests were all the *crème de la crème*, topped by the golden seal of the Windsors. However, domestic arrangements were unorthodox: I, an English girl, supervised a team of servants from Mexico, headed by Bernadina the cook. I learned some useful kitchen Spanish, as well as *Almanac de Gotha* tastes in cooking.

One day, Florence decided to offer her guests a real American rib roast of beef. The butcher required instruction, mystified by such a crude, expensive cut which made no demand on his skills in boning and tying. Finally, two massive, seven-rib roasts arrived. Never having cooked anything larger than a fillet, I decided that an hour in a hot oven would suffice – cooked at the last minute, of course, for finest flavour. My timing left no room for error, but what an error I made. The purple meat, still stone cold at its centre, struck terror to my heart. My job was on the line and forty guests awaited their main course beyond the panelled door, emblazoned with the arms of Colbert, Louis XIV's Minister of Finance. It was Bernadina, veteran of a dozen years' cooking for Wells Fargo, who saved the day. She simply sliced the raw meat, set it on trays and baked it. Not even the waiters were the wiser.

Every cook has a story like this, but not every cook has the good fortune to work for people like the van der Kemps. Florence showed me the way when I moved to the States in 1965, and became a good friend. After Versailles she and her husband have turned their talents to restoring Monet's home and garden in Giverny, with results that all may enjoy.

When I was at *Gourmet* magazine in 1964, Beef Wellington was still the recipe most demanded by readers. One touching letter from a closed order of monks explained that such treats were allowed 'for festivities'.

After my disaster with roast beef, I developed this foolproof recipe in which the beef is sliced and sandwiched with a mushroom, bacon and tomato stuffing, calling it immodestly by my married name.

SERVES 8

3–4lb (*about 1.8kg*) fillet of beef, trimmed and tied
salt and pepper
1 tablespoon vegetable oil
8 medium tomatoes
bunch of watercress (for garnish)
For the stuffing
2 shallots, cut into pieces
4oz (*125g*) sliced streaky bacon, cut into pieces

1lb (*500g*) mushrooms, finely chopped
2lb (*1kg*) tomatoes, peeled, seeded and chopped*
For the Madeira sauce
1¼ pints (*750ml*) veal stock*
½oz (*15g*) arrowroot* or potato flour, mixed to a paste with 2 tablespoons Madeira
3fl. oz (*90ml*) Madeira

1 Heat the oven to Gas 8/230°C/450°F. Sprinkle the beef with salt and pepper. Heat the oil until very hot and brown the meat well on all sides. Roast it in the oven for 11 minutes. Remove it and leave it to cool. Discard any fat from the pan. Add half the veal stock and boil, stirring to dissolve the pan juices. Strain the juices back into the remaining stock.

2 *For the stuffing.* In a food processor, chop the shallots and bacon to a paste, or chop by hand as finely as possible. Heat the paste in a frying pan, stirring, until it begins to brown: 1–2 minutes. Add the mushrooms, chopped tomatoes, salt and pepper, and cook over a high heat, stirring occasionally, until all the moisture has evaporated: 15–20 minutes. Taste the stuffing for seasoning, then leave it to cool completely.

3 When the meat is cool, discard the strings. Slice the meat ¾in (2cm) thick, cutting not quite right through the meat, so that the underside is still attached. Spread a tablespoon of stuffing between each slice and press the fillet back into its original shape. Reserve the remaining stuffing. Wrap the beef in two layers of foil.

4 Discard cores from the tomatoes. Cut off the tops to form a lid and slice the bases so that the tomatoes sit flat. Set them in an oiled baking dish. Top each with a tablespoon of stuffing and the tomato lid.

5 *For the Madeira sauce.* Bring the stock to a boil. Whisk in the arrowroot paste to thicken the sauce. Add the Madeira and taste for seasoning. The meat, tomatoes and sauce can be kept for up to a day in the refrigerator, providing the stuffing was cold before adding to the beef.

6 *To finish.* Heat the oven to Gas 7/220°C/425°F. Roast the beef, still wrapped in foil, in the oven until a skewer inserted in the centre of the meat is warm to the touch when withdrawn (60°C/140°F on a meat thermometer): about 25 minutes for medium rare meat, or 10 minutes longer for medium well-done meat (71°C/160°F on the meat thermometer). Bake the tomatoes in the same oven until tender when pierced with a skewer: 15–20 minutes.

7 Transfer the beef to a heated serving dish and remove the foil. Allow the beef to rest briefly before serving. Arrange the stuffed tomatoes down one side of dish. Bring the sauce to a boil, spoon a little over the beef and serve the rest separately. Garnish the serving dish with watercress.

Cook's Comment. If the beef is too underdone for your taste when sliced, simply cook it longer when reheating in foil.

Entrecôte Marchand de Vin

ENTRECOTE STEAK IN RED WINE SAUCE

Steak Marchand de Vin, that Parisian bistro quickie, seems now to be sadly eclipsed by the American imports of chef's salad and microwaved hamburger in a plastic bag. Around Les Halles or the meat market at La Villette, you could once have been sure of a substantial, juicy steak cooked to your taste and topped with fresh herbs, shallots and garlic. *Frites* were the standard accompaniment or, in grander establishments, you might have been lucky enough to find *pommes soufflées*.

SERVES 2

1 tablespoon vegetable oil
1 tablespoon butter
2 steaks cut ¾in (*2cm*) thick
salt and pepper
2 shallots, chopped
1 clove garlic, crushed

6fl. oz (*175ml*) red wine
2 tablespoons chopped, mixed
    fresh herbs – tarragon,
    chives, parsley, thyme or
    oregano
bunch of watercress

1 Heat the oil and butter in a heavy frying pan until foaming. Sprinkle the steaks with salt and pepper, add to the pan and sauté until browned, allowing not more than 2–3 minutes on each side to keep the steak rare. Remove them and keep them warm.

2 Add the shallots to the pan and cook until soft but not brown. Add the garlic and cook for 1 minute longer. Add the wine and boil, stirring to dissolve the pan juices, until the sauce is reduced by half. Remove from the heat, add the herbs, taste for seasoning and spoon over the steaks. Garnish with watercress and serve at once.

Cook's Comment. Any steak tender enough to pan fry is improved by a little wine sauce. I suggest using rump or sirloin in the UK, and ribeye or Delmonico in the USA.

Fricandeau à l'Oseille

BRAISED VEAL WITH SORREL PUREE

No one else has ever had quite the gift of Madame Saint Ange for describing a dish so that you can taste it on the palate. *Le Livre de Cuisine de Madame Saint Ange* is a sixty-year-old classic that was rare and high priced until the advent of facsimile reprints. Her vivid and exhaustive text can run to five pages on a single recipe, and you know that she herself has experienced every step. A cook's cook – or perhaps, to be sexist, a woman cook's cook: Elizabeth David on one side of the Atlantic and Julia Child on the other have both paid homage to her. Listen to Madame Saint Ange on the subject of this simple little braised veal with sorrel. 'Fricandeau is the archetypal braise, slow and methodical, which renders meat soft and gleaming with succulent amber juices, until it can be "cut with a spoon," as the saying goes.' Sorrel purée is traditional with *fricandeau*, but spinach purée can be substituted.

SERVES 4–6

2½–3lb (*1.3kg*) rump of
veal
4–5 slices fat bacon
2 carrots, thinly sliced
2 onions, thinly sliced
6fl. oz (*175ml*) white wine

12fl. oz (*375ml*) veal stock,* or
more if needed
salt and pepper
*bouquet garni**
Sorrel or Spinach Purée (see
page 99) (for serving)

1 Heat the oven to Gas 3/160°C/325°F. Roll the veal into a cylinder and tie it with string. Lay the bacon slices in the bottom of a heavy casserole just large enough to hold the meat. Add the carrots and onions, set the veal on top and pour over the wine. Simmer over the heat until the wine has reduced to 2–3 tablespoons.

2 Add 5–6 tablespoons of the stock and reduce to a glaze.* Add enough stock to half cover the meat, season with salt and pepper, and add the *bouquet garni*. Cover the casserole, bring to a boil and braise in the oven until the meat is very tender: 1½–2 hours. It can be refrigerated for up to 3 days.

3 Heat the oven to Gas 7/220°C/425°F. Reheat the meat on top of the stove, if necessary. Remove it and keep it warm. Boil the cooking liquid until reduced to about 8fl. oz (*250ml*). Cut the veal into ¾in (*2cm*) slices. Overlap the slices in a shallow baking dish and pour over the cooking juices. Cook the veal in the oven, basting often, until the liquid evaporates to a few spoonfuls of shiny glaze: 20–25 minutes.

4 Meanwhile, make the Sorrel or Spinach Purée and mound it down the centre of a serving dish. Set the veal on top and spoon over the glaze.

Cook's Comment. Just the kind of old-fashioned dish that deserves revival!

Rôti de Veau Jardinière

ROAST VEAL WITH SPRING VEGETABLES

How I miss the grand classics like this! A great serving dish set before the host, whether carved in the kitchen or at the table, is in itself a celebration of the new season. The glossy brown meat surrounded by mounds of baby spring carrots, peas, green beans, onions and potatoes is a feast to the eye and the nose before it even reaches the plate.

Contrast this with the new-style equivalent: a medallion of veal with vegetables presented on individual plates. Of course it looks pretty, but instead of being roasted in one piece to retain the juices, the veal is sautéed or grilled in a single slice and easily gets dry. The vegetables, arranged one by one in a contrived still life to show off the meat, lose all individuality. Even the sauce is usually spooned under the meat and vegetables to highlight their colour, rather than coating to moisten and marry their juices. Flavour is subordinated to show – a fundamental mistake.

SERVES 6–8

4–5lb (*about 2kg*) boneless veal
  roast
2–3 sprigs fresh or dried thyme
  or rosemary
1oz (*30g*) butter
salt and pepper
1¼ pints (*750ml*) veal stock,* or
  more if necessary

For the garnish
1lb (*500g*) baby or medium carrots
1 teaspoon sugar
salt and pepper
1½oz (*45g*) butter
1lb (*500g*) baby green beans
  or shelled fresh green peas
2lb (*1kg*) baby potatoes
2 tablespoons chopped parsley

1 *To prepare the garnish*. Peel and trim baby carrots, leaving some green stem; quarter medium carrots. Put them in cold water, to just cover, with the sugar, salt, pepper and 1 tablespoon of butter. Boil until tender and all the water has evaporated, leaving a shiny glaze: 15–20 minutes.

2 Trim the green beans, put them in a large pan of boiling salted water and boil until tender but still firm: 8–12 minutes. Drain, rinse with cold water and drain again thoroughly. Cook the peas in the same way, allowing 6–8 minutes.

3 Put the potatoes in cold salted water, cover and boil until just tender: 15–20 minutes. Drain and peel, or leave unpeeled, as you like. All the vegetables can be refrigerated for up to 8 hours.

4 *About 2 hours before serving.* Heat the oven to Gas 6/200°C/400°F. Tie the veal in a neat cylinder with the herbs. Set the meat in a roasting pan, spread with the butter, sprinkle with salt and pepper and pour in about a third of the stock. Roast in the oven, basting often, allowing 20 minutes per lb (*45 minutes per kg*) for slightly pink meat (71°C/160°F on a meat thermometer). Add more stock to the pan as it becomes dry. Remove the meat from the pan and keep it warm.

5 Boil the pan juices to reduce to a glaze and discard any fat. Add the remaining stock and boil, stirring to dissolve the juices. Boil until the gravy is well reduced, taste for seasoning and strain.

6 Reheat the carrots over a low heat, shaking the pan occasionally. Melt 1 tablespoon of butter in a pan, add the green beans or peas and heat gently. Melt the remaining butter in a pan, add the potatoes and reheat them also.

7 Carve the meat in slices and arrange them overlapping on a large serving dish, or carve the meat at the table. Add the parsley to the carrots and potatoes and arrange the vegetables in 'bouquets' or neat piles around the meat, alternating the colours. Spoon a little gravy over the meat and serve the rest separately.

Cook's Comment. I have found that a boned loin of the very best new lean pork, trimmed of all fat and neatly tied with string, prompts most of our guests to say 'What excellent veal.' At half the price, a little deception is justified!

Rôti de Veau Orloff

ROAST VEAL WITH MUSHROOM DUXELLES, HAM AND CHEESE SAUCE

Every chef has a party piece and this has long been one of mine. Like Kulebiak and Pojarski (see pages 60 and 120), Rôti de Veau Orloff is a grand nineteenth-century classic from the days when the Russian court was more French than the French, borrowing the fashions, language and, of course, the cooks of *la belle France*. The original Veal Orloff featured a whole side of veal on the bone, which was roasted, sliced, sandwiched with purées of onion (*soubise*) and wild mushrooms, then reshaped on the bone and coated with Mornay sauce. Mine is a simplified version, with the veal sandwiched with ham and mushroom purée, then coated with Mornay sauce.

SERVES 10

5lb (*2.3kg*) boneless veal roast
salt and pepper
1oz (*30g*) butter
1 onion, coarsely chopped
1 carrot, coarsely chopped
8fl. oz (*250ml*) white wine
12fl. oz (*375ml*) veal stock,* or
   more if needed
*bouquet garni**
14–16 thin slices smoked ham,
   weighing about 12oz (*375g*)
3–4 tablespoons grated Gruyère
   cheese
For the duxelles
1oz (*30g*) butter
1 onion, finely chopped

1½lb (*750g*) mushrooms, finely
   chopped
salt and pepper
1 clove garlic, crushed
2 shallots, finely chopped
2 tablespoons chopped parsley
For the Mornay sauce
5oz (*150g*) butter
3oz (*90g*) flour
2⅓ pints (*1.5 litres*) milk, or
   more if needed
pinch of grated nutmeg
salt and pepper
3 egg yolks
1 teaspoon Dijon mustard
2oz (*60g*) grated Parmesan cheese

1 *To braise the meat.* Heat the oven to Gas 4/175°C/350°F. Roll the veal in a neat cylinder and tie with string. Sprinkle it with salt and pepper. In a large casserole, heat the butter and brown the veal on all sides. Add the onion and carrot to the bottom of the casserole and cook until lightly browned. Add the white wine and boil until reduced by half. Add the stock, *bouquet garni*, salt and pepper and bring to a boil.

2 Cover the casserole and cook in the oven until a skewer inserted in the centre of the meat is hot to the touch when withdrawn after 30 seconds: about 2–2½ hours. Baste the meat from time to time and add more stock if the casserole gets dry. Let the meat cool to tepid, then strain the gravy and, if necessary, boil it until it is reduced and concentrated.

3 Meanwhile, make the *duxelles*. Melt the butter in a frying pan and sauté the onion until soft but not brown. Add the mushrooms, season with salt and pepper, and cook, stirring occasionally, until all the moisture has evaporated: 15–20 minutes. Add the garlic and shallots, and cook for 2–3 minutes longer, stirring. Take from the heat, stir in the parsley and taste for seasoning.

4 *To assemble the dish*. Discard the strings from the veal and cut it into ⅜in (*1cm*) slices. On a heatproof serving dish or tray reassemble the slices, spreading one slice with *duxelles* and sandwiching the next with ham until the roast is complete. Spread any leftover *duxelles* on top. (*Note*: Prop up the first slice with leftover ends of meat so that it sits up well like a sliced loaf.)

5 *For the Mornay sauce*. Melt the butter in a saucepan, stir in the flour and cook until foaming. Add half the milk and bring to a boil, stirring constantly until the sauce thickens. Season with nutmeg, salt and pepper and simmer for 2 minutes. Take it from the heat and beat in the egg yolks. Stir in the mustard and Parmesan cheese and taste for seasoning. The sauce should thickly coat a spoon; if necessary, add a little more milk.

6 Spoon about a third of the Mornay sauce over the meat to coat it well. (*Note*: This layer of coating sauce should be thicker than usual, as it softens during reheating.) Thin the remaining sauce with milk until it lightly coats a spoon and use it to coat the meat and the surrounding dish. Sprinkle the meat with the grated Gruyère cheese. Veal Orloff can be refrigerated for up to 24 hours.

7 *To finish*. Heat the oven to Gas 4/175°C/350°F. Bake the veal until the sauce is bubbling and browned and a skewer inserted in the meat is hot to the touch when withdrawn after 30 seconds: about 30–40 minutes. Skim fat from the gravy, bring the gravy to a boil and serve separately.

Cook's Comment. Veal Orloff calls for a full-bodied accompaniment like Kasha (buckwheat grains – see page 107).

Cive de Veel

MEDIEVAL SPICED VEAL STEW

In the early 1970s, when I first began to explore old cookbooks, little culinary research had been done. Few cooks appreciated the potential of medieval or Renaissance recipes. Since then '*cuisine ancienne*' has become something of a fad. The three-star restaurant Archestrate in Paris is named after a cook of classical Greece, and its most famous dish of duck topped with spiced honey nougat comes from the Roman cook Apicius.

Personally, my interest in this kind of thing begins with Taillevent, cook to the French King Charles V in the late fourteenth century. (Taillevent is also the name of a top Paris restaurant.) Taillevent's *Le Viandier* is one of the first cookbooks to give detailed instructions for a highly spiced, complex cuisine. When first I tried this recipe, it was with some misgivings that I followed his directive: 'Take toasted bread softened in wine and beef bouillon, or a purée of peas, and bring to a boil with your meat.' Bread as a liaison made me shudder, for I knew of it only in that porridge-like mixture called bread sauce. However, I found Taillevent's instructions just right. His way of thickening a sauce with bread made it light as well as smooth and my concern about the apparently heavy spicing and sharp flavouring of vinegar and *verjus* (sour grape or crabapple juice) was equally misplaced. The result closely resembles a good Indian curry.

Unhappily, Taillevent has become such a target of overcharged academic research that we are now being told that *Le Viandier* is not an original work. I daresay this is correct, but in the cookery field it should be no great surprise. No recipes are of virgin birth, and all cookbook writers owe a greater or lesser debt to their peers.

SERVES 10

3lb (*1.4kg*) boneless leg or shoulder of veal	salt and pepper
	2–3 tablespoons lemon juice
1oz (*30g*) lard or vegetable oil	2–3 tablespoons wine vinegar
2 medium onions, chopped	*For the thickening mixture*
1 tablespoon ground ginger	4 slices white bread, crusts removed
1 tablespoon ground cinnamon	
½ teaspoon ground cloves	8fl. oz (*250ml*) red or white wine
½ teaspoon ground cardamom	
pinch of saffron, soaked in 2–3 tablespoons boiling water	8fl. oz (*250ml*) beef or veal stock,* or more if needed

1 *For the thickening mixture.* Heat oven to Gas 2/150°C/300°F. Bake the bread until very dry and lightly browned: 25–30 minutes. Grind it to crumbs in a food processor or rotary cheese-grater. Stir in the wine and allow to stand for 5 minutes until the crumbs are soft, then stir in the stock.

2 Cut the veal into 1½in (*4cm*) cubes, discarding any sinew but leaving a little fat. Heat the oven to Gas 3/160°C/325°F. In a flameproof casserole, heat the lard or oil and brown the pieces of veal on all sides, a few at a time. Remove them, add the onions and brown them too. Replace the veal, stir in the bread mixture and bring to a boil.

3 In a small bowl, mix the ginger, cinnamon, cloves, cardamom, and the saffron and its liquid. Add enough water to make a soft paste. Stir the paste into the veal stew and season with salt and pepper. Cover and cook in the oven until the meat is tender: 1–1½ hours. Add more stock during cooking if the casserole gets dry.

4 Stir in the lemon juice and vinegar and taste for seasoning, adding more spices, salt, pepper or lemon juice if necessary. The stew can be refrigerated for up to 3 days, or frozen. For serving, reheat on top of the stove or in a Gas 4/175°C/350°F oven.

Cook's Comment. Given its spiced sauce, I would follow the Indian example and serve this stew with boiled rice and side dishes like chutney, toasted almonds and lentil purée.

Pojarski

GROUND VEAL CUTLETS

The best Pojarski I know are cooked by Linda Collister, who lived with us for three years, lapping us in kindness and good cooking. She acquired the recipe at Clarence House, where she had been *sous-chef* for the Queen Mother. So far as state banqueting goes, it would seem that the contrast between the Elysée in Paris and Buckingham Palace is roughly that between the Ritz and a British boarding school. However, Linda did introduce us to Pojarski, a nineteenth-century classic of the Russian court that was said to have been added to the repertoire of the Hanover family when their Romanoff cousins came to stay at Sandringham. Departing from tradition, the royal Pojarski are shaped as a round rather than a cutlet, and their airy succulence comes from coating them with finely diced brioche or white bread.

SERVES 3–4

4fl. oz (125ml) milk
10 slices dry white bread, crusts
    discarded
1lb (500g) minced lean veal
3 tablespoons single cream
pinch grated nutmeg
salt and pepper

2oz (60g) flour, seasoned with
    salt and pepper
1 egg, beaten to mix
fat or vegetable oil (for deep
    frying)
Tomato and Mushroom Sauce
    (see opposite) (for serving)

1 Pour the milk over two slices of the bread and leave to soak for 5 minutes. Cut the remaining bread into tiny dice and reserve. Squeeze excess milk from the soaked bread.

2 Work the veal through the fine blade of a mincer with the soaked bread, or work them briefly in a food processor. Beat in the cream, with nutmeg, salt and pepper. Fry a small piece of the mixture and taste – it should be lightly seasoned. Using wet hands, shape the mixture into four balls and flatten them slightly. Roll them in seasoned flour, coat with the beaten egg and, finally, roll them in the diced bread. Chill for 30 minutes. Pojarski can be refrigerated for up to 12 hours.

3 *To finish.* Heat the oven to Gas 5/190°C/375°F. Heat deep fat to 185°C/350°F. Add the Pojarski to the fat and fry until brown: 2–3 minutes. Transfer them to a baking sheet and bake in the oven until a skewer inserted in the centre is hot to the touch when withdrawn: 25–30 minutes. Transfer to individual warm plates or to a serving dish and serve the Tomato and Mushroom Sauce separately.

Cook's Comment. The Russian court would probably have regarded Kasha (buckwheat grains – see page 107) as peasant food, but it is delicious with Pojarski.

Tomato and Mushroom Sauce

A sauce that embellishes grilled fish, poultry or meat.

MAKES 16fl. oz (500ml) SAUCE TO SERVE 4–6

1 small onion, finely chopped
2 tablespoons vegetable oil
1lb (*500g*) tomatoes, peeled,
   seeded and chopped*
1 tablespoon tomato purée

1 clove garlic, crushed
bouquet garni*
salt and pepper
4oz (*125g*) mushrooms, sliced

1 In a frying pan, fry the onion in half the oil until browned. Stir in the tomatoes, tomato purée, garlic, *bouquet garni*, salt and pepper, and cook, stirring occasionally, until fairly thick: 8–10 minutes.

2 Strain the tomato mixture into a bowl, pressing well to extract all the pulp. Wipe out the frying pan, heat the remaining oil and fry the mushrooms until tender. Stir in the tomato sauce and taste for seasoning. The sauce can be refrigerated for up to 3 days, or frozen.

Costolette di Vitello alla Griglia

GRILLED VEAL CHOPS WITH LEMON MARINADE

One happy spring I discovered Venice and the Gritti Palace Hotel. The aristocratic ladies who came to cooking class were interested in French cuisine, but I was interested in Italian. At lunch every day, overlooking the Grand Canal, I indulged in hot and cold hors-d'œuvre by the dozen – little vegetable and fish salads dressed only, it seemed, in olive oil, lemon and herbs. The same treatment was given to *coda di rospo* (baby monkfish) and meats cooked on the grill, yet without a trace of monotony. Everything tasted bright, lively, and of itself.

SERVES 2

2 veal chops, cut ¾in (2cm) thick
2 tablespoons olive oil
grated rind and juice of 1 lemon

1 clove garlic, crushed
1 sprig fresh or dried rosemary
salt and pepper
½ lemon, cut into wedges

ridged frying pan or barbecue

1 Set the chops in a shallow, non-reactive tray. In a small bowl, whisk together the oil, lemon rind and juice and garlic. Pour the marinade over the chops and sprinkle with rosemary, stripping the leaves from the stem. Turn the chops so that they are thoroughly coated in marinade, cover and refrigerate them for at least 2 and up to 6 hours.

2 *To finish.* Heat a ridged frying pan or barbecue. Sprinkle the chops with salt and pepper and set them, seasoned side down, on the grill. Cook for 2–3 minutes, turn 90 degrees to mark with a lattice pattern, and continue cooking for a further 1–2 minutes, pressing with a metal spatula so that the pattern is clearly marked. Sprinkle with salt and pepper, turn and repeat on the other side. Transfer to individual plates and serve with lemon wedges.

Cook's Comment. With this chop, I would serve little vegetables tossed in butter, or green salad with a few tart leaves of radicchio.

Pennsylvania Dutch Pork Stew with Dried Fruits

I took to Pennsylvania Dutch cooking at once, for the generous spread of seemingly unrelated dishes reminded me of an English farmhouse tea. The German (Deutsch or 'Dutch') immigrants to the area liked to serve 'seven sweet and seven sour' accompaniments to a meal, a tradition which continues. Our host was Betty Groff, the only cook I know who also entertains her guests on a trumpet. The table was spread with a heavy white cloth on which were crowded creamed chicken, baked ham, pickled peppers, sauerkraut, coleslaw, brownie cake, sweet and sour dill pickles and apple rings with beets. Never mind that the cheese pastries somehow got involved with the spiced herring – there was more to come. Glazed sweet potatoes, carrots with raisins, creamed marrow, Fried Onions and Apples with Bacon (see page 157), cranberry muffins, pumpkin pie and shoofly pie (made with molasses) were all offered at one stage or another, plus the following stew.

SERVES 4–6

4oz (125g) stoned prunes
3oz (90g) dried apricots
1½oz (45g) raisins
2lb (1kg) boned pork shoulder
1½oz (45g) flour
½ teaspoon nutmeg
salt and pepper

1 tablespoon vegetable oil
12fl. oz (375ml) veal stock* or
  water, or more if needed
juice of ½ lemon
1oz (30g) butter, cut into pieces
  (to finish)

1 Soak the dried fruits in enough hot water to cover. Meanwhile, heat the oven to Gas 3/160°C/325°F. Cut the pork into 1½in (4cm) cubes. Season the flour with nutmeg, salt and pepper, and toss the pork cubes in it until well coated. In a flameproof casserole, heat the oil and fry the pork cubes, a few at a time, until well browned. Return all the pork to the casserole and add the stock or water. Cover the casserole, bring to a boil and cook in the oven for 1 hour.

2 Drain the dried fruits, add them to the casserole and simmer until pork and fruits are very tender: ½–¾ hour longer. Add the lemon juice and taste the sauce for seasoning. The stew can be refrigerated for up to 3 days, or frozen.

3 To finish. Reheat the stew on top of the stove. Add the butter, off the heat, shaking the pan so that it melts and is mixed into the sauce.

Cook's Comment. The lemon juice is my addition – a Pennsylvania cook would probably have added a tablespoon of brown sugar, a common flavouring of theirs. As accompaniment, try the Pennsylvania dish of Fried Onions and Apples with Bacon (see page 157). Then be eclectic and add as many other side dishes as you can muster.

Irish Stew with Leeks

In England in 1947 food was at its shortest and rationing at its most severe. Ireland seemed a land of plenty, and the first grand dinner of my life was at Jammet's restaurant in Dublin. I was astonished at the choice of dishes. Back home, restaurants were forbidden to serve more than one protein ingredient in a dish, so even eggs with bacon were proscribed. In Dublin my parents ordered their first steak for six years, then found themselves unable to finish it off, so diminished were their appetites. I tucked in to fried fillets of plaice, which had none of those tiresome fish bones.

In the countryside, food was simpler but no less abundant for those who could pay. Crossing to the west coast, we stopped for lunch at a large country town on market day. Motor vehicles were a rarity – the wide main street was jammed with cattle, horses, donkeys and goats. At the hotel we stepped from the reek of tethered animals into the musty warmth of Guinness and stale cigars.

The high Georgian dining room was set with white-clothed tables occupied by half a dozen other diners, many in the tweeds and gaiters of the prosperous farmer. My parents soon grew restive – in Ireland everything is late – and sighed when the huge bowls of boiled potatoes and turnips, the wet cabbage and the thick slices of mutton in gravy finally arrived. For my part, I rather liked it, particularly the hefty helping of pudding and custard for dessert.

Sometime in Ireland I must have had Irish stew, for I know just what it *should* taste like – the lamb tender enough to fall from the bone, the gravy lightly thickened by the potatoes to be rich and not soupy, the top an agreeable brown. Yellow onions, of course, are the traditional third main ingredient, but I'm fond of this version with leeks.

SERVES 6

3lb (*1.4kg*) ribs, neck or shoulder chops of lamb, cut into 1½in (*3cm*) pieces
1½lb (*750g*) leeks

4lb (*1.8kg*) potatoes, peeled and thickly sliced
salt and pepper
1⅔ pints (*1 litre*) water, or more if necessary

1 Heat the oven to Gas 3/160°C/325°F. Trim the meat of sinew, leaving the bones and a little fat for richness. Trim the leeks, leaving some green top, split them lengthwise and wash them thoroughly. Cut them into ⅜in (*1cm*) slices.

2 Spread a layer of potatoes in a deep baking dish or shallow casserole. Sprinkle with salt and pepper and add a layer of meat followed by a layer of leeks, sprinkling each layer with seasoning. Continue adding layers until all ingredients are used, ending with a layer of potatoes. Arrange the top layer neatly, overlapping the slices. Pour in the water, adding enough just to cover the top layer of potatoes.

3 Cover the dish tightly with foil or a lid and cook in the oven until the potatoes and meat are almost tender when pierced with a two-pronged fork: 1½–2 hours. During cooking, add more water if the pan gets dry.

4 Remove the lid and continue cooking until the top of the stew is lightly browned and the meat is very tender: about 1 hour. The finished stew should be moist and creamy but not soupy. Irish stew can be refrigerated for up to 3 days. Reheat it, covered, in a Gas 4/175°C/350°F oven for 30–40 minutes.

Cook's Comment. Neck of lamb (or better still, mutton) is the classic cut for Irish stew, but a few shoulder chops add more meat, while ribs, with their high proportion of bone, give flavour to the gravy.

Satés

INDONESIAN GRILLED KEBABS

Rarely in my life have I risen at 4 a.m. as I did to see the Indonesian temples of Borobudur. After scrambling the precipitous steps and roaming terraces lined with nearly 1500 *bas-relief* panels illustrating the life of Buddha, by mid-morning I was ravenous. Luckily, in Indonesia you cannot go far without passing a stall serving fritters, dumplings, fruits or tasty little *saté* kebabs like these, served with peanut sauce.

MAKES 12 KEBABS TO SERVE 6 AS A MAIN COURSE

3 shallots, finely chopped
2 cloves garlic, crushed
3 tablespoons dark soy sauce
½ teaspoon dried chillies
2 teaspoons ground coriander
2 teaspoons ground ginger
2 tablespoons white malt
  vinegar

2 tablespoons vegetable oil
3lb (*1.4kg*) boneless beef or
  lamb, cut into ¾in (*2cm*)
  cubes
Peanut Sauce (see opposite) (for
  serving)

12 wooden or metal skewers

1 In a large, deep, non-reactive bowl, combine the shallots, garlic, soy sauce, red pepper, coriander, ginger, vinegar and oil. Add the meat cubes and mix until well coated with spices. Cover and refrigerate for at least 3 hours, or up to 12 hours.

2 *To finish.* Light the barbecue or heat the grill. Thread the meat on skewers and grill 2–3in (5–7cm) from the heat, until the meat is browned on the outside but still pink in the centre: 4–6 minutes on each side. Serve with Peanut Sauce.

Cook's Comment. These *saté* kebabs are just one of the dozen or more dishes that would be part of a *rijstafel* (see page 92), but they are excellent on their own with a rice pilaf and Peanut Sauce. Little ones make good cocktail hors-d'œuvre.

Bumbu Saté

PEANUT SAUCE

The food processor or blender of the modern kitchen is a boon when making this sauce, which traditionally is pounded laboriously in a mortar and pestle.

MAKES 16fl. oz (500ml) SAUCE TO SERVE 6–8

6oz (*175g*) shelled raw peanuts
1½ tablespoons peanut oil
½ onion, chopped
1 clove garlic, peeled
½ teaspoon dried hot red
   peppers

2 teaspoons ground ginger
1 teaspoon brown sugar
1½ tablespoons lemon juice
12fl. oz (*375ml*) hot water, or
   more if needed
salt and pepper

1 In a frying pan, fry the peanuts in the oil, stirring constantly until browned. Transfer them to a food processor or blender with the onion, garlic, hot peppers, ginger, brown sugar and lemon juice. Purée until very smooth, adding a little hot water if necessary so that the mixture churns well.

2 Work in more hot water, adding enough to make a sauce that is thick enough to coat a spoon. Transfer the sauce to a saucepan and simmer it for 2 minutes, stirring. Taste it for seasoning. Peanut Sauce can be made up to 2 weeks ahead and kept covered, in the refrigerator.

Epaule d'Agneau Farcie Bayonnaise

STUFFED SHOULDER OF LAMB WITH HAM

Lamb shoulder is the butcher's choice, sweet-tasting and less expensive than leg. In cooking demonstrations, it offers a handy lesson in boning, as well as an exercise in presentation as a roll or a plump stuffed cushion. But I've learned another lesson with it too. Lamb shoulder is never the same twice. In France, it can be so small you have to halve the other ingredients. When I was in Texas, lamb shoulder came in halves, split down the centre so that for stuffing it had to be sewn together again. In Australia, I learned that sheep bred for their wool don't make convenient eating. Despite my pleas, all the butcher could produce was a shoulder so massive it covered the whole chopping board. Boning it took an hour of hard physical labour instead of the 10 minutes you'll need for this recipe.

SERVES 6–8

a 4–5lb (*2kg*) shoulder of lamb
2 cloves garlic, chopped
1 teaspoon fresh or dried thyme
1 teaspoon fresh or dried
    rosemary
salt and pepper
4 thin slices raw or cooked
    ham, about 2oz (*60g*)
1 tablespoon vegetable oil
1 onion, quartered

1 carrot, quartered
1 tablespoon softened butter
½ pint (*300ml*) veal stock,* or
    more if needed
4fl. oz (*125ml*) white wine
Ratatouille (see page 152) or
    Roasted Garlic and Shallots
    (see page 153) (for serving)
watercress (for garnish)

1 *To bone the lamb shoulder.* Pull any skin from the shoulder, cutting it away with a knife where necessary. Trim off most of the fat, leaving just enough to keep the meat moist. With the fat side of the shoulder on the board, make a slit in the broad end of the meat and outline the blade bone with the point of the knife. Scrape the meat completely from the blade bone with the knife until you reach the joint. Cut through the joint and strip out the blade bone by grasping the joint end and pulling it sharply up and towards you. Turn the shoulder around and remove the arm bone by scraping downwards with short, sharp strokes to free the bone from the meat. With the point of the knife, find the joint connecting the arm bone to the centre bone and cut through the joint. Finally, cut the tendons around the centre bone and scrape the bone clean, working from each end until it can be pulled out. Cut the shoulder through one side of the pocket and lay it skin side down on the board. Reserve the bones.

2 Sprinkle the meat with garlic, thyme, rosemary, and a little salt and pepper. Set the ham slices on top. Roll up the meat in a cylinder and tie it neatly with string. It can be refrigerated for up to 24 hours. Let it return to room temperature before cooking.

3 *To roast the meat.* Heat the oven to Gas 8/230°C/450°F. Heat the oil in a roasting pan and add the lamb bones, onion and carrot. Spread the meat with the butter, sprinkle with salt and pepper and set it on the vegetables. Roast in the oven for 50–60 minutes for rare lamb (71°C/160°F on a meat thermometer) or 1–1¼ hours for medium done meat (80°C/175°F on a meat thermometer). Baste the meat during cooking and, if the pan becomes dry, add half the stock.

4 Remove the meat and keep it warm. If necessary, boil the cooking juices until reduced to a glaze.* Discard the fat from the pan, add the wine and boil until reduced by half, stirring to dissolve the juices. Add the remaining stock, bring to a boil, strain and taste for seasoning. Set the meat on a serving plate, spoon the Ratatouille or Roasted Garlic and Shallots around it and garnish with the watercress. Spoon over a little gravy and serve the rest separately.

Cook's Comment. Bayonne borders the Basque country, so roasted peppers, whether hot or in a salad, would be an appropriate accompaniment for the lamb as an alternative to Roasted Garlic and Shallots. The meat cuts into attractive spiral slices and is good cold as well as hot.

Daube d'Agneau Provençale

LAMB STEW WITH OLIVES AND TOMATO

Though really only a stew made with Mediterranean ingredients, *daube* is one of those warm Earth Mother dishes which attract literati of shy, inward-looking temperament. It even won over Virginia Woolf: 'An exquisite scent of olives and oil and juice rose from the great brown dish as Marthe, with a little flourish, took the cover off. She must take great care, Mrs Ramsey thought, diving into the soft mass, to choose a specially tender piece for William Bankes. And she peered into the dish, with its shiny walls and its confusion of brown and yellow meats and its bay leaves and its wine. . . . "It is a triumph," said Mr Bankes, laying down his knife for a moment. He had eaten attentively. It was rich; it was tender. It was perfectly cooked. How did she manage these things in the depths of the country? he asked her. She was a wonderful woman. All his love, all his reverence, had returned, and she knew it.' (*To the Lighthouse*).

After that, who could resist trying a *daube*!

SERVES 6–8

4lb (*1.8kg*) boned shoulder of
  lamb
1 calf's or pig's foot, split
½lb (*250g*) green olives, stoned,
  or mixed black and green olives
¾lb (*375g*) piece of lean bacon,
  cut into lardons*
1lb (*500g*) onions, sliced in thick
  rounds
1lb (*500g*) carrots, sliced in thick
  rounds
2lb (*1kg*) tomatoes, peeled,
  seeded and chopped*

3 cloves garlic, chopped
ground pepper
1¼ pints (*750ml*) water
For the marinade
large *bouquet garni**
2 strips of orange rind
2in (*5cm*) cinnamon stick
3 whole cloves
1 teaspoon black peppercorns
2 bay leaves
1 bottle (*750ml*) dry red wine

1 Cut the lamb into 2in (*5cm*) cubes, discarding sinew and fat. Layer it in a non-reactive bowl with the marinade ingredients and pour over the wine. Cover and refrigerate for at least 12 and up to 24 hours, stirring occasionally.

2 Heat the oven to Gas 6/200°C/400°F. Blanch the calf's or pig's foot: cover it with cold water, bring to a boil for 5 minutes and drain. Blanch the olives too if they are salty. Drain the meat, strain and reserve the marinade. Tie the flavourings in muslin or cheesecloth.

3 In a large deep casserole, layer the ingredients in the following order: lamb, bacon, olives, onions, carrots, tomatoes, garlic, ground pepper. Tuck the calf's or pig's foot down one side. Pour over the reserved marinade and water and add the bag of flavourings. Cover and bring to a boil in the oven.

4 Turn the oven heat to Gas 2/150°C/300°F and cook the *daube* until the lamb is so tender it can be cut with a spoon: 2–2½ hours. Remove the meat and vegetables with a slotted spoon. Discard the bag of flavourings. Boil the sauce to reduce it by about a third.

5 Meanwhile, pull the meat from the calf's or pig's foot, cut it into pieces, discarding the bones, and add to the lamb. When the sauce is well reduced, replace the meats and vegetables and season the *daube* to taste. It can be refrigerated for up to 3 days, or frozen.

Cook's Comment. *Daube* takes its name from *daubière*, the rotund earthenware pot in which it is cooked. Beef or veal can be used, though beef will take up to an hour longer to cook. Reflecting the influence of their Italian neighbours, Provençaux usually serve *daube* with pasta, particularly macaroni. Leftover *daube* can be shredded to stuff ravioli, or mixed with the gravy to form a meat sauce for pasta.

Jambon Normande

BAKED HAM WITH APPLES

Ham, I am happy to say, is a recurrent theme in my life. As a child, a 20-pounder swathed in muslin hung in a chilly back pantry called 'the bottom place'. My mother inspected the ham for maggots every few weeks and we consumed portions, little by little. At the first sign of rot around the bone, into the pot went the remaining meat. That was that for six months, until the next pig was killed.

Moving to Washington DC introduced me to Virginia hams. Dry, heavily smoked and often peppered, they were designed to keep well in the hot climate and had to be eaten differently. Served cold and plainly boiled, we often found them salty, so I took to adding them to dishes like Stuffed Shoulder of Lamb or Potted Ham and Beef (see pages 128 and 20). Back in Normandy, hams were milder again, smaller and less fatty than the York giants. A whole baked ham reappeared on our table for large parties and was eagerly consumed by French guests. The following recipe, which can be served hot or cold, is typically Norman, with its cider-and-cream sauce and its garnish of baked apples.

SERVES 12

a 12–16lb (*5.5–6.5kg*) cooked or
  uncooked country ham
4 tart apples, quartered and
  cored
1 onion, peeled and stuck with
  4 whole cloves
large *bouquet garni**
1 tablespoon peppercorns
1⅔ pints (*1 litre*) unsweetened
  apple juice, or more if serving
  the ham hot
4oz (*125g*) honey

For the apples
12–14 small, tart apples
1½oz (*45g*) dark raisins
1½oz (*45g*) golden raisins
1½oz (*45g*) chopped mixed
  candied citrus peel
4oz (*125g*) butter
For the apple-cream sauce
1¼ pints (*750ml*) reserved
  liquid from baking ham
16fl. oz (*500ml*) single cream
salt and pepper

1 If using an uncooked country ham, scrub it under cold water and trim off some of the fat. If the ham is salty, soak it in cold water for 12–24 hours, changing the water two or three times. Drain the ham and put it in a large pot with the quartered apples, onion, *bouquet garni* and peppercorns. Cover with cold water and bring to a boil, skimming occasionally. Cover the pot, reduce the heat and simmer the ham for 12 minutes per pound, plus 12 minutes more. Leave the ham to cool to lukewarm, then drain it, discarding the liquid. Cooked hams do not need this boiling step.

2 Use a knife to remove the skin from the ham. Trim off all but a thin layer of fat. Heat the oven to Gas 4/175°C/350°F. Put the ham in a deep roasting dish and add the apple juice. Cover loosely with foil and bake for 45 minutes.

3 Meanwhile, prepare the apples. Wash the apples and core them. Split the skin horizontally around the middle of each apple to prevent bursting and put them into a shallow buttered baking dish. Combine the raisins and candied fruits and stuff them into the apple cavities. Top each apple with a piece of butter. Pour about 4fl. oz (*125ml*) water into the baking dish and bake the apples in the oven with the ham, basting occasionally, until the apples are tender when pierced: 20–25 minutes. Remove them.

4 Uncover the ham and spoon the honey on top. Increase the oven temperature to Gas 8/230°C/450°F and continue baking, basting often until the ham is golden brown: 20–25 minutes. Transfer the ham to a serving dish.

5 *For the apple-cream sauce.* Strain the ham cooking liquid into a saucepan and skim off the fat. Simmer until reduced to about a teacupful. Add the cream, season to taste with salt and pepper, and bring to a boil; taste for seasoning. Ham, apples and sauce can be cooked 2 days ahead, covered and refrigerated.

6 If serving the ham cold, leave it with the apples to come to room temperature: 1–2 hours. Arrange the ham and apples on a serving dish.

7 If serving hot, put the ham in a roasting dish with about 4fl. oz (*125ml*) of apple juice, cover loosely with foil and heat in a Gas 4/175°C/350°F oven until a skewer inserted in the centre of the ham for 30 seconds is hot to the touch when withdrawn: about 45 minutes. Reheat the apples in the oven for the last 10–15 minutes of reheating. Bring the sauce to a boil on top of the stove. Arrange the ham and apples on a large serving dish and serve the sauce separately.

Cook's Comment. Cures for whole raw country hams on the bone vary so that it is hard to give precise cooking instructions. If the ham looks dry or salty, be sure to soak it in cold water for 12 hours or more, changing the water several times before boiling it with the apples and seasonings. After baking with apple juice and honey, Jambon Normande would be accompanied, if served hot, by small fried potatoes or, if cold, with potatoes vinaigrette.

Jambon Chablisienne

BAKED HAM WITH WHITE WINE AND CREAM

Most small towns in rural France still harbour a distant memory of the desperate human losses which the First World War visited on their fighting sons. But few, like Chablis, have also had to cope with two other blows: the nineteenth-century phylloxera plague, which crippled the local wine economy for a couple of generations, and the senseless bombing of the town by German aircraft in the Second World War. Not to be cowed into defeat, however, Chablis is now a sprightly wine centre with side streets that hide some notable cellars and a good kitchen or two. I was particularly taken by this recipe when I first tasted it at the Hôtel Etoile, just off the town square. Perhaps a glass, fresh from the cask, of the flinty, green-tinged local vintage helped. Certainly when I tried the idea at home the marriage of ham with juniper, pepper, cream, well-reduced vinegar and Chablis did seem particularly successful.

SERVES 4

2oz (60g) butter
1oz (30g) flour
12fl. oz (375ml) dry white
  Chablis wine
12fl. oz (375ml) veal stock*
5 juniper berries, crushed
5 black peppercorns, crushed
4 shallots, finely chopped
2½fl. oz (75ml) white wine
  vinegar

4fl. oz (125ml) crème fraîche or
  double cream
salt (optional)
4 thick slices cooked country
  ham, weighing about 1½lb
  (750g)
2 tablespoons Madeira
1 tablespoon mixed chopped
  tarragon and parsley
Pommes Duchesse (see opposite)

1 In a saucepan, melt half the butter, whisk in the flour and cook until foaming. Whisk in the wine, stock, juniper berries, peppercorns and half the shallots. Bring to a boil, stirring until the sauce thickens. Simmer for 10 minutes.

2 In a heavy pan, boil the vinegar with the remaining shallots until reduced to 1 tablespoon. Whisk in the wine sauce and simmer for 5–10 minutes until the sauce is well flavoured and lightly coats a spoon: 5–10 minutes. Strain, whisk in the cream and add salt to taste. The sauce can be kept in the refrigerator for up to 2 days, or frozen.

3 *To finish.* Heat the remaining butter in a frying pan and fry the ham slices until hot and lightly browned on both sides: 1–2 minutes. Arrange the ham on a serving dish and pipe Pommes Duchesse around the edge. Add the Madeira to the pan and stir to dissolve the pan juices. Pour in the sauce and heat until bubbling. Spoon half the sauce over the ham and sprinkle with the chopped herbs. Serve the remaining sauce separately.

Cook's Comment. For an interesting variation, omit the juniper berries and pepper-corns. Add 1 more tablespoon butter and stir in 1½ tablespoons paprika, cooking it over a very low heat for 2–3 minutes to mellow the flavour. Then stir in the flour and make the sauce as above. The paprika colours it a glowing red-gold.

Pommes Duchesse

PIPED POTATOES

Fickle French foodies, having recently rediscovered the joys of *'pommes purée'*, will surely soon return to Pommes Duchesse!

SERVES 6–8

2lb (*1kg*) potatoes, each cut into
2–3 pieces
1½oz (*45g*) butter
pinch of nutmeg

salt and white pepper
4 egg yolks

pastry bag and large star tube

1 Put the potatoes into a large pan of cold salted water, cover and bring to a boil. Simmer until tender: 15–20 minutes. Drain, return the potatoes to the pan and dry over a very low heat, stirring, for 2–3 minutes. Remove from the heat and work the potatoes through a sieve while still hot.

2 Return the purée to the pan with the butter, nutmeg, salt and pepper, and beat over a low heat until fluffy. Take from the heat and beat in the egg yolks. Taste the potatoes for seasoning. If not using immediately, rub the surface with butter to prevent a skin from forming.

Cook's Comment. As well as forming a decorative border, Duchesse Potatoes can be prepared ahead and piped in rosettes or mounds on a buttered baking sheet. When baked in a hot oven until brown, they form an attractive accompaniment to any dish in sauce.

Ris de Veau Sautés la Vénerie

SAUTEED SWEETBREADS WITH POTATOES, MUSHROOMS AND HAM

From a gastronomic viewpoint, the two years we spent in Luxembourg were a dead end. Crayfish and freshwater fish had long since disappeared from the Moselle, 'mountain' trout came from the hatchery, and game seemed to have fled over the border into the French and Belgian Ardennes. One dish I do remember was a substantial square of tripe, breaded and deep fried, which I later found the Lyonnais call 'a fireman's apron'. Dry but tough, the texture was certainly not unlike asbestos. Luckily France was not far away, with dishes like these sweetbreads, a speciality of the one-star restaurant La Vénerie in Sierck-les-Bains.

SERVES 4–6

1½lb (750g) (two pairs) calf's
  sweetbreads
½ lemon
4–5 tablespoons flour
salt and pepper
3oz (90g) butter
2 medium potatoes, peeled,
  boiled and cut into ½in
  (1.25cm) cubes

½lb (250g) smoked ham, finely
  diced
½lb (250g) mushrooms, sliced
2 large tomatoes, peeled,
  seeded and chopped
1 tablespoon chopped parsley
  (for sprinkling)

1 Soak the sweetbreads for 2–3 hours in cold water, changing the water once or twice. Drain and put them into a pan of cold salted water with the lemon half. Bring slowly to a boil, skimming occasionally, and simmer for 10 minutes. Drain, rinse the sweetbreads and peel them, removing the ducts and membranes. Press them between two plates with a weight on top and refrigerate for up to 24 hours.

2 Cut the sweetbreads into 'escalopes' – diagonal slices ½in (1.25cm) thick. Season the flour with salt and pepper and sprinkle on the sweetbreads, patting so that they are well coated. Heat half the butter in a large frying pan until foaming. Sauté the sweetbreads, in two batches if necessary, until tender and golden brown, allowing 4–5 minutes on each side. Keep them warm.

3 Melt the remaining butter in the pan. Add the potatoes, ham and mushrooms, and sauté until thoroughly browned: 5–8 minutes. Add the tomatoes, salt and pepper, and continue cooking until the tomatoes are pulpy and most of the moisture has evaporated: 2–3 minutes. Taste for seasoning. Place the sweetbreads on top and cover. If serving at once, heat gently for 2–3 minutes to blend the flavours. The sweetbreads can be refrigerated for up to 2 days.

4 If necessary, reheat the sweetbreads on top of the stove. Arrange them overlapping on a warm serving dish or individual plates and spoon the garnish down one side. Sprinkle with the parsley and serve.

Cook's Comment. I hold old-fashioned opinions about sweetbreads, for I cannot stand them undercooked and chewy. That's why I blanch them longer than usual, and when cleaning them I often pull away so much membrane that they start to fall apart. So much the better – the little bits fry in the butter until deliciously crisp. Some sweetbreads tend to fall apart anyway, because they come in pairs, one compact lobe, called the *'pomme'* (apple), and the other a looser lobe which is supposed to be less desirable.

Grilled Devilled Kidneys

Kidneys and sweetbreads are one of the secret sources of good eating in the USA. Few people buy them. A Gallup poll has recently revealed that 35 per cent of Americans would never eat kidneys, 24 per cent would not touch sweetbreads and almost half the population rejects brains. Gallup doesn't descend to mentioning testicles, but I was offered them once in Kansas under the sobriquet 'prairie oysters' – an item in plentiful supply on a cattle ranch.

SERVES 2

2 veal kidneys or 6–8 lamb's kidneys, weighing about 1lb (500g)
2 tablespoons vegetable oil
2 tablespoons Madeira
2 teaspoons Dijon mustard
1 teaspoon Worcestershire sauce

pinch of cayenne
salt and pepper
bunch of watercress
Light Béarnaise Sauce (see opposite)

4 kebab skewers

1 Peel the kidneys if necessary and cut out the cores with scissors. Cut veal kidneys into 1in (2.5cm) chunks and lamb kidneys in half. Thread the kidneys on skewers and put them on a shallow tray.

2 Whisk the oil with the Madeira, mustard, Worcestershire sauce and cayenne. Brush the mixture over the kidneys, cover and leave to marinate in the refrigerator for at least 30 minutes and up to 3 hours, turning occasionally.

3 Light the grill. Sprinkle the kidneys with salt and pepper and grill them 3–4in (7.5–10cm) from the heat, until browned outside but still pink in the centre: 3–4 minutes on each side. Set the skewers on individual plates, decorate with the watercress and serve the Light Béarnaise Sauce separately.

Cook's Comment. Kidneys must be eaten very fresh and they should smell sweet.

Light Béarnaise Sauce

Fresh herbs are vital in a delicate sauce like this. Basil, chervil, chives, mint or parsley could all be substituted for the tarragon.

MAKES 12fl. oz (375ml) SAUCE TO SERVE 4–6

6fl. oz (*175ml*) plain yoghurt
2fl. oz (*60ml*) white wine
  vinegar
2fl. oz (*60ml*) white wine
2 shallots, finely chopped

1 tablespoon chopped fresh
  tarragon
3 egg yolks
juice of 1 lemon, or more to taste
salt and pepper

1 Whip the yoghurt until smooth. In a small, heavy, non-reactive saucepan combine the vinegar, wine, shallots and tarragon. Boil until reduced to 1 tablespoon and allow to cool.

2 Whisk in the egg yolks and continue whisking until the mixture is pale: about 30 seconds. Set the pan over a low heat and whisk constantly until the mixture is creamy and thick enough for the whisk to leave a trail on the bottom of the pan. (*Note*: This should take 2–3 minutes; the base of the pan should be quite warm but never burning to the touch or else the mixture may separate.)

3 Take the pan from the heat and whisk in the yoghurt a tablespoonful at a time. Season the sauce to taste with lemon juice, salt and pepper. The sauce can be kept warm for up to 30 minutes in a *bain marie*.* (*Note*: The water should never be hotter than tepid, or the sauce may curdle.)

[139]

Medallions of Venison with Onion Confit

Why can't *nouvelle cuisine* chefs leave well alone! The current tendency to dress up dishes with trendy flavourings like ginger, pink peppercorns, chilli and lime shows its worst in game dishes. The flavour of most game is already so distinctive that it needs a suave background, not a sharp contrast. In this recipe the sauce is softened with cream and redcurrant jelly, while the onions bake gently until they are meltingly soft and transparent – an old-fashioned preserve or *confit* which can be kept for months if sealed with wax in a jar.

SERVES 6

6 medallions or steaks of
   venison, weighing about 2lb
   (1kg)
1 tablespoon vegetable oil
1 tablespoon butter
salt and pepper
2 tablespoons brandy
4fl. oz *(125ml) crème fraîche** or
   double cream
2–3 teaspoons redcurrant jelly
6 round *croûtes,** 3in *(7.5cm)* in
   diameter
bunch of watercress (for
   garnish)

For the marinade
8fl. oz *(250ml)* fruity red wine
1 teaspoon crushed juniper
   berries
½ teaspoon black peppercorns
1 tablespoon oil
2–3 sprigs fresh or dried thyme
For the onion confit
2 tablespoons butter
30 baby onions, peeled
1 tablespoon sugar
salt and pepper
3 tablespoons red wine

1 Put the venison medallions in a shallow tray. For the marinade, mix the wine, juniper berries and peppercorns, and pour over the venison. Spoon over the oil and set the thyme on top. Cover and refrigerate for 24 hours, turning the meat from time to time.

2 *For the onion confit.* In a frying pan, heat the butter and add the onions. Sprinkle with the sugar, salt and pepper and fry until well browned, shaking the pan so that they colour evenly: 5–7 minutes. Add the wine, cover the pan tightly and cook over a very low heat until the onions are glossy and meltingly soft: 25–30 minutes. If the onions start to stick before they are tender, add a few tablespoons of water. They can be refrigerated for up to 3 days. Fry the *croûtes*.

3 *To finish.* Drain the medallions, reserving the marinade, and pat them dry with paper towels. Heat the oil and butter in a frying pan until foaming. Sprinkle the venison with salt and pepper and sauté until browned outside but still pink in the centre: 4–5 minutes on each side. Add the brandy and flame. Remove the medallions and keep warm.

4 Add the marinade to the pan and boil until reduced by half, stirring to dissolve the pan juices. Whisk in the cream and redcurrant jelly and bring the sauce to a boil. Strain it into a saucepan, bring just back to a boil and taste, adding more redcurrant jelly or pepper if needed – the sauce should be quite highly seasoned. Meanwhile, reheat the onions on top of the stove and warm the *croûtes* in a low oven.

5 Set the medallions on the *croûtes* on individual plates, spoon over the sauce, set the onions on one side, and garnish with watercress.

Cook's Comment. Medallions, from the saddle of venison, are the most expensive cut but they are always tender and leave no waste. The trend now is towards mild-flavoured game, either because it is farmed or because wild animals are not hung long enough for the taste to develop. Therefore, to intensify flavour I suggest marinating the meat, though this step can be omitted and the marinade ingredients can be added directly to the pan to make the sauce.

Pâté de Chevreuil en Croûte

VENISON PATE IN PASTRY

It's Friday morning at La Varenne in Paris, and Chef Chambrette has just completed his favourite ritual – the end-of-the-week cleaning of the cold-store. Tired vegetables are cast in the stockpot, leftover fish makes one of his famous soups. *'Débarrasse moi de tout ça!'* he yells, thrusting in front of a student a motley collection of baby onions beginning to sprout, a scrag end of bacon, a pot of chicken livers and a little bit of venison left from class the day before. The result may be a snazzy fricassée with a touch of vinegar, or deep-fried rissoles with a ground-meat filling, or a full-blown pâté like this one. Whatever the outcome, it is bound to be memorable. A chef is as preoccupied as anyone else with using up the bits – he just does it better.

SERVES 10

1½lb (750g) venison
½lb (250g) slice of cooked ham,
cut into strips
2 tablespoons white wine
4 tablespoons brandy
1 egg, beaten to mix, with
½ teaspoon salt (for glaze)
For the sour-cream pastry dough
1lb (500g) flour
6oz (175g) unsalted butter
2 teaspoons salt
2 eggs
5 tablespoons sour cream, or
more if needed

For the stuffing
2lb (1kg) ground pork, equal
parts of fat and lean
4oz (125g) chicken livers,
trimmed and very finely
chopped
2 eggs, beaten to mix
2 teaspoons ground allspice
1 teaspoon ground nutmeg
1 teaspoon salt, or more if
needed
1 teaspoon pepper, or more if
needed

1 Make the sour-cream pastry as for *pâte brisée,** substituting sour cream for water. Chill the pastry for 30 minutes.

2 Slice half the venison into ⅜in (1cm) strips and cut the rest into small pieces. Put the venison and ham strips into a shallow dish, pour over the wine and half the brandy and leave to marinate for 30 minutes.

3 *For the stuffing.* Work the pieces of venison with the pork through the fine plate of a mincer into a large bowl. Add the remaining brandy, chicken livers, the 2 eggs, allspice, nutmeg, salt and pepper. Drain the marinade from the meat strips and add these too. Beat the mixture well with your hand or a wooden spoon until it comes away from the sides of the bowl: 2–3 minutes. (*Note*: This gives the pâté body so that it slices well.) Fry a small piece of stuffing in a frying pan and taste, adding more seasoning if necessary – it should be quite spicy.

4 Roll out the pastry on a floured work surface to a 14 × 20in (*35 × 50cm*) rectangle. Divide the stuffing in four. Spread one portion lengthwise on the dough in a 4 × 14in (*10 × 35cm*) strip. Top with half the strips of venison. Cover with a second portion of stuffing, then add the strips of ham and a third layer of stuffing. Cover this with the remaining venison strips and top with the remaining stuffing. Mould the filling with your hands so that the rectangle is as neat and tall as possible.

5 Cut a 2in (*5cm*) square from each corner of the pastry and brush the edges of the rectangle with the egg glaze. Lift one long edge of dough over the top of the filling, then fold over the opposite edge to enclose the filling completely. Fold the ends to make a neat package and press gently to seal. Lightly grease a baking sheet and roll the pâté on to it so that the seam is underneath.

6 Brush the pâté with egg glaze. Cut leaves from leftover pastry and attach them to the top of the pastry with glaze. Brush the leaves with glaze. With a sharp knife, cut three holes in the top of the pâté. Insert a roll of foil in each hole to form a 'chimney' for steam to escape. Cover and refrigerate until firm: ½–1 hour.

7 Heat the oven to Gas 6/200°C/400°F. Bake the pâté until the pastry is set and starts to brown: 15–20 minutes. Reduce the heat to Gas 4/175°C/350°F and continue baking until a skewer inserted in the centre of the pâté is hot to the touch when withdrawn after 30 seconds: 1¼–1½ hours. If the pastry browns too quickly during baking, cover it loosely with foil. Let the pâté cool on the baking sheet for 5 minutes before transferring it to a serving dish.

8 The pâté can be made up to 3 days ahead and refrigerated, or frozen. If serving cold, let it come to room temperature. If serving warm, reheat it in a Gas 4/175°C/350°F oven for 25–35 minutes. Cut the pâté into thick slices for serving.

Cook's Comment. What a chance to offer interesting accompaniments! Hot pâté asks for a Madeira sauce, glazed chestnuts, potato pancakes, Fried Onions and Apples with Bacon (see page 157) – possibly all at once. If the pâté is cold, you could go the English route with Cumberland sauce made with redcurrant jelly, and potato salad, or opt for a French accompaniment of Celeriac in Mustard Mayonnaise (see page 188) and Onion Confit (see page 140). If you cannot get venison, any game meat will do, including rabbit.

Vegetables, Pasta and Rice

It's worth remembering that, compared with herbs, vegetables are relative newcomers to the table. Four hundred years ago, most were regarded as food for the poor, a penance to be swallowed only on days of fast. Herbs were the major preoccupation. The herbalist Thomas Tusser recommended no less than forty-two seeds and herbs for the kitchen, twenty-two herbs and roots for salads and sauce, eleven for boiling and buttering, seventeen herbs for the still, and twenty-five for the physic garden, with others for strewing (on floors) and for windows and pots. He certainly puts modern plant catalogues to shame!

In her classic *Vegetable Book*, Jane Grigson points out that it was not until the mid-eighteenth century that vegetables acquired their own identity as 'herbs and roots grown for food'. Before that the word vegetable denoted a class of objects as in 'animal, vegetable, mineral'. New vegetables like the tomato, potato, bell pepper and squash – all imports from the Americas – were slow to catch on. Even now, prejudices about the vegetable kingdom die hard. Americans still don't think much of Brussels sprouts, seem unable to grow their own chicory, yet turn out megatons of low-cost green asparagus for which the French pay such extortionate prices. In fact, whenever I go to Europe in winter it strikes me how little green stuff is available even now. Until the jet engine got Europe moving with imports of *haricots verts* from Burkina Faso and lettuce from the Levant, the winter provisioning in northern climes was limited to roots and cabbage. There's no substitute for living on the same continent as California, which seems to assure American supermarkets of bountiful supplies year round.

My most vivid picture of Jane Grigson is of a sturdy figure in rubber boots planted firmly in the middle of the vegetable garden at Le Fey, with Monsieur Milbert beside her, leaning, as always, on his hoe with yesterday's hand-rolled cigarette still affixed to his lips. The planter's moon had risen early that year – an inauspicious start. What of the apple trees, whose buds had fallen prey to a tardy frost? Would the baby lettuces survive the unseasonably wet and chilly May? In that 250-year-old garden, I wonder how many times precisely the same circumstantial encounter has not taken place. But rarely, I think, between two such experts.

Petits Pois à la Française

GREEN PEAS WITH BACON AND LETTUCE

My husband Mark collects old menu cards. Some are displayed in a big picture frame and our guests like to invent stories about the occasions they were printed for. Was the marriage a success? Did the baby being christened grow up well? What battle was the regiment remembering? Our American guests particularly relish the menu perpetrated by one R.B. Saft, 'cosmopolitan refreshment contractor', as he called himself, for an Independence Day celebration on 4 July 1879 in Baden, Switzerland. The *pièce montée*, or centrepiece, was Plymouth Rock with the landing of the Pilgrims in 1620 rendered, I like to think, in marzipan. The *soupe du jour* was 'Boston Tea Party' consommé. With 'Capon Abraham Lincoln' and 'Galantine of Pheasant Ulysses S. Grant' among the entrées, the menu displayed the typical European bias toward the Northern, or Union, side in America's recently concluded Civil War. In America, besides patriotic speeches, the Fourth of July meant salmon served with the season's new peas. The Swiss menu obliged with Chesapeake salmon and 'green peas in the plain Ben Franklin fashion'. It is not out of the question that Franklin, during his long (1776–85) residence in France on behalf of the American colonies, ate something like this braise of peas with bacon.

SERVES 6–8

6 thin slices streaky bacon, diced
1oz (*30g*) butter
6–8 spring onions, cut into lengths
1 head cos lettuce, coarsely shredded

2–3 pints (*about 1 litre*) shelled fresh peas (4–5lb (*2kg*) peas in the pod)
½ pint (*300ml*) water
2 teaspoons sugar
salt and pepper
*bouquet garni**
2 tablespoons kneaded butter*

1 In a heavy pan fry the bacon in the butter until the fat runs. Add the spring onions, lettuce and peas. Stir until all are coated with fat.

2 Add the water, sugar, salt, pepper and *bouquet garni*. Cover and cook over a low heat for 15–20 minutes or until the peas are tender.

3 Taste the peas for seasoning. Discard the *bouquet garni*. If a good deal of liquid has been produced, thicken it by adding small pieces of kneaded butter, shaking the pan over the heat so that the butter melts and thickens the sauce. Bring just to a boil, to cook the flour. (*Note*: Add only enough butter to thicken lightly. If the peas are moist but not watery, kneaded butter may not be necessary.) The peas can be refrigerated for up to 2 days.

Cook's Comment. Braised peas go with any dish as a substitute for frozen.

Burnt Green Beans

All families have codenames and burnt beans is one of ours. When our daughter, Emma, was small I would invariably reheat for her supper the food from dinner the night before. Green beans fried in butter until scorched a bit around the edges were her favourite, soon adopted by the rest of us. The beans acquire a melting, old-fashioned richness which the French call *confit* – a style which suits all but the finest of baby *haricots verts*.

SERVES 4

2lb (*1kg*) green beans   salt and pepper
2–3 tablespoons butter

1 Cook the beans in a large pan of boiling salted water until tender but still firm: 8–10 minutes, depending on age and variety of the beans. Drain the beans, rinse them with cold water and drain again well. If possible, leave them to cool thoroughly.

2 *To finish.* Melt the butter in a wok or large frying pan. Add the beans and toss until coated. Leave to cook over a very low heat, stirring occasionally, until the beans are soft: 15–20 minutes. Season to taste with salt and pepper.

Cook's Comment. Brussels sprouts and cabbage also benefit from the *confit* method, though they do not approach the perfection of green beans.

Stir-fried Cabbage

If you think a wok is for Chinese cooking only, you're missing a lot. I discovered the wok two years ago and it rapidly became indispensable. Its thin shell and smooth surface brown vegetables much more efficiently than a Western frying pan, and a wok is spacious enough for stirring large quantities. The pan is cheap, easy to clean (once the surface is thoroughly proved) and the economy of its design, with the companion stirrer nicely curved to its contours, is a delight.

SERVES 3–4

1 small head (about 1lb (*500g*))
    Savoy or white cabbage,
    shredded
2 tablespoons peanut oil
1 tablespoon finely chopped
    fresh ginger

1 spring onion, thinly sliced
1 clove garlic, finely chopped
1 tablespoon dark soy sauce
a few drops sesame oil

1 Blanch the cabbage by plunging it into a large pan of boiling water for 2 minutes. Drain and rinse the cabbage with cold water and drain it again thoroughly. It can be blanched several hours ahead.

2 *To finish.* Heat the peanut oil until very hot, add the ginger, spring onion and garlic and fry for 30 seconds, stirring constantly. Add the cabbage and fry over a very high heat, tossing and stirring constantly until the cabbage is very hot: 2–3 minutes. Add the soy sauce and toss well. Take from the heat, sprinkle with a few drops of sesame oil, toss and serve at once.

Cook's Comment. Other blanched vegetables, such as broccoli or green beans, also do well finished this way and they certainly are not limited to a Chinese meal; they are an ideal accompaniment to grilled meats, poultry or fish.

Champignons Sauvages en Persillade

WILD MUSHROOMS WITH GARLIC AND PARSLEY

When I was a child, mushrooms grew by the basketful in the neighbouring paddock
– not only little pink-and-white field mushrooms but also big 'horse' mushrooms
which supposedly gave you stomach-ache, though I never believed it. Sadly, within
a couple of decades, the mushrooms were wiped out by chemical fertilisers. Today's
children rarely awaken to find a field dotted with white mushrooms, popped up
overnight as if by magic.

In fact, many of today's varieties of so-called wild mushrooms are often cultivated,
their origin betrayed by their cleanliness and large size. But in the right place at the
right time – Oregon in April for morels; the Ardennes in August for yellow-and-
black *girolle* trumpet mushrooms; or the Alps in October for boletus – you will find
the genuine wild fungi, freshly picked and with a heady aroma and taste. (If you
pick them yourself, be sure to call in an expert to identify them with absolute
certainty.) Boletus, *girolles*, oyster mushrooms, or eye-catching orange chicken-in-
the-woods, you cannot do better than to cook them like this, with a shower of garlic
and parsley. Only the princely morel needs the gentler background of butter and
cream.

SERVES 4–6

1lb (*500g*) wild mushrooms	3–4 cloves garlic, finely
1oz (*30g*) butter	chopped
2 tablespoons vegetable oil	3–4 tablespoons chopped
salt and pepper	parsley

1 Pick over the mushrooms and trim the stems. Rinse them quickly in a bowl of cold
water, lifting them out with your hands so that any sand or grit is left behind.

2 In a frying pan, heat half the butter and half the oil. Add the mushrooms, season
with salt and pepper and cook over a high heat for 5 minutes. (*Note*: Some
mushrooms, particularly boletus and oyster mushrooms, can produce a great deal of
liquid. If they do, drain them and put them back in the pan.) Add the remaining
butter and oil with the garlic, and continue frying, tossing constantly, until the
mushrooms begin to brown. Stir in the parsley, taste for seasoning and serve.

Cook's Comment. You can cook just one kind of wild mushroom, or a glorious
medley of black, white and gold fungi. They are the perfect accompaniment to game
and red meats, and make a wonderful first course, served on toast or on a bed of tart
greens like curly endive with radicchio.

[149]

Epinards et Champignons Gratinés Ali-Bab

GRATIN OF SPINACH AND MUSHROOMS

There's a limit to the number of times you can serve leaf spinach at the height of the growing season, but I decline to purée it because of the mess. So once again Ali-Bab (see page 65) comes to the rescue with this little number.

SERVES 6

2lb (1kg) spinach
3oz (90g) butter
½lb (250g) mushrooms,
   trimmed and sliced

salt and pepper
2oz (60g) grated Gruyère cheese

1 Cook the spinach* and coarsely chop it. Melt half the butter in a pan and sauté the spinach, stirring constantly, until it is very dry: 4–5 minutes. Melt another tablespoon of butter in a saucepan and sauté the mushrooms with salt and pepper until tender: 2–3 minutes. Mix the mushrooms and spinach and taste for seasoning.

2 Spread the vegetables in a buttered baking dish, smoothing the top. Melt the remaining butter, drizzle it over the vegetables and sprinkle with the grated cheese. The *gratin* can be refrigerated for 48 hours, or frozen.

3 *To finish.* Heat the oven to Gas 5/190°C/375°F. Bake the *gratin* until very hot and browned: 20–25 minutes.

Cook's Comment. This recipe is a good disguise for frozen spinach.

Artichokes with Tarragon and Lemon Sauce

From childhood I've loved globe artichokes. My aunt grew a special variety with prickly leaves and a more pronounced flavour than the soft-leaved commercial type. The only other place I have come across it was halfway around the world in Rio de Janeiro, so imagine my delight when we moved to Burgundy and I found the same variety growing in the garden. The sauce I owe to an American associate whose Greek background led to this variation on *avgolemono*.

SERVES 6

6 globe artichokes
½ lemon
For the lemon and tarragon sauce
3 tablespoons lemon juice
8oz (*250g*) cold unsalted butter,
   cut into pieces

4 tablespoons chopped fresh
   tarragon
white pepper

1 Bring a large pan of salted water to a boil. Trim the artichoke stems so that the artichokes will sit flat and rub the cut surface with the lemon half to prevent discoloration. Trim about 1in (*2.5cm*) of the top leaves parallel with the base. Trim the remaining leaves to remove spines.

2 Put the artichokes in the pan of boiling water and lay a teatowel on top to keep the artichokes completely immersed. Simmer them until the leaves pull out easily: 30–40 minutes.

3 Drain the artichokes thoroughly, remembering to drain them upside down; leave them to cool slightly. With your fingers pinch the cone of central leaves and lift it out. Using a teaspoon, scoop out the choke which is hidden inside the outer leaves and discard. Replace the cone upside down on top of the artichoke. Keep them warm.

4 *For the sauce.* In a small saucepan, bring the lemon juice to a simmer. Remove from the heat and whisk in the butter, a few pieces at a time, working on and off the heat so that the butter softens and thickens the sauce but does not melt to oil. Whisk in the tarragon and white pepper to taste. Serve the sauce separately from the artichokes.

Cook's Comment. Particularly good with asparagus, this sauce is handy with most green vegetables.

Ratatouille

Now, two generations later, it is easy to identify the French dishes brought to Britain in the 1950s by Elizabeth David and to the USA in the 1960s by Julia Child. They stand without translation – quiche lorraine, bœuf bourguignon, cassoulet, bouillabaisse, and of course, ratatouille, for which both authors give authoritative recipes. Their difference of approach clearly illustrates how no recipe can ever be definitive.

Julia Child is writing for the novice. She measures ingredients exactly and cautions against the danger of scorching pans. She warns that all the vegetables should 'retain their own shape and character', and goes to considerable trouble to fry them one by one. Elizabeth David is more freewheeling, taking two of this and three of that, with coffee cups of oil (after-dinner size!). She can assume her readers have a certain skill, so she combines everything cheerfully in the pan and cooks until 'quite soft, but not too mushy'. You can take your pick of styles, but for me the clincher is in the choice of ingredients, with David's use of sweet red peppers and crushed coriander giving the authentic Mediterranean flavour.

In my recipe for ratatouille I've added yet another dimension by cooking in a wok. Not only can the vegetables be fried quickly with a minimum of fat, but a wok allows large quantities to be cooked rapidly and stirred without crushing them to purée.

SERVES 6–8

2 medium aubergines weighing about 1lb (*500g*)
4 small courgettes, weighing about ¾lb (*375g*)
salt and pepper
5–6 tablespoons olive oil, or more if needed
3 red peppers, weighing about ¾lb (*375g*), cored, seeded and cut into strips

3 medium onions, sliced
1lb (*500g*) tomatoes, peeled, seeded and chopped*
2 cloves garlic, crushed
½ teaspoon ground coriander
2–3 sprigs fresh thyme
2 tablespoons coarsely chopped fresh basil or parsley

1 Wipe the aubergines and courgettes, trim the ends and cut them into ⅜in (*1cm*) slices. Sprinkle them with salt, turn, sprinkle the other side and leave them on a tray for 30 minutes so that the juices are drawn out. Rinse the vegetables and dry them on paper towels.

2 Heat 2–3 tablespoons of the olive oil in a wok and fry the aubergine slices until brown on both sides. Remove them, and fry the courgette slices until brown too, adding more oil if necessary. Take them out, add the peppers and fry them in a little more oil until just limp. Remove them also.

3 Fry the onion in a tablespoon more oil until soft and lightly browned. Add the aubergine, courgette, tomatoes, garlic, coriander, thyme, salt and pepper, and stir until mixed. Cover and cook until the vegetables are tender: 10–15 minutes. If they are very moist, cook them uncovered for 3–5 minutes to evaporate the liquid, stirring often. Stir in the basil or parsley and taste for seasoning.

4 Ratatouille can be refrigerated for up to 3 days and it improves on standing. It can be reheated on top of the stove or served at room temperature.

Cook's Comment. This short cooking time leaves the vegetables firm *à la* Julia Child, so if you prefer them softer, keep cooking for 10–15 minutes longer. A more traditional heavy casserole can be used instead of a wok.

Roasted Garlic and Shallots

Round about mid-June, the first garlic and shallots of the season arrive on our kitchen table in Burgundy. What a treat – the shallots juicy and fragrant, the garlic so mild you can practically eat a whole clove raw. By August the soft outer skins have dried to the more familiar papery brown or white. Although the flavours are assertive, we continue to roast them both, blanching the garlic first to mellow its pungency.

SERVES 8

¾lb (*375g*) garlic heads, divided into cloves
2 tablespoons olive oil, or more if needed

salt and pepper
1½lb (*750g*) shallots, peeled

1 Heat the oven to Gas 3/160°C/325°F. If the skin on the garlic is dry, the cloves should be blanched: put the cloves in a pan of cold water, bring to a boil and simmer 3 minutes; drain and peel the cloves. If the garlic is very fresh, peel without blanching.

2 Put the garlic in a shallow baking dish with a tablespoon of the oil. Sprinkle with salt and pepper and stir until coated. Repeat in a separate dish with the shallots, adding oil, salt and pepper. Bake the garlic and shallots uncovered in the oven until they are tender and golden brown, allowing 20–25 minutes for the garlic and 30–40 minutes for the shallots, depending on size. Stir them occasionally and sprinkle with more oil if either starts to char.

3 The garlic and shallots can be refrigerated for up to 2 days. Reheat them in the oven or on top of the stove.

Cook's Comment. Roasted Garlic and Shallots are addictive, particularly when served with roast lamb or beef.

Fresh Maize or Corn Pudding

My one regret about spending summer in France, as we have for the last fifteen years, is missing the American season for corn on the cob. By tradition, corn should be picked in the backyard and rushed to the kitchen on winged feet. Only once have we had that opportunity, at a summerhouse on the Delaware shore. Sam Sloan, the farmer, grew a small patch of maize for friends, and each weekend evening he would make deliveries for the supper table. The ears of corn were indeed impressively tender and sweet – almost too sweet to be true. The rest of the menu was equally predictable: roast chicken with huge, juicy beefsteak tomatoes baked in the oven, baked potatoes, and a Peach Pie (see page 254), all of it locally grown.

SERVES 8

8 ears of fresh maize or corn
1½oz (45g) flour
16fl. oz (500ml) milk
4 eggs, separated

2oz (60g) melted butter
salt and pepper

about 5-pint (3-litre) shallow baking dish

1 With a sharp knife, cut the maize or corn kernels from the ear, pressing out the milk. Measure the kernels and liquid – there should be 1⅔ pints (*1 litre*).

2 In a bowl, stir the flour into the maize or corn kernels, followed by the milk, egg yolks, butter, and salt and pepper to taste. The maize or corn mixture can be refrigerated for up to 6 hours.

3 *To finish.* Heat the oven to Gas 4/175°C/350°F and butter the baking dish. Stiffly whip the egg whites and fold them into the maize or corn mixture. Spoon the mixture into the baking dish and bake in the oven until firm and golden brown: 20–25 minutes. Serve as soon as possible.

Cook's Comment. Good with ham, pork, or any dish well-suited by a sweet accompaniment.

Haricots à la Vigneronne

BAKED RED KIDNEY BEANS WITH RED WINE

One of the most curious weeks I have ever spent was as part of a team from La Varenne teaching twenty chefs from US Army mess halls in Frankfurt. The aim was to revive flagging staff enthusiasm and introduce a few new dishes among the hamburgers and club sandwiches. We worked eighteen hours a day but the students had a ball, concocting an innocuous-looking cocktail with Madeira and cream designed to look like coffee. Cooking difficulties were compounded by a chef who kept disappearing to the red-light district just when he was needed most. At the final banquet, the Seafood Newburg burned and the kidney beans in the cassoulet fermented overnight, despite having been chilled in the cold-store. Ever since, I cannot eat baked beans without remembering the whole episode.

SERVES 8

1½lb (*750g*) dried red kidney
  beans
1 onion, studded with 1 clove
large *bouquet garni**
4 cloves garlic, peeled

½lb (*250g*) piece of streaky
  bacon
16fl. oz (*500ml*) fruity red wine
salt and pepper

1 Cover the beans generously with water and let them soak overnight. Drain them.

2 Heat the oven to Gas 3/160°C/325°F. Put the beans, onion, *bouquet garni* and garlic into a large pan and bury the bacon in the beans. Add the wine and enough water to cover. Cover with the lid, bring to a boil on top of the stove and bake in the oven until the beans are very tender: 1–1½ hours. If necessary, add more water. At the end of cooking, the liquid should just cover the beans, but if they are soupy, boil uncovered to evaporate some liquid. Take out the bacon, dice it and stir it back into the beans. Season with salt and pepper.

3 Despite my unfortunate Frankfurt experience, baked beans can usually be refrigerated for 2 days and the flavour mellows on keeping. Reheat them on top of the stove.

Cook's Comment. This recipe was suggested in a Languedoc cookbook as part of a vineyard feast to include snails, spicy sausage, and lamb barbecued with herbs.

Bubble and Squeak

I still cannot approach the town of Cheltenham without a shudder. This is where I was at school for six miserable years. Given my vocation, it might have been the execrable food that did me in, but there was much more to it than that. Do physical cruelty and an unfeeling environment always go hand in hand with a classical education? Calvinist principles of self-denial permeated the menus and our suppers followed a leaden cycle of Yorkshire pudding and gravy but no meat, baked beans with boiled rice, baked potato, Welsh rarebit without the cheese, and sausage custard, followed by a dozen or more slices of bread and margarine, as much as we could cram down in the allotted time. For thirteen weeks we never saw a piece of fresh fruit.

I note that even that Victorian superman, Sir Richard Burton, complained bitterly about conditions at his boarding school in Richmond, where a reign of terror prevailed and 'Saturday was a day to be feared on account of its peculiar pie, which contained all the waifs and strays of the week'. The only dish I remember with any pleasure from Cheltenham is Bubble and Squeak, with its crispy browned bits of potato hidden among the cabbage.

SERVES 6 AS A MAIN COURSE, 8 AS AN ACCOMPANIMENT

1 small (1½lb) (750g)) Savoy cabbage, coarsely shredded
salt and pepper
2lb (1kg) potatoes

4–5 tablespoons dripping from roast meat, or lard or butter
1 medium onion, thinly sliced

1 *To cook the cabbage.* Bring a large pan of salted water to a boil. Add the cabbage and boil, uncovered, until tender but still firm: 5–8 minutes. Rinse with cold water and drain thoroughly.

2 *To cook the potatoes.* Put them, unpeeled, in a large pan of salted water and bring to a boil. Simmer until just tender: 15–20 minutes. Drain them, let them cool slightly and peel them. Return them to the pan and mash with a masher or fork – a few lumps do not matter.

3 *To finish.* In a large frying pan, heat a tablespoon of the fat and fry the onion until soft but not brown. Add the remaining fat and heat well. Mix in the cabbage and potatoes and season with salt and pepper. Pack down lightly and fry without stirring until the bottom is crisp and nicely browned. Stir to mix the crust into the vegetables, then fry again to make another crust. Continue until the crisp brown pieces are thoroughly mixed with the vegetables: 15–20 minutes. Serve very hot.

Cook's Comment. The best Bubble and Squeak is made with leftover potatoes and cabbage, because they brown much more satisfactorily than when freshly cooked. The name is said to have come from the noise made as the vegetables fry in the pan, though they have never done it for me.

Fried Onions and Apples with Bacon

It is no accident that this Pennsylvania Dutch recipe so closely resembles Alsatian *Schnitzen* made with dried apples and pears, potatoes and bacon. Part of the heritage of both regions is German.

SERVES 4

4 firm apples, such as Granny
   Smiths, unpeeled
1 tablespoon vegetable oil
4 slices streaky bacon, diced

1 teaspoon sugar
3 onions, cut into thick rings
salt and pepper

1 Core the apples and cut them into ⅜in (*1cm*) slices.

2 Heat the oil in a large frying pan and fry the bacon until crisp. Remove it with a draining spoon and dry on paper towels. Discard all but 2 tablespoons of the fat from the pan. Add the apple rings to the pan, sprinkle with half the sugar, turn, and fry briskly until browned. Sprinkle the apples with the remaining sugar, turn and brown the other side.

3 Remove the apples from the pan; add the onions, salt and pepper, and cook until brown, stirring occasionally. Return the bacon and apples to the pan, stir lightly to mix and taste for seasoning.

4 The mixture can be kept at room temperature for a few hours, but it loses its fresh flavour if refrigerated. Undercook it slightly to allow for reheating and warm it quickly in a frying pan.

Cook's Comment. This original alternative to fried onions has the same affinity for rich meats like duck, pork and liver.

Gratin Dauphinois

GRATIN OF POTATOES

The true glory of Gratin Dauphinois, the French version of scalloped potatoes, was revealed to me by Chef Chambrette, who used to make them by the vat in his restaurant. Wildly rich, the potatoes are first simmered in milk to remove their acidity (potatoes are surprisingly acid), then in cream. After that kind of treatment, with or without a topping of grated cheese, they are almost impossible to spoil.

SERVES 6–8

2lb (*1kg*) potatoes
2 pints (*1.25 litres*) milk
12fl. oz (*375ml*) double cream
12fl. oz (*375ml*) *crème fraîche** or
    more double cream

salt and pepper
pinch of grated nutmeg
3oz (*90g*) grated Gruyère cheese

1 Peel the potatoes, thinly slice them and add them to the milk at once to prevent them from discolouring. Bring to a boil and simmer until almost tender: 15–20 minutes. (*Note*: Potatoes take longer to cook in milk than in water.)

2 Drain the potatoes and wipe out the pan. Return the potatoes to the pan with the double cream and *crème fraîche*. Season to taste with salt, pepper and nutmeg, cover, bring to a boil and simmer until the potatoes are very tender: 10–15 minutes.

3 Butter a baking dish and spread the potatoes and cream in it. Sprinkle the top with the grated cheese. The *gratin* can be refrigerated for up to 48 hours.

4 *To finish.* Heat the oven to Gas 4/175°C/350°F. Bake the *gratin* until very hot and browned on top: 25–30 minutes.

Cook's Comment. Without parboiling the potatoes in milk, I find that the cream in Gratin Dauphinois invariably curdles in the oven.

Madame Milbert's Potatoes with Garlic

Plump little Madame Milbert, whose chickens supply our Burgundian table with such an abundance of eggs, is a remarkably good cook. She has that gift for seasoning and cooking ingredients to just the right extent so that they taste their best. It was she who suggested I add whole unpeeled cloves of fresh garlic to perfume fried potatoes.

SERVES 6–8

2lb (*1kg*) potatoes
8fl. oz (*250ml*) vegetable oil
8oz (*250g*) butter

16–20 whole garlic cloves,
   unpeeled
salt

1 Heat the oven to Gas 6/200°C/400°F. Peel the potatoes, cut them into 3–4 pieces each and trim any sharp edges. Heat the oil and butter in a shallow flameproof baking dish and add the potatoes; they should all touch the bottom and be half covered with fat. Heat them on top of the stove until bubbling: 3–5 minutes.

2 Fry the potatoes in the oven for 20 minutes. Add the garlic and continue cooking until the potatoes are very brown and crisp and the garlic is tender: 15–25 minutes. Lift out the potatoes and garlic with a draining spoon and dry them on paper towels. The potatoes can be refrigerated for up to 48 hours and reheated in a low oven, but they will not be quite so crisp.

3 Just before serving, sprinkle the potatoes with salt. When squashed with a knife, the garlic cloves yield a delicious purée to eat with the potatoes.

Cook's Comment. Goose fat makes the very best golden-brown potatoes, and this mixture of oil and butter is next best. The fat left over from frying can be used again and again.

Pommes Darfin

BUTTER POTATO CAKE

The changing role of the chef is an interesting reflection of social patterns. In medieval times the master cook was a quartermaster with a staff of hundreds – at least in a princely household. He controlled the daily provisions for thousands of nobles and retainers, and the lavishness of his food mirrored the power and prestige of his master. By the seventeenth century food was still an important reflection of social status, but the chef was more closely linked to the cooking; he wrote cookbooks and named recipes after patrons like the Marquis Béchamel or the Duc de Soubise, whose names now connote white sauce and onion sauce. It was not until the mid-nineteenth century, when fine dining had switched from private houses to restaurants, that chefs began to qualify their own creations with their surnames. Whoever Chef Darfin was – he is post-war, I think, but I cannot trace him further – he had a way of cooking potatoes that is now part of the modern repertoire.

In the latest change, chefs have become promoters, merchandising their names and, some would say, their integrity by endorsing domestic stoves and frozen foods.

SERVES 4

2lb (*1kg*) potatoes, peeled
2 tablespoons vegetable oil
2oz (*60g*) butter

salt and pepper

*7–8in (18–20cm) frying pan,
preferably non-stick*

1 Heat the oven to Gas 5/190°C/375°F. Cut the peeled potatoes into julienne strips and dry thoroughly on paper towels. (*Note*: Do not soak the potatoes in water as this removes some of their starch, which is needed to stick the cake together.)

2 Spread half the butter over the base and sides of the pan and add the oil. Press in a thick layer of potatoes, dot them with butter and sprinkle with salt and pepper. Add the remaining potatoes and butter, seasoning each layer. Cover the pan with buttered foil and top with a lid and a weight.

3 Cook the potatoes on top of the stove over a low heat until the bottom is browned: about 10 minutes. To check, lift up one side of the potatoes with a metal spatula – you should smell browned butter. Bake the potatoes in the oven until the cake is very tender: 20–30 minutes. Loosen the cake with a metal spatula and turn it out on to a serving dish. It can be refrigerated for up to 24 hours and reheated in a low oven, but will lose some of its crispness.

Cook's Comment. The julienne blade on a food processor does an excellent job on potatoes. Alternatively, slice the potatoes on a mandoline cutter, or slice them thinly by hand, then cut them into strips.

Sunday Night Pilaf

In these days of 'fresh' cuisine, the creative use of leftovers is not regarded as an art. Yet croquettes, creamed fish and poultry, rissoles and even soufflés were all designed to accommodate leftovers, not to mention little concoctions delicately referred to in the more flossy cookbooks as 'rechauffés'. My own solution to using odd bits and pieces is to put them in a pilaf, which often ends up tasting better than the original dish.

SERVES 6–8 AS A MAIN DISH

2 tablespoons vegetable oil
3–4 slices streaky bacon, diced, or 2oz (60g) chopped ham
1 onion, sliced
10oz (300g) long-grain rice
1 pint (600ml) veal stock* or water
3–4 mushrooms, sliced (optional)
*bouquet garni**
salt and pepper
4oz (125g) cooked shredded chicken or flaked cooked fish
4oz (125g) cooked sliced green vegetables such as broccoli, green beans, courgettes or cabbage
2 cloves garlic, chopped
1 tablespoon tomato purée
2–3 tablespoons white wine
large pinch cayenne or ½ teaspoon Tabasco, or more to taste
grated Parmesan or Gruyère cheese (for serving)

1 Heat the oven to Gas 4/175°C/350°F. Heat half the oil in a heavy casserole and fry the bacon (if using) until lightly browned. Pour off all but 1 tablespoon of fat, add the onion and ham (if using) and fry, stirring, until the onion is lightly browned. Add the rice and cook, stirring, until the grains are transparent: 2–3 minutes.

2 Stir in the stock or water with the mushrooms (if using), *bouquet garni*, salt and pepper. Cover with a lid and bring to a boil. Cook the rice in the oven until all the water is absorbed: 18–20 minutes. If the rice is not tender, add a little more liquid and continue cooking. Let the rice cool slightly and firm up: about 10 minutes. Discard the *bouquet garni*. The rice can be refrigerated for up to 2 days.

3 *To finish.* Reheat the rice over a low heat on top of the stove. Heat the remaining oil in a wok or large frying pan and sauté the chicken or fish, vegetables and garlic, stirring and tossing constantly, until very hot. Stir the wine into the tomato purée. Add it to the rice with the vegetable mixture. Cook, tossing over the heat until very hot. Finally, add the cayenne or Tabasco and season to taste with salt and pepper. Serve very hot and pass the grated cheese separately.

Cook's Comment. Additions or subtractions can be made to this recipe at will.

Fettuccine Fresci

FRESH NOODLES

It's rarely that a legend lives up to expectation, but the only time I met gastronome André Simon he more than fulfilled the courtly, cultivated image I had built up from his finely crafted books on wine and food. At ninety-one, his presence still dominated the room. He took from the bookcase a treasure I later came to know well – an early edition of that masterpiece of high Renaissance printing, *Opera* by Bartolomeo Scappi (1570). Though almost blind, André leafed through the book lovingly to the dozen pages of woodcuts showing the tools of the cook's trade. Here are three-legged pots designed to sit level in the ashes, some with a compartment for water so that the contents do not burn on the bottom. One illustration shows a mortar and pestle, another a jelly bag for straining sauces, a third the correct way to handle a sauce whisk. The knives for boning, carving, chopping and slicing have changed not a whit today. And nor has the handling of homemade pasta, shown graphically in the illustration of a working kitchen. When I visited André Simon I was just married and starting on a career in writing. His blend of expertise with an intuitive understanding of the good life seemed a goal that was unattainable. It still does.

MAKES 1½lb (750g) FRESH NOODLES TO SERVE 4 AS A MAIN COURSE

1lb (*500g*) flour	4 eggs, beaten to mix
2 teaspoons salt	3 tablespoons water, or more if
2 tablespoons vegetable oil	needed

1 Sift the flour on to a work surface and make a well in the centre. Beat the salt, oil, eggs and water together with a fork and pour into the well. Gradually draw in the flour, working the dough lightly between the fingers so that it forms large crumbs. If some dry crumbs remain, sprinkle another tablespoon of water on to the dough. Press the dough together to form a ball. It should be soft but not sticky. Knead it on a floured surface until very smooth and elastic: about 10 minutes. Cover it with an upturned bowl and leave it to rest for about 1 hour.

2 Divide the dough in half and roll out each piece on a floured surface to a sheet as thin as possible or, if using a pasta machine, crank the dough through the rollers. Leave the sheets to dry for about 30 minutes, preferably over a broom handle or on a laundry rack so that air will reach both sides. To cut by hand, loosely roll up each sheet of dough and cut crosswise into the desired width. The noodles can be cooked almost immediately or left to dry for an hour or two. They will keep for up to a week if they are left to dry for several hours then wrapped in cling film and refrigerated. They can also be frozen.

3 *To cook the noodles.* Bring a large pan of salted water to a boil. Add the noodles, stir well and return to a boil. Simmer, stirring occasionally, for 2–3 minutes, or until the noodles are just tender but still firm to the teeth; dried noodles will take 7–10 minutes. Drain the noodles, rinse them with hot water to wash away the starch and drain them thoroughly. They can be kept warm for half an hour after rinsing by covering them with an inch of warm water.

Cook's Comment. To make green instead of white noodles, spinach purée is added. Cook 1lb (*500g*) of spinach,* drain it and purée it in a food mill or chop it very finely. Dry the purée in a saucepan over a low heat for 2–3 minutes, stirring constantly. In the noodle recipe, add the spinach purée with the eggs and omit the water.

A Trio of Pastas

It used to be 'chips with everything' but now pasta seems to have taken over. This offers an interesting challenge for contemporary cooks in defining the combinations which work and those which don't. Ravioli stuffed with pumpkin, for instance, uniting as it does two soft, bland ingredients, is bound to be insipid. Nor can I approve of the popular fettuccine with white fish and cream. Two of the cardinal cooking rules – contrast of colour and texture – are broken right there.

The happiest modern marriages, it seems to me, have traditional roots, like noodles with goat cheese and chives, which is basically an update of the time-honoured Fettuccine Alfredo. Almost as classic is pasta with wild mushrooms, here modernised with smoked salmon to provide a touch of colour. As for green fettuccine with venison sauce, even that has an honourable Italian heritage. It's an invention of Margo Miller, a *Boston Globe* writer, whose inquiring mind leads to the kind of gastronomic experimentation much appreciated by her friends. In a typical American cross-fertilisation of cultures, a rather tatty bit of venison supplied by a neighbour in Vermont is combined with a sauce based on the classic *salsa Bolognese*. Its rich, rust-gold colour, the result of 2–3 hours' simmering, made green noodles an obvious colour contrast. Here contemporary improvisation comes out tops.

Fettuccine with Goat Cheese and Chives

SERVES 8 AS A FIRST COURSE, 6 AS A MAIN DISH

2lb (1kg) Fresh Noodles (see
 page 162) or 1½lb (750g)
 dried white or green noodles
1½oz (45g) butter
8fl. oz (250ml) double cream

½lb (250g) soft goat cheese,
 crumbled
4 tablespoons chopped fresh
 chives
salt and pepper

1 Cook the noodles and drain. Melt the butter in the same pan, return the noodles and toss until coated. Add the cream and toss until well mixed. Add the cheese and toss over a low heat for 2–3 minutes until the noodles are hot and the cheese has melted. Remove from the heat and add the chives. Season to taste with a little salt and plenty of pepper. Pile on individual plates for serving.

Fettuccine with Smoked Salmon and Wild Mushrooms

SERVES 8 AS A FIRST COURSE, 6 AS A MAIN DISH

¾lb (375g) fresh wild
 mushrooms or 1½oz (45g)
 dried wild mushrooms,
 soaked and drained
1½oz (45g) butter
1 onion, finely chopped
2 cloves garlic, finely
 chopped

4fl. oz (125ml) veal stock,* or
 more if needed
4oz (125g) smoked salmon,
 coarsely chopped
salt and pepper
2lb (1kg) Fresh Noodles (see
 page 162) or 1½lb (750g)
 cooked white noodles

1 Coarsely chop the mushrooms. In a frying pan, melt half the butter and sauté the onion and garlic until soft but not brown. Add the mushrooms and cook until tender, stirring occasionally: 4–5 minutes. Stir in the stock, bring just to a boil, add the salmon and season with salt and pepper to taste. The mixture should be moist and almost soupy; if necessary, add more stock. The sauce can be refrigerated for up to 2 days.

2 To finish. Cook the noodles and drain. Warm the salmon mixture just until hot. Melt the remaining butter in the noodle pan, add the noodles and toss until coated. Add the salmon and mushroom mixture and toss again over the heat until very hot. Mound the sauced noodles on individual plates and serve.

Green Fettuccine with Venison Sauce

SERVES 8 AS A MAIN COURSE

1½fl. oz (45ml) olive oil
1½oz (45g) butter
2 onions, chopped
3 stalks celery, chopped
3 carrots, chopped
2lb (1kg) ground venison, or
  any other game
16fl. oz (500ml) white wine
8fl. oz (250ml) milk
2lb (1kg) Italian plum tomatoes,
  peeled, seeded and chopped* or
  2lb (1kg) tinned plum tomatoes,
  chopped with their juice

salt and pepper
3lb (1.4kg) Fresh Noodles (see
  page 162) or 1½lb (750g)
  dried green noodles
1oz (30g) butter (to finish)
grated Parmesan cheese (for
  serving – optional)

1 Heat the oven to Gas 4/175°C/350°F. In a heavy casserole, heat the oil and butter and fry the onion until soft but not browned. Add the celery and carrot and cook until soft too.

2 Add the venison and cook, stirring constantly to break up the meat, until it loses its raw red colour: 2–3 minutes. (*Note*: Do not allow the vegetables or meat to brown.) Add the wine and cook until evaporated: about 20 minutes. Add the milk, reduce the heat and cook gently until it too has evaporated: about 15 minutes.

3 Stir in the tomatoes and add salt and pepper to taste. Bring to a boil and cook, uncovered, in the oven for 2–3 hours, stirring occasionally. If the sauce gets very thick, add a little water. At the end of cooking, the sauce should be just thick enough to hold its shape. Taste it for seasoning. The sauce can be refrigerated for up to 3 days, or frozen.

4 *To finish*. Cook the noodles* and drain them. Melt the butter in a pan, add the noodles and toss until coated with butter. Meanwhile, reheat the sauce on top of the stove. Pile the noodles on individual plates and spoon the sauce on top. If you like, serve grated Parmesan cheese separately.

SALADS

Just what constitutes a salad? As a category, salads are remarkably difficult to pin down. They certainly are not limited to lettuce, as all those lovely Mediterranean vegetable salads perfumed with garlic and herbs attest. Meat, fish, poultry and fruit are all perfectly acceptable salad ingredients.

In *The Good Cook*, Richard Olney suggests that 'In its most elementary form, a vegetable salad consists of little more than raw vegetables, seasoned with salt.' Spartan though it sounds, originally salads were precisely that, for the name derives from the Latin *sal*, meaning salt. But by medieval times salads had already acquired modern characteristics; for example, one of the earliest English recipe manuscripts, *The Forme of Cury* (1340) describes a composition of fourteen herbs and vegetables and counsels 'waische hem clene . . . myng hem wel with rawe oile . . . lay on vyneger and salt, and serve it forth.'

Perhaps one clue lies here – the distinguishing feature of a salad is surely its dressing, whether of oil with vinegar, lemon juice or wine, or mayonnaise, or even some esoteric concoction of nuts and soy sauce. Salads are 'usually served cold', remarks one dictionary, but this seems unhelpful, as a hot bacon dressing for tough greens is a time-honoured classic. In new-style restaurants, at least half the dishes labelled salad have hot ingredients or a hot dressing (sometimes resulting in a wilted mélange of no merit at all).

For the best definition of what constitutes a good salad, I proffer two suggestions. One comes from an elusive Dr Bushwhacker, possibly a character in a pastiche novel, who wittily observed that 'A bowl of lettuce is the Venus of the dinner-table. It rises upon the sight, cool, moist and beautiful, like that very imprudent lady coming out of the sea, sir. And to complete the image, sir, neither should be dressed too much.' Or we can heed the words of John Evelyn in his *Discourse on Sallets* (1699): 'In a sallet every plant should come in to bear its part without being overpowered by some herb of a stronger taste, but fall into their places like the notes in music.' Not a bad principle to keep in mind when cooking anything.

Squid and Prawn Salad
with Walnuts

At the age of thirteen, our son Simon was nominated to a juvenile gastronomic research team by Calvin Trillin, the *New Yorker* columnist who makes the most mundane events seem funny. In this case, the job at hand was to evaluate the hamburger joints on the Champs Elysées. It seems the balance at Simon's job interview was tipped by the statement that, though his favourite food was French fries, he also liked squid. I think Bud Trillin appreciated such catholicity of taste; he certainly made a good story of their hamburger quest for the *New Yorker*.

SERVES 6 AS A FIRST COURSE

1lb (*500g*) cleaned squid
12fl. oz (*375ml*) vinaigrette
    dressing* made with olive oil
    and lemon juice
1½lb (*750g*) medium prawns,
    unpeeled
2oz (*60g*) coarsely chopped
    walnuts
3–4 tablespoons chopped Italian
    or regular parsley
juice of ½ lemon (optional)
pinch of cayenne

salt and pepper
2 lemons, cut into wedges (for
    decoration)
For the court bouillon
2 pints (*1.25 litres*) water
4fl. oz (*125ml*) white wine
    vinegar
1 onion, sliced
1 carrot, sliced
*bouquet garni**
2 teaspoons whole peppercorns
1 teaspoon salt

1 *For the court bouillon.* Combine all the ingredients in a large saucepan and bring to a boil. Simmer for 15 minutes and strain.

2 Wash the squid and cut it into ⅜in (*1cm*) slices. Add the squid to the *court bouillon* and simmer until just tender: 2–3 minutes. (*Note*: Do not overcook the squid or it will be tough.) Remove the squid with a draining spoon and, while still warm, toss with half the vinaigrette dressing.

3 Bring the *court bouillon* to a boil, add the prawns and simmer until just tender: 2–3 minutes. Drain and peel them. While still warm, toss the prawns with the remaining dressing. Mix squid and prawns. The salad can be refrigerated for up to 8 hours.

4 Just before serving, stir the walnuts and parsley into the salad. Taste and add lemon juice, cayenne, salt and pepper. Serve the salad chilled, decorated with lemon wedges.

Cook's Comment. Forget the walnuts and you have the classic Italian approach to salad, suited to mussels, clams and any firm fish, such as monkfish. Mussels and clams* should be steamed open, then shelled and tossed with dressing, while monkfish should be cut into thick strips and poached in *court bouillon*.

Curried Mussel Salad

Spices turn up in all sorts of odd places. Who would have expected to find spice bread in Dijon (a reminder that the medieval Burgundian empire was not landlocked, and could use its Low Country possessions to trade with the Orient), or saffron in East Anglia, where it was cultivated from the crocus in the sixteenth century as a dye for wool as well as a medicine and food flavouring. This recipe is a variation of *mouclade* – a recipe found on the French coast just south of Brest, home port to many spice ships trading with the Indies. The flat, sandy coast is ideal for mussel farming, which dates from the thirteenth century.

SERVES 6 AS A FIRST COURSE

6lb (2.7kg) mussels, cleaned*
3 tablespoons chopped fresh
  chives
For the dressing
4fl. oz (125ml) vegetable oil
2 shallots, finely chopped
1 teaspoon curry powder, or to
  taste

pinch of cayenne pepper
1 clove garlic, crushed
4 tablespoons white wine
  vinegar
4fl. oz (125ml) double cream
salt and pepper

1 Steam open the mussels.* Remove them from their shells, discarding the rubbery ring around each. Discard any unopened mussels.

2 *For the dressing.* In a small pan, heat 1 tablespoon of the oil and fry the shallots until soft but not brown. Add the curry powder and cayenne and cook gently, stirring, for 2 minutes. Add the garlic and vinegar and bring just to a boil. Remove from the heat, allow to cool slightly and gradually whisk in the remaining oil. Stir in the cream and taste for seasoning. The mussels and dressing can be refrigerated separately for up to 12 hours.

3 *To finish.* Toss the mussels with the dressing and stir in the chives. Serve the mussels on a bed of lettuce, on individual plates or in a glass bowl.

Cook's Comment. Curried Mussel Salad combines well with Squid and Prawn Salad with Walnuts (see opposite) as a cold main course.

A Trio of Prawn Sauces

Here are three contrasting sauces to serve with cooked prawns: one a lush green with basil, the second pink with salmon caviar, and the third a red tomato sauce which came in handy during a memorable trip to Mexico in an RV (recreational vehicle). Not being a family keen on the great outdoors, we were taught many lessons in self-sufficiency by living in an American-style mobile home. We learned to conserve electricity lest the battery fail in the night, and to ration water from stop to stop. Forced to cook on two burners, I proved you can fry, sauté, boil, steam, poach and even bake in pioneer style with only a cast-iron Dutch oven and skillet. We tried to live off the land but with mixed results south of the border. However, wiggling-fresh prawns from the Gulf were one of the highlights.

Salsa Verde Italiana

ITALIAN GREEN SAUCE WITH BASIL

MAKES 12fl. oz (375ml) SAUCE TO SERVE 6–8

2 slices white bread, crusts
    discarded
4fl. oz (125ml) red wine vinegar
large bunch (1½oz (45g)) fresh
    basil, finely chopped
4 cloves garlic, crushed

3 tablespoons capers, drained
    and rinsed
4 anchovy fillets
5fl. oz (150ml) olive oil
salt and pepper

1 In a small bowl, soak the bread in the vinegar for 5 minutes, then squeeze the bread dry. In a blender or food processor, purée the bread with the basil, garlic, capers and anchovy. If using a blender, add a little olive oil along with the ingredients. If using a food processor, gradually add the olive oil, with the machine on, once the other ingredients are worked. Season to taste with salt and pepper.

2 The sauce can be refrigerated for up to 3 days; it will separate slightly, so let it come to room temperature, then whisk lightly before serving.

Cook's Comment. Good too with hot pasta.

Salmon Caviar Cream Sauce

MAKES 16fl. oz (500ml) SAUCE TO SERVE 8

8oz (*250g*) cream cheese
8oz (*250g*) sour cream
juice of 1 lemon

pinch of cayenne
4oz (*125g*) red salmon caviar
salt and pepper

Beat together the cream cheese and the sour cream until smooth. Beat in the lemon juice, cayenne, and pepper, then fold in the caviar. Season to taste with salt and more pepper. The sauce can be refrigerated for up to 3 days.

Cook's Comment. Thicker than most sauces, this mixture is a classic American dip.

Salsa Roja Picante

MEXICAN TOMATO CHILLI SAUCE

MAKES 1 PINT (600ml) SAUCE TO SERVE 6–8

1½lb (*750g*) tomatoes, peeled, seeded and chopped*
1 onion, finely chopped
1 tinned or fresh green chilli pepper, drained, seeded and finely chopped
2 tablespoons olive oil

2 tablespoons red wine vinegar
1 clove garlic, finely chopped
1 tablespoon chopped fresh coriander or parsley
2 teaspoons chopped fresh oregano
salt and pepper

Stir together all the ingredients until mixed. Taste the sauce for seasoning. Cover and chill for at least 2 hours or up to 3 days. Serve cold.

Cook's Comment. Lacking prawns, any of these sauces is also good with corn chips or vegetable sticks.

To Boil Prawns

For 2lb (*1kg*) medium or large prawns, in a saucepan combine 3¼ pints (2 *litres*) water, 1 sliced onion, 1 sliced carrot, a large *bouquet garni,** 1 teaspoon whole peppercorns, 1 teaspoon salt and ½ teaspoon Tabasco or a large pinch cayenne. Bring to a boil and simmer for 5 minutes. Add the prawns and cook just until they lose their transparency: 3–5 minutes, depending on their size. Drain, cool and then peel them, removing the dark intestinal vein. They are best freshly cooked, though they can be refrigerated for up to 2 days.

A Chicken Salad Partnership

The coronation of Queen Elizabeth II was one of the highlights of my 1953 school year. Here was an event with which a conservative English boarding school could thoroughly identify. We were carefully versed in the symbolism of the pageant, thanks to a film screened at least four times in the school hall, to an off-key background of Handel's 'Water Music'.

Food, of course, had no educational status, so it was not until years later that I learned what the guests of state were offered to eat. Unexpectedly, the London Cordon Bleu Cookery School was asked to do some of the catering and to supply students as cooks and waitresses. In *The Constance Spry Cookery Book*, the Cordon Bleu's innovative founder, Rosemary Hume, describes the details thus: 'The luncheon was for about three hundred and fifty people, the largest party to be seated in the Great Hall (of Westminster School), the rest in a house some distance away. By two o'clock the guests would be very hungry and probably cold. There would be people of many nationalities, some of whom would eat no meat. We knew the kitchen accommodation was too small to serve hot food beyond soup and coffee, and we realised the serving of the food would have to be simple because all the waitresses would be amateurs.'

When I taught at the Cordon Bleu ten years later, the Coronation lunch was already a distant memory. But we still taught Coronation dishes like these two salads, which are an unusually happy marriage of French technique (mayonnaise, vinaigrette) with the typically British flavours of curry and port wine.

Poulet Elizabeth

CHICKEN SALAD WITH CURRY MAYONNAISE

SERVES 4 AS A MAIN COURSE

4–5lb (*about 2kg*) roasting
  chicken
paprika (for serving)
1lb (*500g*) cherry tomatoes,
  peeled*
4fl. oz (*125ml*) vinaigrette
  dressing* made with lemon
  juice and vegetable oil
1 tablespoon chopped fresh
  oregano or tarragon
salt and pepper
To poach the chicken
1 onion, quartered
1 carrot, quartered
2 stalks celery

*bouquet garni**
1 teaspoon whole peppercorns
4 pints (*2.5 litres*) chicken stock*
  or water, or more if needed
For the curry mayonnaise
1 tablespoon vegetable oil
1 small onion, finely chopped
2 teaspoons curry powder
4 tablespoons tomato juice
4 tablespoons red wine
2 tablespoons apricot jam
12 fl. oz (*375ml*) mayonnaise
salt and pepper

trussing needle and string

[172]

1 *To poach the chicken.* Truss the chicken and set it on its back in a deep pan. Add the onion, carrot, celery, *bouquet garni*, peppercorns and enough stock to cover the bird. Bring to a boil, skimming occasionally. Cover the pan and simmer until the bird is tender and the juices no longer run pink when the thigh is pricked with a skewer: 1–1¼ hours. Let the chicken cool to tepid in the stock, then drain it. Keep the stock for another use.

2 *For the curry mayonnaise.* Heat the oil in a saucepan and sauté the onion until soft but not brown. Add the curry powder and cook gently for 2 minutes. Add the tomato juice and red wine and simmer until reduced by half. Stir in the apricot jam, let the mixture cool and strain it, pressing well to extract all the liquid. Stir this mixture into the mayonnaise. If necessary, add a tablespoon or two of warm water to thin the mayonnaise until it just coats a spoon. Season to taste with salt and pepper. The chicken, mayonnaise, peeled tomatoes and vinaigrette can be refrigerated for up to 48 hours.

3 Not more than 2 hours before serving, remove the trussing strings and carve the chicken into 8 pieces,* discarding the skin. Arrange the chicken down one side of a serving dish, coat it with the mayonnaise and sprinkle lightly with paprika. Mix the tomatoes with the vinaigrette and oregano or tarragon and taste for seasoning. Arrange the tomatoes down the other side of the dish and refrigerate until ready to serve.

Cook's Comment. How useful is that decorative pinch of paprika, currently so *déclassé*!

Poulet Philippe
CHICKEN SALAD WITH MUSHROOMS IN PORT WINE

SERVES 4 AS A MAIN COURSE

2–3 sprigs fresh or dried thyme
   or rosemary
4–4½lb (2kg) roasting chicken
1oz (30g) butter, softened
salt and pepper
For the mushroom vinaigrette
1 tablespoon vegetable oil
¾lb (375g) mushrooms,
   quartered if large

4fl. oz (125ml) port wine
4fl. oz (125ml) red wine
2 shallots, finely chopped
2 cloves garlic, crushed
6fl. oz (175ml) vinaigrette*
   made with red wine vinegar
   and salad oil
2 tablespoons chopped parsley

trussing needle and string

1 Heat the oven to Gas 6/200°C/400°F. Put the thyme or rosemary inside the chicken and truss the bird. Set it, breast side up, in a roasting pan, spread with the butter and sprinkle with salt and pepper. Roast the chicken in the oven, basting often, until the juices from the centre of the bird run clear, not pink: about 1–1¼ hours. Rotate the chicken from one side to the other during cooking, finishing it on its back. Let the chicken cool.

2 In a saucepan, heat the oil and sauté the mushrooms for 1 minute. Add the port and red wine and boil until reduced to 2 tablespoons. Allow to cool, then stir in the shallots, garlic and half the vinaigrette and taste for seasoning. The chicken and mushroom vinaigrette can be refrigerated for up to 24 hours.

3 Not more than 2 hours before serving, remove the trussing strings and carve the chicken into 8 pieces.* Arrange the chicken down one side of a dish, and place the mushrooms down the other. Add the parsley to the remaining vinaigrette and spoon it over the chicken. Chill until ready to serve.

Cook's Comment. Cooked with sweet white wine instead of port and red wine, the mushrooms make an excellent accompaniment to cold roast veal.

Hot Pasta Salad

I'm often asked about my own or other people's recipes: 'Is it original?' My inclination is to answer both 'Yes' and 'No'. 'Yes' in the sense that a recipe, like any set of instructions, can be written in a thousand and one different ways according to what the author believes is the clearest and most helpful to a given audience. 'No' in the sense that recipes don't spring full-blown from nowhere – they have roots.

Take this Hot Pasta Salad. Given the craze currently sweeping America, you might think that the idea of mixing vinaigrette dressing with hot pasta is new. Yet as early as 1833 in Alsace a mention appears of a dish called 'totelots', made of squares of homemade pasta mixed with garlic, shallots, herbs, vinegar and sour cream. Modern chefs may create their own variations on Hot Pasta Salad by changing the pasta, adding fish and vegetables, or using a special oil. But the underlying theme is unchanged and certainly dates back to before the nineteenth century.

SERVES 8 AS A FIRST COURSE

1½lb (750g) Fresh Noodles (see page 162), or ¾lb (375g) dried noodles

4 hard-boiled eggs, sliced (for garnish)

For the dressing

2½fl. oz (75ml) white wine vinegar

6 shallots, finely chopped

1oz (30g) chopped parsley

3 cloves garlic, finely chopped

8fl. oz (250ml) vegetable oil

6fl. oz (175ml) sour cream

salt and pepper

Cook the pasta and drain it. Meanwhile, make the dressing. Whisk the vinegar with the shallots, parsley and garlic. Gradually whisk in the oil so that the dressing thickens slightly. Whisk in the sour cream and season to taste with salt and pepper. Return the pasta to the pan with the dressing and toss both together over the heat until very hot: 1–2 minutes. Pile the noodles in a serving bowl. Decorate with the egg slices and serve at once.

Cook's Comment. If you are using fresh noodle dough for this recipe, traditionally it should be cut into little ½in (1.25cm) squares or 'totelots' rather than into strips.

Tomato, Gorgonzola and Mascarpone Salad with Basil

How rapidly the food market is changing in the USA! We eat some variation of this salad at home almost every week, yet even five years ago the main ingredients would have been unobtainable. Ripe, juicy tomatoes would have been limited to June until late October, but now remarkably good (and inexpensive) ones are flown in from the southern hemisphere. The cheese counter in our local supermarket leaves a good deal to be desired, but intermittently it offers mascarpone, buffalo mozzarella, and Gorgonzola which is not inedibly salty. The Stilton is reliable enough to substitute for Gorgonzola and fresh feta, always available, is another possibility. As for herbs, it must have been three years ago that a tray of water-filled pots appeared in the produce section, each holding a flourishing bunch of green. True, they vary in quality with the season, but thyme and chives seem to survive the depths of winter.

SERVES 6–8 AS A FIRST COURSE

2lb (*1kg*) ripe tomatoes, cored
6oz (*175g*) Gorgonzola cheese,
  softened
5oz (*150g*) mascarpone,
  softened

1–2 tablespoons single cream
  (optional)
5–6 tablespoons olive oil
small bunch of fresh basil
pepper

1 Cut the tomatoes into ½in (*1.25cm*) slices; there should be at least twenty-four.

2 Cream the Gorgonzola and mascarpone, thinning the mixture with a little cream, if desired. Spread the cheese on the tomato slices and arrange the slices flat on individual plates. Sprinkle with the olive oil. Cover tightly with cling film and leave at room temperature for at least 1 hour and up to 3 hours.

3 Just before serving, very coarsely chop the basil, trying not to bruise it. Grind fresh pepper on top of the tomatoes and cheese, sprinkle with the basil and serve.

Cook's Comment. An hour's marinating in olive oil and seasoning draws out the juice of tomatoes and improves their flavour.

Salade de Fromage de Chèvre Chaud

HOT GOAT CHEESE SALAD

One of the most curious gastronomic counterpoints I can remember witnessing occurred during a cruise we took one year on a French ship in the Red Sea. The arid, ancient shores of Egypt on the one hand and Jordan on the other slipped by; we went ashore to the shabby port of Aqaba, cheek by jowl across the bay from brashly booming Eilat in Israel, and took a trip to Petra, the red-rose city carved in rock. But on board we ate French cuisine of the utmost sophistication – sautéed fresh *foie gras*, crayfish salad with green beans, *feuilleté* of snails with wild mushrooms – all imported from France. The chef had a talent for grafting new ideas on to familiar favourites and this was the first time I had come across what has now become a new-style classic.

SERVES 8 AS A FIRST COURSE

medium head of curly endive, leaves torn into pieces
2 bunches of watercress, large stems removed
3–4 (300g) small, round goat cheeses, or 1–2 logs

8 slices wholewheat bread
4fl. oz (125ml) vinaigrette* made with olive oil and wine vinegar

2in (5cm) pastry-cutter

1 Wash and dry the endive and watercress. Cut the cheese into sixteen slices. Use the pastry-cutter to stamp out sixteen rounds from the bread, put them on a baking sheet and set a piece of cheese on each round. If preparing up to 4 hours ahead, cover with a damp cloth.

2 Heat the oven to Gas 6/200°C/400°F. Bake the cheese toasts until bubbling and browned: 8–12 minutes. Meanwhile, toss the endive and watercress with the vinaigrette dressing and arrange on individual plates. Top with the toasts and serve at once.

Cook's Comment. Piquant little *crottin de Chavignol* cheeses from Sancerre have become traditional for this recipe, though any fairly soft goat cheese works well. Serve the salad with a glass of matching Sancerre white wine.

Bœuf à la Mode en Gelée

BEEF IN ASPIC WITH VEGETABLES

Here we are, back at the Château de Versailles, the scene a multi-national ladies' luncheon. At Madame van der Kemp's right sits Comtesse Mapie de Toulouse Lautrec, *grande dame*, *directrice* of Maxim's finishing school and famous for the luxuriance of her hats. She raises her lorgnette and inspects the dish of beef in aspic presented by Serge, the *maître d'hôtel*. 'Pretty, but I suspect the presence of artificial gelatine,' is her lapidary judgement. Having learned my lesson, the following recipe contains the requisite amount of calf's or pig's foot to set the aspic naturally!

SERVES 12–14

3oz (*90g*) pork fat or mild
  bacon, cut into lardons*
a 7lb (*3kg*) piece of braising beef
2 calf's or pig's feet, split
3lb (*1.4kg*) veal bones, cracked
2 tablespoons vegetable oil
2 pints (*1.25 litres*) veal stock,*
  or more if needed
salt and pepper
3 tablespoons Madeira
bunch of watercress (for
  garnish)
For the marinade
2 cloves garlic, peeled
large *bouquet garni**
1 tablespoon whole
  peppercorns
4 whole cloves

1lb (*500g*) onions, quartered
1lb (*500g*) carrots, quartered
3 stalks celery, sliced
1 bottle (*725ml*) red Burgundy
  wine
1 tablespoon vegetable oil
For the garnish
3lb (*1.4kg*) carrots, cut into
  sticks
3lb (*1.4kg*) baby onions, peeled
3lb (*1.4kg*) turnips, cut into
  sticks
2lb (*1kg*) green beans, trimmed
  and cut into sticks

about 5-pint (3-litre) terrine
  mould, or two smaller ones;
  larding needle (optional)

1 One or two days before serving, make the marinade. Tie the garlic, *bouquet garni*, peppercorns and cloves in muslin. Put all the ingredients for the marinade except the oil into a saucepan, bring to a boil and simmer for 10 minutes. Let cool until cold.

2 Insert the pork fat or bacon lardons into a larding needle and lard the beef by 'sewing' the fat into the meat. Alternatively, poke holes in the meat with the point of a knife and insert the lardons. Put the meat in a deep bowl (not aluminium), pour over the marinade and spoon the oil over the meat to keep it moist. Cover and refrigerate for 12–24 hours, turning the meat occasionally.

3 *To braise the meat.* Blanch the calf's or pig's feet and veal bones by putting them in cold water, bringing to a boil, simmering for 5 minutes and draining. Drain the beef and pat it dry with paper towels. Strain the marinade; reserve it with the vegetables and bag of seasonings. Heat the oven to Gas 3/160°C/325°F.

4 In a large flameproof casserole, heat the oil and brown the beef thoroughly on all sides. Remove the beef, add the reserved vegetables from the marinade and cook gently until they begin to brown. Replace the beef, add the marinade, bag of seasonings, stock and a little salt. Tuck the bones and feet down beside the meat, cover the pan and bring to a boil. Braise in the oven until the meat is very tender when pierced with a skewer: 2½–3 hours. Baste the meat occasionally and add more stock if the liquid evaporates.

5 Let the meat cool to tepid, then remove it and strain the cooking liquid, discarding bones, feet and vegetables. There should be about 2⅓ pints (*1.5 litres*) of liquid; if too little, add more stock, or if too much, boil to reduce it. Stir in the Madeira, taste the liquid for seasoning and chill it until set. Skim off the fat which sets on the surface.

6 *For the garnish.* Cook the carrots in boiling salted water for 8–10 minutes or until just tender, and drain them. Cook the onions, turnips and green beans in the same way, allowing 12–15 minutes for the onions, 6–8 minutes for the turnips and 6–12 minutes for the green beans, depending on size.

7 *To mould the aspic.* Discard the strings from the beef and carve it into thick slices. Melt the cooking liquid and spoon a thin layer into the terrine. Chill until set. Arrange the slices of meat overlapping down the centre of the terrine. Arrange about a third of the vegetables in lengthwise rows down each side of the beef. Spoon over enough cooking liquid to cover the vegetables completely and almost cover the meat. Chill until set.

8 Add a second layer of vegetables, cover with the cooking liquid and chill again until set. Finally, fill the terrine with the remaining vegetables, pour over the rest of the cooking liquid and chill for at least 6 hours. Beef in aspic can be refrigerated for up to 3 days.

9 To serve, briefly set the mould in hot water, then run a knife around the edge of the mould and turn the aspic out on to a serving dish. Cut a few slices so that the layered pattern of vegetables can be seen, and decorate the dish with watercress.

Cook's Comment. Complex though this recipe is, it can be prepared well ahead and has the advantage of combining meat and vegetables in a single striking dish. For the beef, I would look for a piece which will tie in a neat cylinder and slice well; top rump or topside are good cuts.

Boiled Beef Salad

Exuberant, 6 feet 4 inches and massive with it, the late James Beard epitomised everything a *gourmand* should be. No matter what the time of day, you would be welcomed at his house with a glass of wine and a bite – I remember a freshly baked cheese bread, some ribs barbecued with a different new sauce, a wheel of blue Maytag, one of the few native American cheeses. Towards the end of his life, his doctors would plead with him to lose weight and his longtime friends Paul Kovi and Tom Margittai at The Four Seasons restaurant in New York would send in special meals each day. At one stage even that was forbidden, and his supper when I went to see him one day was a single huge beefsteak tomato. 'Great eating!' he remarked, and he meant it. Jim loved plain food like this beef salad, though he appreciated the finest flights of gastronomic fancy too.

SERVES 8–10

5lb (*2.8kg*) boneless stewing
  beef, rolled and tied
*bouquet garni**
1 teaspoon whole peppercorns
1 teaspoon salt
4 pints (*2.5 litres*) water, or
  more if needed
2lb (*1kg*) carrots
2lb (*1kg*) medium onions
4lb (*1.8kg*) small potatoes,
  unpeeled
Hot Pepper Mayonnaise (see
  opposite)

For the salad
1¼ pints (*750ml*) vinaigrette
  dressing* made with red
  wine vinegar and olive oil
3–4 shallots, very finely chopped
2–3 cloves garlic, very finely chopped
2–3 tablespoons capers, finely chopped
2 tablespoons chopped gherkins
salt and pepper
1 large head lettuce, divided
  into leaves and washed
2lb (*1kg*) ripe tomatoes

1 *To cook the beef.* Put the beef into a large pan with the *bouquet garni*, peppercorns, salt and water to cover. Cover with a lid and bring slowly to a boil. Simmer, skimming often, for 2 hours.

2 Add the carrots and onions and simmer until the meat is tender: about 1 hour longer. If the water evaporates during cooking, add more so that the meat and vegetables are always covered.

3 Add the potatoes and continue cooking until the meat and vegetables are very tender: 15–20 minutes. Leave them to cool in the liquid. The beef and vegetables can be cooked up to 2 days ahead. Transfer them to a bowl and refrigerate. Keep the broth to use as stock.

4 *To finish.* Cut the beef into thick slices. Slice the carrots, quarter the onions and leave the potatoes whole or cut them in half, depending on their size. Make the vinaigrette dressing and mix half with the shallots, garlic, capers and gherkins. In separate bowls, mix the carrots, onions and potatoes with half the remaining dressing. Season to taste.

5 Arrange the lettuce leaves around the edge of a large tray or serving dish. Slice the tomatoes and lay the slices overlapping on top of the lettuce. Spoon over the remaining vinaigrette dressing. Arrange the beef down the centre of the dish and coat with the shallot and caper dressing. Pile the carrots, onions and potatoes in mounds around the beef. The salad can be prepared up to 2 hours ahead and kept covered. Serve at room temperature, with the Hot Pepper Mayonnaise separately.

Cook's Comment. Boiled beef is the place to use one of those tough cuts with plenty of cartilage which softens so satisfactorily with long, slow cooking. I'd suggest silverside or topside.

Sauce Rouille

HOT PEPPER MAYONNAISE

Rouille, so called because of its rust colour, is commonly served with Provençal fish soups. For serving with beef salad, you can make the pepper lively!

MAKES 16fl. oz (500ml) SAUCE TO SERVE 8–10

1–2 dried or fresh red chillies	12fl. oz (*375ml*) olive oil
8–10 cloves garlic, peeled	2 tablespoons tomato purée
4 egg yolks	cayenne (optional)
salt	

1 If using dried chillies, soak them for 15–20 minutes in hot water, then drain. Discard the stems of fresh or dried chillies and cut them into pieces, removing the cores and seeds. (*Note*: Handle fresh chillies with gloves, as the oil will burn your fingers.)

2 Purée the chillies in a food processor or blender with the garlic, egg yolks and a little salt, with the machine running for at least 2 minutes. Work in the oil a little at a time, as for mayonnaise, until the mixture is quite thick. Then add the remaining oil in a slow steady stream. Finally, work in the tomato purée and taste the mayonnaise for seasoning. If it is not hot enough, add a pinch of cayenne.

Jambon Persillé

PARSLEYED HAM IN WINE ASPIC

I once attended that most ancient of rural festivals – a pig-killing. The setting was an orchard in Normandy. I deliberately missed the actual despatch of the animal, so by the time I arrived the carcass was hanging from an apple tree, surrounded by sturdy peasant figures in boots and aprons that might have stepped out of a Brueghel tableau. Little by little, under the supervision of the local *charcutier*, the innards were removed. The intestines were set aside to be cleaned for the local version of *boudin noir* – blood sausage made with diced fat, fried onions and the blood collected when the pig was killed. Delicacies like the trotters and the spare ribs were despatched to the kitchen for supper, with a sharp eye on the back feet, known to be plumper and more succulent than the front. The shadows grew longer and the swigs of cider more frequent; the warmth of the fire with its huge cauldron for blanching the sausages became more welcome. Finally, the carcass itself was dismembered and the hams and sides borne away to be salted and smoked.

Boudin was pressed upon me for supper, with instructions to eat it with fried apples in Norman style. And a couple of weeks later a salted ham hock appeared on the kitchen table with a little note. I could have baked it with apples and cream *à la Normande* (see page 132), but instead I turned to Burgundy and simmered the ham with white wine, layering it in a bowl with parsley in a glowing mosaic of pink and green.

SERVES 10–12 AS A FIRST COURSE

7–8lb (*about 3.5kg*) shank half of
  a country ham, or the
  equivalent weight in ham
  hocks
2 calf's or pig's feet, split
1lb (*500g*) veal bones
2 onions
large *bouquet garni**
1 tablespoon whole
  peppercorns

1 leek, trimmed and split
3 stalks celery
2 carrots
1 bottle (*725ml*) dry white wine
4 pints (*2.5 litres*) water
5–6 tablespoons chopped
  parsley
6 shallots, very finely chopped
salt and pepper

5–6-pint (3–4-litre) deep glass bowl

1 If the ham is very salty, soak it for 12 hours in several changes of cold water. Blanch the ham, calf's or pig's feet and veal bones by putting them in a large pan of cold water, bringing to a boil and simmering for 5 minutes. Drain and rinse the meats and bones thoroughly under cold running water. Halve the onions and singe them on an electric plate or over a gas burner until very dark to give colour to the aspic.

2 In a large, heavy, non-reactive pan, put the ham, calf's or pig's feet, veal bones, onions, *bouquet garni*, peppercorns, leek, celery, carrots, two-thirds of the wine and enough water to cover. Bring slowly to a boil, skimming often. Simmer until the ham is tender enough to be pulled apart with a fork: 2½–3½ hours. Skim the mixture often during cooking to remove fat and keep the aspic clear. Add more water if necessary to keep the meats and vegetables covered.

3 Let cool to tepid, then lift out the meat, bones and vegetables with a draining spoon. Boil the cooking liquid until it is well flavoured and reduced to about 2⅓ pints (*1.5 litres*). Bring the remaining wine almost to a boil and pour over the parsley to set its bright green colour. Mix in the shallots. Season both liquids with salt and pepper.

4 Remove all the meat from the ham and the feet, discarding any skin but keeping a little fat. Pull the ham into large chunks with two forks. Mix the shallot liquid with the meat and put a layer loosely in the bowl. Strain the cooking liquid through muslin or cheesecloth and pour a layer over the ham barely to cover it. Add the remaining ham and aspic in layers so that the ham is well moistened with aspic.

5 Chill the bowl for several hours until the aspic is set. It can be refrigerated for 3–5 days. Serve the ham directly from the bowl, or turn it out and cut it into slices or wedges.

Cook's Comment. In our home town of Joigny in northern Burgundy, every *charcutier* has a slightly different version of this popular dish. Some add garlic and herbs, such as chives, to the shallots. Some leave out the shallots altogether, with the result that they can keep the aspic for a week or more. One variation, served at Easter, has whole hard-boiled eggs layered with the ham.

Légumes à la Grecque

MARINATED VEGETABLE SALAD

When I first moved to Paris in 1962, vegetables *à la Grecque*, cooked and left to marinate in a supposedly Greek mixture of peppercorns, coriander, wine, lemon, tomato and herbs, were a standard bistro first course beside the *pâte de campagne* and the *œufs mayonnaise*. The better establishments offered a selection in glass bowls for the customer to choose from: mushrooms, cauliflower, cucumber, possibly green beans, and artichokes if you were lucky.

SERVES 8–10

3lb (*1.4kg*) any three of the
   vegetables below
6 tablespoons olive oil
30–40 baby onions, peeled
1lb (*500g*) tomatoes, peeled,
   seeded and coarsely
   chopped*
3 tablespoons tomato purée
4½ tablespoons coriander seeds

1½ tablespoons whole peppercorns
1 pint (*600ml*) veal stock* or
   water, or more if needed
8fl. oz (*250ml*) white wine
3 *bouquets garnis**
juice of 1 lemon, or more if needed
salt and pepper

3 sauté pans or large frying pans

1 Prepare the vegetables as described below. In each of three sauté or frying pans, heat 2 tablespoons of oil. Divide the onions among the pans and fry them until lightly browned: 2–3 minutes. Divide the tomatoes, tomato purée, coriander seeds and peppercorns among the pans and stir equal quantities of the stock and wine into each. Add the individual vegetables and a *bouquet garni* to the pan with a squeeze of lemon juice. There should be enough liquid barely to cover the vegetables.

2 Cover with a lid and boil over a high heat until the vegetables are tender. (Note: Boiling emulsifies the oil and stock so the sauce thickens slightly. If the vegetables produce a great deal of liquid, evaporate it by uncovering the pans for the last 5–10 minutes of cooking.) Let the vegetables cool to tepid, then discard the *bouquets garnis* and taste, adding lemon juice, salt and pepper as needed. Mushrooms and cabbage ribs should be more highly seasoned than, for instance, green beans or artichokes.

3 Vegetables *à la Grecque* should marinate in the refrigerator for at least 12 hours before serving; they can be kept for up to 3 days.

Cook's Comment. Personally, I like the crunch of the occasional peppercorn and coriander seed among my vegetables, but if you prefer to remove them, tie them in a muslin bag during cooking.

Artichokes. Trim the stems and tops of 1lb (*500g*) baby artichokes. Cut them into 2–4 pieces each, depending on their size, and cut out the hairy central choke. Cook them for 20–25 minutes.

Cabbage Ribs. Cut out the cabbage ribs, reserving the leaves for another use. Cut the ribs into 2in (*5cm*) lengths and cook for 10–15 minutes.

Cauliflower. Divide a large cauliflower into florets and cook for 12–15 minutes.

Courgettes. Wash 1lb (*500g*) courgettes and then cut into ½in (*1.25cm*) slices. Add them to the onions after 5 minutes' cooking and continue boiling for 8–10 minutes.

Cucumbers. Peel 2 cucumbers, halve them lengthwise and scoop out the seeds. Cut them into ½in (*1.25cm*) slices and add them to the onions after 8 minutes of cooking. Continue boiling for 8–10 minutes.

Green Beans. Trim 1lb (*500g*) green beans and cut them into 2–3 pieces. Add to the onions after 5 minutes of cooking and continue boiling for 8–12 minutes.

Mushrooms. Trim, rinse and halve or quarter 1lb (*500g*) mushrooms. Cook them for 15–20 minutes.

Pissenlits ou Frisée au Lard

HOT DANDELION OR ENDIVE SALAD WITH BACON

In England, the sight of a figure bent double with a little knife digging dandelions gives rise to the assumption that he or she is improving the landscape. Not so in France, where wispy fronds of baby dandelion are a delicacy.

SERVES 6

8oz (*250g*) dandelion greens, or a small head of curly endive	2 tablespoons vegetable oil
6oz (*175g*) piece of streaky bacon, cut into lardons*	2½fl. oz (*75ml*) red wine vinegar
	salt and pepper

1 Trim the roots from the dandelion greens, leaving the leaves attached, or separate endive leaves. Wash the greens very thoroughly and dry them. If the bacon is salty, blanch it by putting it into cold water, boiling for 5 minutes and draining. The greens can be refrigerated, wrapped in a towel, for 24 hours.

2 *To finish.* Put the greens into a salad bowl. Fry the bacon in the oil until brown. There should be 4–5 tablespoons of fat and any excess should be discarded. Pour the bacon with the hot fat over the greens, tossing until well mixed. Add the vinegar to the pan and boil until reduced to about 2 tablespoons. (*Note*: Stand back, as it will splutter.) Pour over the greens and toss again. Sprinkle with pepper and taste the greens, adding salt only if necessary. Serve at once.

Cook's Comment. An invaluable salad for winter greens, which can be tough.

Gado Gado

INDONESIAN VEGETABLE SALAD

My first taste of Indonesian food was in an unlikely country – Costa Rica – where I spent a few days in 1966 for an even more unlikely reason – to get married. My husband-to-be took it into his head that the further away from home, the easier it would be. So when the World Bank sent him to Central America, he found the ideal location. The British Embassy sprang to life with diplomatic booze and recorded our union on the twenty-ninth certificate issued since the registry began in the days of Lord Curzon. In the afternoon we ascended an active volcano and I was stung by a wasp. By evening we were thankful to relax at the Royal Dutch Hotel, which served a very passable Indonesian *rijstafel* (see page 92), and ever since I have had a weakness for Indonesian food.

SERVES 6 AS A FIRST COURSE

½ small head of cabbage, shredded
6oz (*175g*) bean sprouts
6oz (*175g*) green beans, each cut into
  2–3 pieces
½ medium head of cauliflower,
  divided into florets

¾lb (*375g*) fresh spinach
½ cucumber, peeled, seeded
  and cut into sticks
Peanut Sauce (see page 127)

1 Put the cabbage in a bowl, cover with boiling water and leave for 1 minute. Drain thoroughly. Repeat with the bean sprouts, leaving them for only 10 seconds.

2 Cook the green beans in a pan of boiling salted water until they are just tender: 3–5 minutes. Drain them, rinse with cold water and drain again thoroughly. Repeat for the cauliflower, cooking it for 5–7 minutes. Cook the spinach* and coarsely chop it. All the vegetables can be refrigerated for up to 24 hours.

3 Not more than an hour before serving, arrange the vegetables in piles on a rectangular serving dish, or in pie-shaped wedges on a round dish. Spoon the Peanut Sauce over the vegetables and leave them to marinate at room temperature.

Cook's Comment. This salad is designed for a hot climate, where refrigeration is a luxury.

Melon Salad

Off on the road again. With a sigh I pack the familiar La Varenne red valise with all the paraphernalia of a promotion tour – press kits, brochures, give-away aprons and T-shirts, books, the trusty sauce whisk and the talisman case of knives. I don sneakers for comfort and a scarlet shirt for show. I grab the air tickets which will take us to ten cities in eight days, and hope that my travelling companion will be congenial as well as capable of carrying the bags – people like Steve Raichlen, now restaurant columnist for *Boston* magazine, and ex-*Time-Life* staffer Henry Grossi, whose laconic asides are guaranteed to disperse the worst fit of stage fright. Together we've suffered pre-dawn exposure to the camera's eye and late-night conferences with teetotal sponsors who would not countenance a glass of wine. We've perfumed the aisles of many a housewife show with garlic and introduced more than one charity audience to the nuances of swearing in French. Over the years we've developed a repertoire of ideal road recipes – quick, amusing, easy to make with ingredients to be found anywhere, colourful (for the camera) and tasty (for the audience). This Melon Salad has always proved a winner.

SERVES 8

2 medium cantaloupe or
   honeydew melons
1lb (*500g*) seedless green grapes
3 navel oranges
juice of 3 lemons
1 tablespoon sugar, or to taste

4fl. oz (*125ml*) single cream
2 tablespoons chopped fresh
   mint
8 sprigs of mint

melon-baller

1 Cut each melon into quarters and discard the seeds. Scoop out the flesh with the melon-baller. Scrape the rinds clean and refrigerate them. Separate the grapes from the stems and add to the melon balls. With a serrated knife, cut the skin and pith from the oranges. Cut out segments, discarding the skin, add to the other fruit and chill.

2 In a small bowl, whisk the lemon juice with the sugar until dissolved. Whisk in the cream. (*Note*: The acid in the lemon juice will thicken the cream slightly.) The fruit and lemon dressing can be refrigerated for up to 12 hours.

3 *To finish.* Pile the fruit in the melon shells. Whisk the chopped mint into the dressing and spoon over the fruit, topping each serving with a mint sprig.

Cook's Comment. This dressing is also good with tomato.

Six Salads from the Mediterranean

Like so many Northerners starved of sun, I have a romantic memory of summers in Provence. Roast lamb *à la ficelle* mingles with the perfume of the *maquis* wild herbs of the hillside, while under the trees a shaded table is set with half a dozen vegetable salads flanked by crocks of black and green olives, *cornichon* pickles, round loaves of country bread and, of course, curvaceous bottles of chilled Provençal rosé wine.

This idyll is overlaid by a more substantial image. An elderly, upright lady, clad in a large white apron with her hair set in careful waves, comes into view. It is Simone (Simca) Beck, extraordinary cookery teacher, author of two intensely French cookbooks in English and known to Americans as co-author with Julia Child of *Mastering the Art of French Cooking*. A demanding personality who earns the lifelong allegiance of all students who pass through the kitchen of her Provençal villa, Simca greets me with: 'Ma chère Anne, you are just the person I need to help me . . . peel the potatoes, read the proofs of an article, be off to Mougins to get some squid.' Such is her infectious enthusiasm that one follows eagerly, even to the kitchen sink, for with Simca, life is not only active, it is a perpetual adventure.

Céleri Remoulade

CELERIAC IN MUSTARD MAYONNAISE

SERVES 6

2 medium (2lb (*1kg*)) celeriac
½ lemon
1 tablespoon Dijon mustard, or
   more to taste

½ pint (*300ml*) mayonnaise
salt and pepper

1 Peel the celeriac, cut it into thin slices and then into julienne strips. To avoid discoloration, immerse the strips at once in a pan of cold salted water with half a lemon and its juice. Blanch the celeriac by bringing it to a boil, simmer for 1–3 minutes then drain. It must be cooked lightly so that it retains its crunch.

2 Add the mustard to the mayonnaise and stir into the celeriac. Season to taste with salt and pepper, adding more mustard if needed. Refrigerate Céleri Remoulade for at least 2 hours for the flavours to mellow. It can be kept for up to 24 hours.

Cook's Comment. A classic, much overlooked outside France. When celeriac is not available, you can substitute turnips.

Roasted Pepper Salad

SERVES 4–6

2 red peppers
2 green peppers
2 yellow peppers, or more red
　ones
2 medium onions, unpeeled
salt and pepper

6fl. oz (175ml) vinaigrette
　dressing* made with red
　wine vinegar and olive oil
2 cloves garlic, chopped
2 tablespoons chopped fresh
　oregano, thyme or parsley

1 Heat the grill. Quarter the peppers, discarding the cores and seeds. Line the grill rack with foil. Set the peppers on the foil, skin side up, and grill them until their skins are charred and blistered: 8–12 minutes. Cover the peppers with a wet cloth or paper towel. Leave them to cool, then peel them and cut them into wide strips.

2 Meanwhile, halve the onions crosswise, leaving the peel. Set them cut side up on the grill rack, and grill them until charred, 5–8 minutes. Turn and cook the other side until the onions are tender: 5–8 minutes longer. Peel them, cut them into wedges and add them to the peppers.

3 Mix the peppers and onions with the vinaigrette, garlic, herbs and salt and pepper to taste. (The onions will break up.) The salad can be refrigerated for up to 24 hours. Serve it at room temperature.

Cook's Comment. Perfect with grilled fish or lamb.

Salade Niçoise Escoffier

SALAD OF TOMATO, TUNA AND ANCHOVIES

SERVES 4

1½lb (750g) large ripe tomatoes,
　sliced
6½oz (200g) tin tuna in oil,
　drained and flaked
2 tablespoons chopped mixed
　fresh chervil, chives and tarragon

4fl. oz (125ml) vinaigrette
　dressing* made with white
　wine vinegar and olive oil
1 tin anchovies, drained and
　coarsely chopped

Arrange the tomato slices overlapping in a shallow dish. Spread the tuna on top. Whisk the herbs into the vinaigrette and spoon over the tuna and tomatoes. Sprinkle with the chopped anchovies, cover and marinate for 1 hour at room temperature.

Cook's Comment. Auguste Escoffier came from Villeneuve-Loubet, just outside Nice, so this simple little recipe must be authentic, though it is unlike any other I have seen.

Salade Italienne Escoffier

RICE SALAD WITH PEAS AND CARROTS

Escoffier's relatively little-known household cookbook, *Ma Cuisine*, was published the year before his death at the age of eighty-nine in 1935. He wrote it under pressure from his publisher, Henri Flammarion, whose son once told me that the great chef was reluctant to claim such simple ideas as full-blown recipes. He was too modest, for *Ma Cuisine* is full of attractive recipes like this salad which he describes as having '*couleurs italiennes*'.

SERVES 6

6½oz (*200g*) long-grain rice
½ lemon
4oz (*125g*) shelled fresh or
    frozen peas
8oz (*250g*) diced carrots

6fl. oz (*175ml*) vinaigrette*
    dressing made with olive oil
    and lemon juice
1 tablespoon chopped oregano
salt and pepper

1 Bring a large pan of salted water to a boil. Add the rice and lemon half and simmer, stirring occasionally, until the rice is just tender: 10–12 minutes. Drain, rinse with cold water to wash away the starch and drain again thoroughly. Discard the lemon.

2 Cook fresh peas in a pan of boiling salted water until tender: 8–15 minutes; cook frozen peas according to the packet directions. Drain the peas, rinse with cold water and drain again thoroughly. Cook the carrots in boiling salted water until tender – 4–6 minutes – then drain. The vegetables and rice can be refrigerated for up to 24 hours.

3 Not more than 2 hours before serving, stir the vinaigrette into the vegetables and rice using two forks. Add the oregano. Season with salt and pepper to taste and serve.

Cook's Comment. Other colourful vegetables to add to rice salad are tomato, celery and peppers, but then the salad is no longer 'Italian'.

Salade de Courgettes au Safran

COURGETTE SALAD WITH SAFFRON

SERVES 4

3 tablespoons olive oil
1lb (*500g*) small courgettes,
    thinly sliced
2 cloves garlic, crushed
1 medium onion, finely chopped

1 teaspoon fennel seeds
pinch of saffron infused in
    2 tablespoons boiling water
salt and pepper
3–4 tablespoons white wine vinegar

1 Heat the oil in a large frying pan. Add the courgettes, garlic and onion and cook over a low heat for 5 minutes, stirring occasionally. Put the fennel seeds in a thick envelope and crush with a rolling pin. Alternatively, crush the fennel seeds in a mortar and pestle.

2 Stir in the saffron and its liquid, crushed fennel seeds, salt, pepper and vinegar, and continue cooking until the courgettes are just tender: about 5 minutes. Let the salad cool, then taste for seasoning. The salad can be refrigerated for up to 24 hours. Serve at room temperature.

Cook's Comment. Recipes like this, coloured with saffron and spiced with vinegar, date back even earlier than the Renaissance.

Salade aux Aubergines et Tomates
BAKED AUBERGINE AND TOMATOES

SERVES 4

2 aubergines (about 1lb (500g)), unpeeled
salt and pepper
1½lb (750g) ripe tomatoes
2 cloves garlic, crushed
7–8 tablespoons olive oil

2 sprigs fresh or 1 teaspoon dried rosemary
2 bay leaves
3–4 tablespoons red wine vinegar

1 Cut the aubergines, including skin, into ⅜in (1cm) slices. Sprinkle with salt, turn, sprinkle the other side and leave for 30 minutes to draw out the juices. Rinse thoroughly with cold water and pat dry on paper towels.

2 Heat the oven to Gas 4/175°C/350°F. Thickly slice the tomatoes. Oil a large shallow baking dish, sprinkle it with the garlic and add the rosemary and bay leaves. Arrange the aubergine and tomato slices in the dish, alternating and overlapping the slices. Sprinkle them with remaining olive oil, salt and pepper.

3 Cover the dish and bake in the oven until the vegetables are tender: 20–25 minutes – removing the cover for the last few minutes' cooking so that the vegetables brown. While still hot, sprinkle with the vinegar. The vegetables can be refrigerated for up to 24 hours. Serve at room temperature.

Cook's Comment. Such a simple recipe depends on the quality of the vegetables, particularly the tomatoes. I've often added courgettes and thinly sliced onions to this vegetable mix.

[191]

DESSERTS

Desserts lodge longer in our affections than any other foods. Not long ago I was talking to two of New York's most innovative chefs, Gérard Pangaud of Aurora and Larry Forgione of An American Place. Both keep changing their menus as a matter of course, but when it comes to desserts, they cannot budge. Customers who are happy to experiment with savoury dishes baulk when it comes to sweets. Look at the line-up in this chapter: fools and syllabubs date back at least three centuries without the smallest change. Nineteenth-century favourites like trifle, *'riz impériale'*, chocolate soufflé and Crêpes Suzette continue to flourish. What is more, they do not take kindly to adaptation. You've probably had 'light' versions of a fruit fool made with yoghurt, or ice-cream without egg yolks – they simply cannot match the originals. What are the most popular desserts today on restaurant menus? Bread-and-butter pudding, snow eggs, *crème brûlée*, and anything made with chocolate. I'm constantly urging everyone to look back, not forward, for some real food. With desserts, at least, we all seem to agree.

Charlotte Malakoff aux Fraises

STRAWBERRY ALMOND CHARLOTTE

Many nations name streets and railway stations after battles, but only the French give such national recognition to a dessert! Malakoff was a key bastion of Sebastopol in the Crimea and when it fell to French troops, the fortress followed. War, however, was still a gentlemanly occupation and Alexis Soyer, chef at London's Reform Club, happened to be on a tour of the battlefield during the action. When a couple of officers expressed their hunger, Soyer took the opportunity to whip up supper on a handy camp stove he had invented. 'I set my Zouave to lay the table; and with my magic stove I cooked some ration-mutton, made an omelette, brought out a piece of boiled beef, bread etc. and gave them a bottle of ale and a glass of sherry'. There is no record that it was Soyer who invented Charlotte Malakoff, an imposing tower fortified with butter, sugar, almonds and cream, but it is typical of the elaborate desserts of his time.

SERVES 8

14–16 sponge fingers
3 tablespoons kirsch
6oz (175g) unsalted butter, softened
6oz (175g) sugar
6oz (175g) ground almonds
8oz (250g) strawberries, hulled and cut into pieces
6fl. oz (175ml) double cream, whipped to hold soft peaks

Strawberry Salad with Mint (see opposite) or Strawberry Sauce (see page 261) (for serving)
8–10 whole strawberries (for decoration)
For the Chantilly cream
6fl. oz (175ml) double cream
1 tablespoon icing sugar
a few drops vanilla essence

3¼-pint (2-litre) charlotte mould or soufflé dish; pastry bag and medium star tube

1 Butter the mould or dish and line the base with a round of greaseproof paper. Line the sides of the mould with ladyfinger sponges, trimming them so that they fit snugly. Sprinkle the remaining ladyfingers with half the kirsch.

2 Cream the butter, add the sugar and beat until light and fluffy: 3–5 minutes. Stir in the ground almonds, strawberries and the remaining kirsch. Fold in the lightly whipped cream. (*Note*: Do not beat the mixture or the cream will curdle and separate.) Spoon half the almond mixture into the mould and add a layer of soaked ladyfingers. Add the remaining mixture and smooth the top. Cover and chill the charlotte until firm: at least 4 hours. It can be refrigerated for up to 4 days. Make the Strawberry Salad with Mint (see opposite).

[194]

3 *To finish.* Not more than 4 hours before serving, trim the sponge fingers level with the almond mixture. Unmould the charlotte on to a shallow dish. Make the Chantilly cream* and scoop it into a pastry bag fitted with a star tube. Decorate the top and base of the charlotte with rosettes of whipped cream and top with the strawberries. Serve the Strawberry Salad with Mint separately. Alternatively, leave the base of the charlotte undecorated and spoon the salad or sauce around the edge. Chill the charlotte until serving.

Cook's Comment. Charlotte Malakoff sets when the butter in the mixture solidifies, avoiding the need for gelatine, which makes most charlottes so tricky when set in the traditional tall, bucket-shaped mould. With too little gelatine, a charlotte wobbles tremulously when unmoulded, or collapses altogether, particularly on a hot day. With a safe quantity of gelatine to hold the shape, it can be unpleasantly chewy. Charlottes are back in fashion but, if you notice, crafty chefs now often mould them in a much wider, shallower ring.

Salade de Fraises à la Menthe

STRAWBERRY SALAD WITH MINT

Keep a few mint sprigs to decorate the charlotte.

SERVES 8

2lb (1kg) strawberries, hulled
and cut into pieces
sugar to taste

2 tablespoons kirsch
bunch of mint

1 Mix the strawberries gently with kirsch and sugar to taste. Cover and leave to marinate in the refrigerator for at least 2 hours and up to 12 hours.

2 Not more than 2 hours before serving, strip the leaves from the mint and coarsely chop them without bruising. Reserve a few sprigs for decoration. Stir the chopped mint into the strawberries and top with sprigs.

Raspberry Fool

Over the derivation of the dessert 'fool' I beg to differ with the *Oxford English Dictionary*. The OED cites a late sixteenth-century definition of fool as 'a kinde of clouted creame called a foole or trifle', rejecting its derivation from the French *fouler* as 'not only baseless, but inconsistent with the early use of the word'. Clearly OED wordsmiths have never made the dessert. *Fouler* means to purée a mixture through a strainer with a ladle – precisely what is done in making a fool, as I know from experience. Our garden in Burgundy is awash with berries – strawberries, raspberries, red-, white- and blackcurrants, and gooseberries (which are another member of the currant family). We've planted mulberry trees and surreptitiously imported loganberry canes from the USA. During July it is almost impossible to keep apace with supply, so quick recipes like fruit fools are imperative.

SERVES 8

3lb (*1.4kg*) fresh raspberries, or two 10oz (*300g*) packets unsweetened frozen raspberries, drained

4fl. oz (*125ml*) double cream, whipped until it holds soft peaks

sugar to taste

ground cinnamon (for sprinkling) or 8 fresh mint sprigs

For the pastry cream

½ pint (*300ml*) milk

vanilla pod or a few drops vanilla

3 egg yolks

2oz (*60g*) sugar

½oz (*15g*) flour

1 *For the pastry cream.* Scald the milk with the vanilla pod, if using. Beat the egg yolks with the sugar until thick and light: 2–3 minutes. Stir in the flour. Whisk the milk into the egg mixture, then return it to the pan. Bring to a boil, whisking constantly until the cream thickens. Simmer it for 1–2 minutes, stirring until it thins slightly. (*Note:* Be sure that the pastry cream is smooth before letting it boil; if any lumps form, work it through a strainer.) Stir in the vanilla extract, if using, or remove the vanilla pod (it can be used again). Transfer the cream to a bowl, rub the surface with a lump of butter to prevent a skin forming, and let it cool.

2 Reserve 8 raspberries for decoration. In a blender or food processor, purée the remaining raspberries. Strain them through a sieve to remove the seeds. There should be 16fl. oz (*500ml*) purée.

3 Beat the raspberry purée into the pastry cream and add sugar to taste. Fold in the lightly whipped cream. Spoon the fool into stemmed glasses, cover and chill. The dessert can be refrigerated for up to 2 days. Just before serving, sprinkle each fool with cinnamon or top with a sprig of mint, then add a raspberry.

Cook's Comment. Besides berries, any tart fruit which is not too juicy makes good fool. Rhubarb and currants should be cooked with sugar (and, if you like, a countryside flavouring of elderflowers or geranium leaves) until very soft before puréeing.

Oranges and Grapefruit with Caramel

I was once asked to lunch by Lord Forte (then Sir Charles) at the Georges V in Paris, which was under his control at the time. This was my first experience of big business at work and I viewed the table of bland-faced executives with trepidation. I need not have worried. Sir Charles devoted his time to a motherly Italian lady who had been plucked, it transpired, from the hotel laundry – one can only suppose to make him feel at home. Our business project did not prosper, but I still retain the Dior scarf presented with ceremony after lunch, one for me, one for the laundress. The cooking was indifferent. Only the simplicity of the dessert remains in my mind.

SERVES 6–8

6 navel oranges	*For the caramel*
3 tablespoons sugar	6½oz (200g) sugar
3 tablespoons water	8fl. oz (250ml) water
	4 grapefruit

1 With a vegetable peeler, thinly pare the rind from 4 oranges. With a sharp knife, cut the rind into the thinnest possible julienne strips. Blanch the julienne in boiling water for 2–3 minutes, then drain. To candy them, heat the sugar and water in a small pan until the sugar dissolves, then add the julienne and cook over a very low heat, stirring occasionally, until the liquid evaporates and the julienne are glazed: 10–15 minutes.

2 Oil a baking sheet. Make the caramel* using the sugar and half the water. Remove from the heat and when the bubbles subside pour about half on to the baking sheet, leaving it to cool and set. Add the remaining water to the pan. (*Note*: Stand back as it will splutter.) Heat gently, stirring until the caramel dissolves, then boil until reduced to a thick syrup. Squeeze the juice from 1 grapefruit, strain and stir into the syrup.

3 Lift the hard caramel from the baking sheet and crush it in a bowl with a pestle or the end of a rolling pin. The candied julienne and crushed caramel can be kept for up to 3 days in air-tight containers. The caramel syrup should be stored in a jar.

4 Not more than 2 hours before serving, cut the rind, skin and pith from the grapefruits and remaining oranges. Thinly slice the fruits and arrange them overlapping on individual plates. Add any juice to the caramel syrup, spoon it over the fruit and chill. Before serving, top with candied julienne and crushed caramel.

Cook's Comment. Cooking caramel to just the right deep gold is tricky because it continues cooking in the pan even after being removed from the heat. When the syrup starts to change colour, you should lower the heat; the first tendrils of smoke are a good indication that the caramel is done. After that it burns very quickly.

Pears in Port Wine Jelly

As anyone who has styled food for photographs knows, complications increase in geometric proportion to the number of dishes to be featured. So you can imagine the turmoil when a publisher decided to cram no fewer than twelve dishes on to the cover of one of my books. Chef Claude from La Varenne and I, with a couple of helpers, cooked all weekend and lugged the results to a studio in Montmartre. In typical style, the premises lacked a stove, hot plate or hot water, so we fudged it, brushing the chicken with oil (to give it a warm shine) and loading the hollandaise sauce with flour so that it would not dry out under the klieg lights. We floated ravioli like little boats on pieces of cork to stop them from sinking into their broth, but every now and again they would turn turtle, so we had to rush in and right them for the camera. Star of the set was a golden-pink pear jelly. However, I would have hated to eat this specimen, doctored as it was with cochineal to register a glowing hue on film, and with enough gelatine to bounce it out of the window. The following recipe gives the correct proportions for this delightful dish!

SERVES 8–10

16fl. oz (500ml) red port wine
16fl. oz (500ml) water
6½oz (200g) sugar
rind of 1 lemon
vanilla pod

5 large firm pears, weighing
  about 2lb (1kg)
½oz (15g) gelatine

12in (30cm) deep cake tin (3½-
  pints (2-litre) capacity)

1 In a deep saucepan, heat the wine, water, sugar, lemon rind and vanilla pod until the sugar dissolves, then simmer for 2–3 minutes. Peel and halve the pears, scooping out the cores and any stem fibres. Immerse the pear halves at once in the syrup and simmer until tender: 8–15 minutes, depending on the ripeness of the pears. Let them cool slightly in the syrup.

2 Set aside about 4 tablespoons of the syrup in a small pan. Drain the pears and measure the syrup; there should be 1⅔ pints (1 litre). If there is too much, boil the syrup to reduce it; if too little, add more water.

3 Sprinkle the gelatine over the cooled syrup in the pan and let it stand for 5 minutes, until spongy. Melt over a low heat and stir it into the remaining sugar syrup to make the jelly.

4 Pour a ⅜in (1cm) layer of jelly into the mould and chill until set. Arrange the pear halves in the mould, cut sides up, and pour over half the remaining jelly. (Note: Do not add enough for the pears to float.) Chill again until firmly set. Add the remaining jelly to cover the pears completely and chill until firm. Cover and chill for at least 2 hours, or up to 2 days.

5 Not more than 2 hours before serving, unmould the jelly: dip the bottom of the mould in hot water for 5–10 seconds, and wipe off the mould; set a flat plate or tray on top and turn it upside down, gently shaking to loosen the jelly.

Cook's Comment. This recipe derives from Mrs Beeton. There's something very Victorian about port wine jelly. The ideal mould for it is a French *moule à manqué* cake tin with sloping sides.

Peaches in Spiced Red Wine

On my first visit to South Africa I did not have great hopes for the cuisine, beyond a few English afternoon teas and perhaps a traditional Dutch cake or two. I found much more. The vigorous, spicy cooking of the Cape Malays includes stews like *bobotie*, a curry flavoured with lemon leaves, *sosaties* or kebabs, and a multitude of chutneys. Chilli powder, called *peri-peri*, is an important ingredient. From the African kitchen come vegetable casseroles and mealie bread. Most important is the abundance of good ingredients, leading to recipes like these fresh peaches marinated in spiced wine.

SERVES 6

3¼ oz (*100g*) sugar, or to taste	1 cinnamon stick
4fl. oz (*125ml*) water	8 ripe peaches
12fl. oz (*375ml*) dry red wine	vanilla ice-cream (for serving –
1 tablespoon peppercorns	optional)

1 In a saucepan, combine the sugar, water and wine. Tie the peppercorns and cinnamon in a piece of muslin or cheesecloth and add to the pan. Heat gently until the sugar dissolves, then simmer for 10–15 minutes. Transfer to a large bowl and cool.

2 Peel the peaches,* slice them and add them to the syrup at once. Taste the syrup, adding more sugar if needed. Cover and leave to marinate in the refrigerator for at least 1 hour and up to 24 hours.

3 Discard the spice bag from the peaches and serve very cold, with vanilla ice-cream if you like.

Cook's Comment. In a fit of new-style inspiration, I once served these peaches sprinkled with pine nuts and passion fruit seeds – rather to my surprise it proved a happy combination.

[199]

Pear and Hazelnut Soufflé

In the days before Chef Anton Mosimann of The Dorchester Hotel hit the headlines, we collaborated on the launch of the *Observer French Cookery* series. To illustrate the value of French cooking techniques as taught at La Varenne in Paris, Anton created an alphabet of soufflés from Apple to Zingara (chicken with paprika). Thanks to The Dorchester's revolving oven, which can accommodate soufflés for 800 – one of the wonders of the culinary world – all twenty-six soufflés were served simultaneously with an accompanying sauce. As far as I am concerned, when it comes to gastronomic spectaculars, you can keep *pièces montées* and bouquets of roses in sugar. Technically and visually, two baker's dozen of hot soufflés provide the finest culinary display.

SERVES 4

5fl. oz (*150ml*) milk	1 large (½lb (*250g*)) ripe pear
2 egg yolks	1 tablespoon pear liqueur or kirsch
1½oz (*45g*) sugar	4 egg whites
½oz (*15g*) flour	icing sugar (for sprinkling)
2oz (*60g*) hazelnuts, toasted and ground*	*1⅔-pint (1-litre) soufflé dish*

1 Scald the milk in a saucepan. Beat the egg yolks with half the sugar until thick and pale: 2–3 minutes. Stir in the flour. Whisk in the hot milk, return the mixture to the pan and bring to a boil, whisking constantly until the mixture thickens. Simmer, stirring, for 1 minute. Allow to cool slightly.

2 Stir the hazelnuts into the mixture. Peel and core the pear. Grind it to a coarse purée in a food processor or chop it very fine with a knife and stir at once into the soufflé mixture with the liqueur. (*Note*: Work quickly as the pears will discolour.) The soufflé can be prepared 3–4 hours ahead to this point; if doing so, rub a lump of butter on top of the mixture to prevent it from drying out. Cover tightly and refrigerate.

3 *To finish*. Heat the oven to Gas 7/220°C/425°F and thickly butter the soufflé dish. Stiffly whip the egg whites. Add the remaining sugar and continue whipping until the egg whites are glossy and form a light meringue: 30 seconds. Reheat the soufflé base until hot to the touch. Stir in about a quarter of the meringue until thoroughly combined. Add this mixture to the remaining egg whites and fold together as lightly as possible. Spoon the soufflé mixture into the prepared dish – it should come to within ¾in (*2cm*) of the rim. The soufflé can be refrigerated for up to 1 hour.

4 Bake the soufflé low down in the oven until puffed and brown: 15–18 minutes. When gently shaken, it should wobble. Sprinkle with icing sugar and serve at once.

Cook's Comment. The taller and narrower the dish, the higher the soufflé will rise, but the greater the risk that the sides may collapse. As a precaution, some cooks wrap a collar around the dish, but French-trained chefs never seem to bother, and nor do I.

Three Flourless Soufflés

In that irritating way that evangelists have of pushing logical precepts to extremes, about ten years ago many new-style chefs banished flour from their kitchens. The flourless soufflé posed a problem because something is still needed to stabilise the mass of whipped egg whites. However, the three following recipes meet the new criterion, for chocolate provides its own glue, and lemons can be cooked with egg yolks to make lemon curd.

Chocolate Soufflé

SERVES 4

4oz (125g) semi-sweet
    chocolate, chopped
4fl. oz (125ml) double cream
3 egg yolks
a few drops vanilla essence

1 tablespoon brandy
5 egg whites
1½oz (45g) sugar
icing sugar (for sprinkling)

1⅔-pint (1-litre) soufflé dish

1 In a heavy saucepan, melt the chocolate in the cream over a low heat, stirring constantly. Cook, stirring, until the mixture is thick and just falls from the spoon. Remove from the heat and beat in the egg yolks so that they cook and thicken the mixture slightly. Stir in the vanilla essence and brandy. The soufflé mixture can be kept covered for 3–4 hours in the refrigerator.

2 To finish. Heat the oven to Gas 7/220°C/425°F and thickly butter the soufflé dish. Stiffly whip the egg whites, add the sugar and continue whipping until the egg whites are glossy and form a light meringue: 30 seconds. Reheat the chocolate mixture until just hot to the touch. Stir in about a quarter of the meringue until thoroughly combined. Add this mixture to the remaining egg whites and fold together as lightly as possible. Spoon the soufflé mixture into the prepared dish – it should come to within ¾in (2cm) of the rim. The soufflé can be refrigerated for up to 1 hour.

3 Bake the soufflé low down in the oven until puffed: 15–18 minutes (when gently shaken, it should still wobble slightly, showing that the centre is soft). Sprinkle with caster sugar and serve immediately.

Cook's Comment. Once at La Varenne a chocolate soufflé was forgotten in the refrigerator not for an hour or two, but for the whole night. We baked it anyway and it rose without a tremor, proving that whipped egg whites can, after all, be kept waiting. Now we no longer think much of leaving soufflés for an hour or two before baking, thus demolishing a hoary culinary myth.

Hot Lemon Soufflé

SERVES 4

2oz (*60g*) unsalted butter
4½oz (*135g*) sugar
3fl. oz (*90ml*) lemon juice
4 egg yolks
grated rind of 2 lemons

5 egg whites
icing sugar (for sprinkling)

1⅔-pint (*1-litre*) soufflé dish

1 In a heavy pan, heat the butter with half the sugar and the lemon juice until the sugar dissolves. Take from the heat and beat in the egg yolks, one by one, and then the lemon rind. Heat very gently, stirring constantly, until the mixture thickens to the consistency of double cream: 5–7 minutes. (*Note*: Do not let it get too hot or it will curdle.) Remove from the heat and cover the mixture with cling film. It can be kept for up to 6 hours at room temperature.

2 *To finish*. Heat the oven to Gas 7/220°C/425°F and thickly butter the soufflé dish. Stiffly whip the egg whites. Add the remaining sugar and continue whipping until the egg whites are glossy and form a light meringue: 30 seconds. Stir about a quarter of the meringue into the lemon mixture until thoroughly combined. Add this mixture to the remaining meringue and fold together as lightly as possible. Spoon the soufflé mixture into the prepared dish – it should come to within ¾in (*2cm*) of the rim. The soufflé can be refrigerated for up to 1 hour.

3 Bake the soufflé low down in the heated oven until puffed and brown: 15–18 minutes. Sprinkle with icing sugar and serve at once.

Cook's Comment. I prefer sweet soufflés to be lightly baked so that the centre forms a soft sauce for the firmer outside. At this stage, the soufflé will be slightly concave on top and when gently shaken it will still wobble slightly. When firm with a flat top, the soufflé is cooked through to the centre.

Cold Lemon Soufflés

Hot and cold lemon soufflés play quite different roles in a menu. Hot soufflé, the essence of lightness, is the ideal note on which to end a rich meal, whereas cold lemon soufflé is so rich in itself that it demands simple dishes to precede it.

SERVES 8

½oz (15g) gelatine
6 tablespoons cold water
6 eggs, separated
11½oz (350g) sugar
6fl. oz (175ml) lemon juice
grated rind of 4 lemons
½ pint (300ml) double cream, whipped until it holds a soft peak

1 lemon, cut into 8 thin slices (for decoration)
For the Chantilly cream
8fl. oz (250ml) double cream
2 tablespoons icing sugar
a few drops vanilla essence

8 ramekins (8fl. oz (250ml) capacity each); pastry bag and small star tube

1 Wrap a double strip of foil around each ramekin to form a collar about 1in (2.5cm) above the rims and fasten with tape or pins. In a small pan, sprinkle the gelatine over the water and leave until spongy: 5 minutes.

2 In a large bowl, beat the egg yolks, two-thirds of the sugar, lemon juice and rind until mixed. Set the bowl over a pan of hot but not boiling water and whisk until the mixture is thick enough to leave a ribbon trail when the whisk is lifted: 5–7 minutes. Take it from the heat.

3 Melt the gelatine over a low heat and whisk into the lemon mousse. Continue whisking until the mousse is cool. Whip the egg whites until stiff, add the remaining sugar and continue whipping until the egg whites are glossy and form a light meringue: 30 seconds.

4 Set the bowl of lemon mousse over ice and stir constantly until it starts to set. Take it from the ice and fold in the meringue, followed by the lightly whipped cream. (*Note:* Work fast, as it sets quickly.) Pour the mixture into the ramekins; it should come 1in (2.5cm) above the rims. Cover and chill for at least 3 hours, or up to 2 days.

5 *To finish.* Make the Chantilly cream* and scoop it into a pastry bag with a small star tube. Remove the collars from the ramekins. Cover the tops of the soufflés with tiny rosettes of cream. Make a cut into the centre of each lemon slice and twist it in a spiral. Set a slice on each soufflé. Chill the soufflés until serving or, if they have been refrigerated for several hours, let them stand at room temperature to soften slightly.

Cook's Comment. If the mixture is moulded as one big soufflé, it makes a grand entrance, though it can be tricky to serve.

Petites Iles Flottant

LITTLE FLOATING ISLANDS

When I was studying cooking at the Cordon Bleu in Paris in the early 1960s, I learned almost as much from the family I lived with as I did at school. The Charpentiers, with their seven children, followed a programme of discipline which must go back generations. Each day Monsieur came home for a two-hour ritual lunch at which all the children, from the age of two onwards, were expected to behave impeccably. This was the time of day when full parental control was expected and exercised. The food was severely plain – dried salami sausage, celery root remoulade, radishes with butter (pâté was regarded as too rich for infants' stomachs), followed by roast meat and a single vegetable (fish on Fridays), then cheese and fruit.

No backsliding on cleaning the plate was permitted. On name-days and birthdays – which occurred with happy frequency, since the Charpentiers formed part of a vast extended family – we had *gâteau* – a simple *génoise* sponge with a flavoured icing chosen by the honoré.

Only on Sundays were rules relaxed to include delicacies like the first scallops of the season baked in garlic butter, or baby sole in Madame Charpentier's own butter sauce. Chicken was always the main course, but what chickens! They came from a special poulterer, the finest in all Paris, it was claimed. Dessert, too, was a festival for young tastes. We might have fritters with honey, or chocolate snowball, or an almond apple tart. Most popular of all was floating island – an island of meringue, floating in vanilla custard and topped with crisp caramel. Children's paradise, with a place for adults too.

SERVES 6

6 egg whites
10oz (300g) sugar
a few drops vanilla essence
For the vanilla custard sauce
1⅔ pints (1 litre) milk
vanilla pod or a few drops
    vanilla essence

10 egg yolks
3¼oz (100g) sugar
For the caramel
3¼oz (100g) sugar
2½fl. oz (75ml) water

6 custard cups or ramekins (7fl. oz
    (200ml) capacity each)

1 Make the vanilla custard sauce* and chill. Heat the oven to Gas 4/175°C/350°F. Butter the custard cups or ramekins and sprinkle with sugar, discarding the excess.

2 *For the meringue.* Stiffly whip the egg whites, add 6 tablespoons of the sugar and continue whipping until the mixture is glossy and forms long peaks when the whisk is lifted: 30 seconds. Fold in the remaining sugar and the vanilla essence. Spoon the meringue into the prepared cups and set them in a *bain marie.**

3 Bring the *bain marie* to a boil on top of the stove and cook in the oven until the meringue is firm and starts to shrink from the sides of the mould: 20–25 minutes. Remove from the *bain marie* and leave to cool. (*Note*: The meringues will shrink as they cool; press the puffed sides inwards so that they shrink evenly back into the cups.) The custard and meringues can be refrigerated for up to 8 hours.

4 Not more than 2 hours before serving, run a knife around the edges of the meringues and turn them into shallow serving bowls. Pour the custard around the edge. With a wide spatula gently lift the meringue 'islands' so that they float.

5 Make the caramel.* Let the bubbles subside before pouring it over the meringues, drizzling the caramel down the sides. (*Note*: It will splutter if it reaches the custard.) Chill until serving.

Cook's Comment. For a dessert that is easier to serve, but less crispy, trail the hot caramel in a lattice rather than pouring a solid layer over the meringues.

Pineapple Pavlova

It seems to me that cooks are born either cuisine or pastry chefs, but never both. The character traits required are quite different. Great cuisine is not a matter of fixed measures and quantities but rather of instinctive adjustments to master recipes to suit the ingredients from day to day and to allow for an individual style. Pastry, on the other hand, demands meticulous care. Chef Jorant at La Varenne reminds me of a Swiss watchmaker as he measures and mixes and shapes with rigid discipline. Perhaps it is no coincidence that the Swiss are such excellent *pâtissiers*.

As a cuisine cook by nature, making meringues is not my forte. They weep sticky syrup, glueing themselves like limpets to the baking sheet; they bubble at the edges and scorch on the bottom. In vain has Chef Jorant instructed me in all the cures – flour the sheet, don't over- (or under-) mix the meringue, keep the oven low, and so on. Meringues remain my Waterloo. It took an Australian to teach me a meringue dessert I know I can get right. The little bit of cornflour and vinegar in Pavlova give the meringue a marshmallow-like texture and seem to render it much more amenable to my ministrations.

SERVES 6–8

1 fresh pineapple	*For the Chantilly cream*
2–3 tablespoons sugar	12fl. oz (*375ml*) double cream,
2 tablespoons kirsch	stiffly whipped
For the meringue	1–2 tablespoons sugar
6 egg whites	a few drops vanilla essence
12oz (*375g*) sugar	
1 tablespoon cornflour	
1 teaspoon distilled white vinegar	*pastry bag and medium star tube*

1 Heat the oven to Gas ½/120°C/250°F. Butter and flour a baking sheet, discarding the excess, or line it with silicone paper. Mark a 10in (*25cm*) circle with a flan ring or pan lid.

2 *For the meringue.* Stiffly whip the egg whites, add 6 tablespoons of the sugar and continue whipping until the mixture is glossy and forms long peaks: 30 seconds. Sift the cornflour with the remaining sugar and fold it into the egg whites, followed by the vinegar. Pile the mixture on to the baking sheet and spread to a round, hollowing the centre slightly.

3 Bake the pavlova in the oven until it is cream coloured and firm, but still soft inside: 1¼–1½ hours. The pavlova will become crisp as it cools. (*Note*: If it starts to brown during cooking, lower the heat and cover loosely with foil.) Let the pavlova cool to lukewarm, then lift it off the baking sheet or peel off the paper. It can be stored for up to a week in an air-tight container, or frozen.

4 Not more than 2 hours before serving, peel, core and slice the pineapple. Reserve 2–3 slices for decoration and cut the rest into chunks. Sprinkle the chunks with sugar and kirsch. Make the Chantilly cream.* Set the pavlova on a serving dish or tray and spoon in half the cream. Spread the pineapple chunks on top. Scoop the remaining cream into the pastry bag with a star tube and top the pineapple with rosettes. Cut the pineapple slices into wedges and set them attractively on top of the cream. Chill the pavlova until serving time.

Cook's Comment. Kiwi is, of course, the traditional fruit for Pavlova, but I've never cared for it (dislike is too strong a word for such a bland fruit). Tropical fruits like mango and papaya are good, with some orange for tartness. And since New Zealand lays claim not only to Pavlova but to excellent raspberries as well, they are another alternative.

Crème Brûlée with Fruit

I shall always think of Robert Carrier as lord of Hintlesham Hall, the grand Georgian mansion near Ipswich that he restored. Bob did not just restore Hintlesham – he brought it to life, installing a restaurant, giving concerts in the great hall and cooking classes in the stables. His canopied bed was so large that, once assembled, he was told it could never be removed. I've often wondered if it is still there! Best of all was Bob himself. Of imposing stature and given to velvet coats, he was the perfect host, with a beaming smile which belied his barbed wit. When we first bought Château du Feÿ in Burgundy, Bob's example was often in my mind as we struggled to adapt a graceful old property to the realities of the twentieth century. I would like to think that we achieved half his flamboyant *élan*. As for Bob Carrier's cooking, it has always been just my style – rather rich, with an unerring flair for valid new ideas like this Crème Brûlée sharpened with fruit.

SERVES 6

½lb (*250g*) raspberries, sliced strawberries or sliced peeled peaches*
1 tablespoon brandy
1 pint (*600ml*) double cream
1 vanilla pod, split, or a few drops vanilla essence

6 egg yolks
3¼oz (*100g*) sugar

6 ramekins (6fl. oz (175ml) capacity each)

1 Heat the oven to Gas 6/200°C/400°F. Mix the fruit with the brandy and spread it in the ramekins. Scald the cream with the vanilla pod, if using, cover and leave to infuse for 10 minutes. Beat the egg yolks with 2 tablespoons of the sugar in a bowl until slightly thickened. Stir in the cream and vanilla essence, if using. Strain this custard into the ramekins.

2 Set ramekins in a cold *bain marie** and cook in the oven until a thin skin forms on top of the custard: 10–12 minutes; underneath it should remain liquid. Chill the ramekins in the refrigerator for at least 1 hour, or up to 8 hours.

3 *To finish.* Heat the grill. Sprinkle each custard with 1 tablespoon of sugar to form a thin layer. Grill as close as possible to the heat until the sugar melts and caramelises: 2–3 minutes. (*Note:* Do not overcook the custard or it will bubble through the sugar.) Allow to cool; the caramel will form a crisp layer on the custard. Serve them within 2–3 hours.

Cook's Comment. Some cooks bake the custard for Crème Brûlée until it sets, but I like the surprise when the caramel topping is broken and sinks into the liquid cream. In winter, tangerine segments or halved grapes can be substituted for the raspberries.

Orange Caramel Cream

It was in Spain that I came across this agreeably tart version of caramel custard, a dessert I've always found insipid. This recipe appeals to me – so simple, but concealing the surprise taste of orange instead of milk. When the cream is turned out, you will see that the colour is even prettier than plain caramel custard.

SERVES 8

10 eggs
4¼oz (135g) sugar
1⅔ pints (1 litre) fresh orange juice

For the caramel
5oz (150g) sugar
4fl. oz (125ml) water

8 ramekins (8fl. oz (250ml) capacity each)

1 Make the caramel.* Let the bubbles subside, then pour the caramel into the ramekins, tilting them so that the base and sides are coated with a thin, even layer. Set aside to cool. Heat the oven to Gas 4/175°C/350°F.

2 Beat the eggs with the sugar until well mixed, then stir in the orange juice. Strain the mixture into the prepared ramekins and set them in a *bain marie*.* Bring the water to a boil on top of the stove.

3 Bake the creams in the oven until they are just set and a knife inserted in the centre comes out clean: 17–20 minutes. (*Note:* Do not overcook or they will curdle.) Take the ramekins from the *bain marie* and leave to cool. They can be kept in the refrigerator for up to 2 days.

4 Not more than 30 minutes before serving, run a knife around the edge of the creams and turn them out on to individual plates. The caramel will have dissolved to form a sauce. Serve them at room temperature.

Cook's Comment. For a French version of this recipe (from the chestnut country of the Ardèche to the west of the Rhône), milk should be reinstated for orange juice. When the cream begins to set in the oven, sprinkle with crumbled pieces of cooked chestnuts sprinkled with a tablespoon of rum. (Tinned chestnuts cooked in water are fine for this.) Then continue cooking until the cream is set. You'll be surprised how much this version differs from plain caramel custard.

Crêpes Suzette

Crêpes Suzette is a good example of how a bastardised recipe can supersede the real thing. Do you remember those overpriced versions made with marmalade and served in Trust House hotels in the 1950s? It is high time that the original Escoffier dish, in which the crêpes are spread with orange butter, fried until they caramelise (a vital touch), and then flamed with brandy and Grand Marnier, came into its own again. Flaming is fun, and it serves the legitimate purpose of burning off harsh alcohol so that only the flavouring essence is left. Cynical chefs point out that the boiling alcohol evaporates anyway, with or without a flame, but I've noticed that even so they are all for a bit of show if given the chance.

SERVES 6

crêpes (see opposite)
4oz (*125g*) unsalted butter,
  softened
4½oz (*135g*) sugar

grated rind of 2 oranges
3–4 tablespoons Grand Marnier
  or orange liqueur
3–4 tablespoons brandy

1 Make the crêpes. Cream all but a tablespoonful of the butter with the sugar and orange rind until very soft and light. Beat in a tablespoon of Grand Marnier or orange liqueur. Spread butter on the underside (spotted side) of each crêpe and pile them one on top of another. The crêpes can be kept covered at room temperature for up to 8 hours.

2 Melt the remaining butter in a chafing dish or frying pan. Add 2–3 crêpes, butter side down, and fry until very hot: 30 seconds. Fold each one in four, move them to the side of the pan and continue until all the crêpes are hot and folded. Towards the end of cooking, the butter and sugar will caramelise at the bottom of the pan.

3 Heat the brandy and the remaining Grand Marnier or orange liqueur in a small pan. Pour over the crêpes and flame by tipping the pan to catch a gas light, or lighting with a match if using electricity. Cook, basting the crêpes, until the flame dies. Serve at once.

Cook's Comment. Don't play pyrotechnics and overdo the alcoholic spirits in Crêpes Suzette. I once saw a chef at La Varenne caught red-handed. Prattling on about his expertise in the kitchen, he tossed a generous slug of brandy into the hot pan, tipped it to the gas light – and woosh, up shot a powerful pillar of flame. As a large hole slowly crinkled its way across the mylar mirror above his head, the expressions which crossed his face were almost worth the repair bill.

Crêpes

The butter for these crêpes goes into the batter, so that at most a brushing of butter is needed for frying.

MAKES 16–18 6in (15cm) CREPES

4oz (125g) flour
½ teaspoon salt
3 eggs

8fl. oz (250ml) milk, or more if needed
2oz (60g) unsalted butter

1 Sift the flour and salt into a bowl and make a well in the centre. Add the eggs and half the milk. Gradually whisk in the flour to make a smooth batter, then stir in the remaining milk. Cover and leave in the refrigerator for at least 30 minutes, or overnight. The batter will thicken on standing.

2 Melt all but 1 tablespoon of the butter and stir it into the batter. Heat the crêpe pan, brush it with butter and add a small ladleful of batter to cover the bottom of the pan, shaking and turning the pan so that it is evenly coated. Fry over a medium heat until brown, turn and brown the other side. If the crêpe is heavy, add a little more milk to the batter.

3 Fry the remaining crêpes in the same way, piling them one on top of another to keep them moist. Crêpes can be kept in the refrigerator, tightly wrapped, for up to 3 days, or they can be frozen.

Riz à l'Impératrice

CREAMED RICE WITH CANDIED FRUITS

In everybody's infancy there must have been rice pudding, for I've noticed its appeal is universal. At our local *relais routier* lorry stop at Villevallier in Burgundy – one of the better ones, by the way – caramelised rice mould is a prime favourite, while Savoy Hotel habitués certainly did not disdain the following classic version offered by Escoffier.

SERVES 6–8

2oz (*60g*) round-grain rice
16fl. oz (*500ml*) milk, or more if needed
vanilla pod
pinch of salt
2oz (*60g*) sugar
1 tablespoon butter
¼oz (*7g*) gelatine
3 tablespoons water
2oz (*60g*) chopped mixed candied peel
1oz (*30g*) candied cherries, chopped
2 tablespoons apricot jam
2 tablespoons kirsch
4fl. oz (*125ml*) double cream, whipped until it holds soft peaks

Dried Apricot Sauce (see opposite)
For the vanilla custard sauce
8fl. oz (*250ml*) milk
vanilla pod
2 egg yolks
1oz (*30g*) sugar
For decoration
1 tablespoon sugar
a few drops vanilla essence
4fl. oz (*125ml*) double cream, stiffly whipped
3–4 candied cherries, halved
a few leaves cut from angelica

2⅓-pint (*1.5-litre*) tall mould; pastry bag and medium star tube

1 Blanch the rice by putting it in enough cold water to cover generously, boiling for 7–8 minutes and draining. Rinse it with cold water and drain again thoroughly. In a heavy pan combine the milk with the vanilla pod, salt and rice. Bring to a simmer and cook, stirring occasionally, until all the milk is absorbed and the rice is tender: 30–40 minutes. The rice should be thick, but still soft enough to fall from the spoon. If it thickens too much during cooking, add more milk.

2 When cooked, take the rice from the heat, stir in the sugar and remove the vanilla pod. Rub the butter on the surface of the rice to prevent a skin forming. Sprinkle the gelatine over the water in a small pan and leave until spongy: 5 minutes. Make the vanilla custard sauce.* Stir in the softened gelatine until melted. Stir the custard into the rice with the candied peel, candied cherries, apricot jam and kirsch.

3 Set the rice mixture over ice and chill, stirring occasionally, until it starts to set. Fold in the lightly whipped cream and pour the mixture into the mould. (*Note*: Do not over-mix or the cream will lose its lightness.) Cover and refrigerate until firmly set: at least 4 hours, and up to 3 days. Make the Dried Apricot Sauce.

4 *To finish.* Run a knife around the edge of the mould. Dip the mould in hot water for 10–20 seconds, set a plate on top, turn the mould upside down and shake sharply downwards. If the rice continues to stick, wrap the mould briefly in a hot, damp cloth.

5 *To decorate.* Stir the sugar and vanilla essence into the whipped cream and scoop it into the pastry bag with a star tube. Decorate the top of the mould with rosettes, topping them with candied cherries and angelica leaves. Spoon the Dried Apricot Sauce around the edge and serve the rest separately. Chill the mould until serving.

Cook's Comment. A tall, peaked mould or a charlotte mould is *de rigueur* for Riz à l'Impératrice. The dessert is named after Empress Eugénie and, with a bit of imagination, should recall an imperial crown. A decoration of whipped cream and candied cherries may seem hackneyed, but that is the way it should be.

Sauce aux Abricots Secs

DRIED APRICOT SAUCE

Look for deep-yellow, shiny apricots with plenty of taste.

MAKES 12fl. oz (375ml) SAUCE TO SERVE 6–8

8oz (*250g*) dried apricots	16fl. oz (*500ml*) water, or more
2 strips of rind and the juice of	if needed
1 lemon	2 tablespoons kirsch
	sugar (optional)

1 In a saucepan, combine the apricots with the lemon rind, juice and water. Cover and simmer until the apricots are tender: 15–20 minutes, or as directed on the packet. If all the water is absorbed during cooking, add more.

2 Discard the lemon rind and purée the apricots and liquid in a food processor or blender. Stir in the kirsch and add sugar if needed. The sauce should just pour easily; if it is too thick, add more water. It can be refrigerated for up to a week, or frozen.

Sherry Syllabub

Old recipes can provide a welcome jolt to one's preconceived ideas. I had always dismissed as flights of fancy the eighteenth-century recipes for syllabub in which the cow is milked directly into wine and fruit juice, but to my astonishment it works! At Williamsburg, the reconstructed early colonial capital of America, this technique is being field-tested with the co-operation of a cow called Hannah, after cookbook author Hannah Glasse. The warmth and force of the jet of milk, it turns out, helps the syllabub to froth and thicken. To obtain the same result in the kitchen, unpasteurised milk must be warmed, then poured from a height into the wine.

SERVES 6

6fl. oz (175ml) medium dry
  sherry
3fl. oz (90ml) brandy
3fl. oz (90ml) lemon juice
5oz (150g) sugar, or more to
  taste

16fl. oz (500ml) double cream
ground nutmeg or cinnamon
  (for sprinkling)

6 stemmed syllabub or wine glasses

1 Mix the sherry, brandy, lemon juice and sugar in a bowl and stir to dissolve the sugar partly. Set the bowl over ice. Beat in the cream and continue beating until the mixture thickens enough to hold a soft peak for a few seconds when the beater is lifted: 4–5 minutes.

2 Spoon the mixture into stemmed glasses and chill. The syllabub can be refrigerated for up to 3 days. Just before serving, sprinkle with a little ground nutmeg or cinnamon.

Cook's Comment. On standing, the syllabub separates into a top layer of lemon–sherry mousse and a bottom layer of clear wine punch – two treats in one.

Trifle

Foreigners find the English dessert of trifle hard to understand. To begin with, the name is misleading, for you could hardly find anything less trifling. Then trifle is so often bad, made with stale cake, cheap sherry, jelly and commercial custard. When I made the real thing for Chef Chambrette, he refused to credit its authenticity and marched round to Marks and Spencer on the Boulevard Haussmann, returning to dump a plastic cup on my desk, insisting, *'Voila, ça c'est un vrai tri-fell!'*

SERVES 6–8

8oz (*250g*) sponge cake or
   pound cake
6–8 tablespoons raspberry jam
5–6 tablespoons medium sweet
   sherry
1lb (*500g*) tin sliced pears or
   peaches, drained
3–4 tablespoons whole
   blanched almonds, toasted
   (for decoration)
For the vanilla custard sauce
16fl. oz (*500ml*) milk

vanilla pod or a few drops
   vanilla essence
2 tablespoons cornflour
6 egg yolks
2oz (*60g*) sugar
For the Chantilly cream
6fl. oz (*175ml*) double cream
1 tablespoon sugar
a few drops vanilla essence

4²⁄₃-pint (3-litre) glass serving
   bowl; pastry bag and medium
   star tube

1 Cut the cake in two horizontally; sandwich it with raspberry jam and cut it into 1in (*2.5cm*) squares. Put the cake squares in the bottom of a glass serving bowl, sprinkle with the sherry and press down lightly. Top with an even layer of the drained fruit.

2 Make the vanilla custard sauce,* stirring the cornflour into the egg yolk and sugar mixture. Bring the custard almost to a boil to cook the cornflour thoroughly. Allow to cool slightly, pour the custard over the fruit and leave it in the refrigerator to set. Cover and refrigerate the trifle for at least a day and up to 3 days so that the flavour matures.

3 Not more than 3 hours before serving, make the Chantilly cream* and scoop it into the pastry bag with a star tube. Pipe a lattice of cream on top of the trifle so that the custard shows through. Decorate the edge of the trifle with rosettes, topping them with browned almonds. Chill the trifle until serving time.

Cook's Comment. Trifle is godfather to *zuppa inglese*, or English soup – that Italian dessert of cake moistened with rum and filled with pastry cream, then topped with meringue. Apparently the concoction was developed in the mid-nineteenth century to please English visitors to Italy.

Chocolate Snowball

'Dessert should be cool, light and slightly sweet, and should be served preferably on a table in front of the sofa, so it serves physically and gastronomically as a transition from the pleasures of the table to those of the bed, and enables you to manœuvre into closer quarters for the very best reasons.' So advises Mimi Sheraton in *The Seducer's Cookbook*, written twenty-five years ago before Mimi rose to great heights as the *New York Times'* redoubtable restaurant critic. Her presence in a Manhattan restaurant became so feared that she plied her trade disguised in wig and dark glasses. A current photograph of Mimi is as rare as one of Elizabeth David or Greta Garbo.

Seduction has become sexist, but in the hope that the ancient art may be revived, I offer the following hints: procure a copy of Mimi's book before it becomes as rare as the first edition of Casanova's memoirs. Ignore legends about oysters and other aphrodisiacs since they have never been authenticated in the laboratory or elsewhere. Concentrate instead on superb cooking and suggestive presentations as the ultimate lure for body and mind. This chocolate snowball, topped with a nipple of whipped cream, is one suggestion.

SERVES 8

8oz (*250g*) semi-sweet chocolate, chopped
6fl. oz (*175ml*) strong black coffee
8oz (*250g*) unsalted butter, cut into pieces
6½oz (*200g*) sugar
4 eggs
fresh mint sprigs or candied violets

For the Chantilly cream
8fl. oz (*250ml*) double cream, stiffly whipped
1 tablespoon sugar
a few drops vanilla essence

1⅔-pint (1-litre) charlotte mould; pastry bag and small star tube

1 Line the mould with a double thickness of foil. Heat the oven to Gas 4/175°C/350°F.

2 In a heavy pan, heat the chocolate gently with the coffee, stirring until melted. Cook, stirring until the mixture is thick but still falls easily from the spoon. Add the butter and sugar and heat, stirring until melted. Bring the mixture almost to a boil and remove from the heat. Whisk in the eggs, one by one. (*Note*: The eggs will cook and thicken from the heat of the mixture.)

3 Strain the mixture into the mould and bake in the oven until a thick crust forms on top: 45–55 minutes. The mixture will rise slightly, but fall again as it cools. Cover and refrigerate for at least 24 hours and up to a week, so that the flavour mellows. The snowball can also be frozen.

4 *To finish.* Not more than 2 hours before serving, run a knife around the mould, turn the snowball on to a serving plate and peel off the foil. (*Note*: The mixture tends to stick and look messy.) Make the Chantilly cream* and scoop it into the pastry bag and star tube. Pipe small rosettes over the chocolate mixture to cover it completely. Top the centre of the mould with a single large rosette. Decorate with mint sprigs or candied violets and chill until serving.

Cook's Comment. Dissolving chocolate in black coffee instead of water takes the edge off its sweetness.

A Trio of Ice-creams

It is impossible to judge which country makes the best ice-cream, for all use the same basic mixture of milk and sugar, usually enriched with eggs and cream. Proportions, however, can vary enormously. Given my extravagant tastes, I would never have thought too rich an ice-cream was possible until the day we started to experiment at school, loading mixtures with egg yolks, sugar and high-butterfat cream. Ten egg yolks to a litre of cream (or milk and cream) we discovered was the limit – beyond that the ice-cream started to resemble frozen butter.

It is in the flavourings that national characteristics emerge. Ginger ice-cream, for instance, has to be English, while only the French would think of dressing up prunes by freezing them in custard after a generous soaking in armagnac. Most creative of all are American cooks, with their rum raisin, chocolate mint chip and even bubble gum ice-creams. From the old favourite, butter pecan, it is only a short step to the caramel pecan which flavours the third ice-cream in this trio.

Ginger Ice-cream

MAKES 2 PINTS (1.25 LITRES) ICE-CREAM TO SERVE 6

2oz (60g) candied ginger
6fl. oz (175ml) single cream
For the custard sauce
1¼ pints (750ml) milk
2 teaspoons ground ginger

6 egg yolks
6½oz (200g) sugar

ice-cream maker

1 Pour boiling water over the candied ginger and leave it to soften for 10–15 minutes. Drain, dry and chop.

2 Make the custard sauce,* substituting ground ginger for vanilla. Strain, stir in the candied ginger and leave to cool. Stir in the cream and chill until very cold.

3 Freeze the mixture in an ice-cream maker until stiff. The ice-cream can be stored for up to a month. Let it soften in the refrigerator for 30 minutes before serving.

Cook's Comment. An excellent accompaniment to melon, strawberries, and tropical fruits like mango.

Caramel Pecan Parfait

MAKES 2 PINTS (1.25 LITRES) ICE-CREAM TO SERVE 6

For the caramel pecan mixture
6½oz (*200g*) sugar
5oz (*150g*) coarsely chopped
   pecans
For the meringue italienne
5oz (*150g*) sugar
4fl. oz (*125ml*) water
4 egg whites

12fl. oz (*375ml*) double cream,
   whipped until it holds a soft
   peak
For decoration
6 tablespoons double cream,
   stiffly whipped
6 whole pecans

pastry bag and medium star tube

1 *To make the caramel pecan mixture.* Oil a baking sheet. In a heavy pan, melt the sugar, stirring occasionally, until it starts to caramelise. Stir in the chopped pecans and cook the caramel, stirring constantly, to a rich golden brown. Immediately pour it on to the baking sheet and leave it until cooled and hard. Lift it off the baking sheet and coarsely grind it in a food processor, or pound it in a bowl with the end of a rolling pin. (*Note*: A few larger pieces of nut will add texture to the *parfait*.)

2 *For the meringue italienne.* Heat the sugar with the water until it dissolves. Boil the syrup without stirring until it forms a sticky thread between forefinger and thumb when a little is lifted on a spoon (116°C/239°F on a sugar thermometer). Meanwhile, stiffly whip the egg whites. Let the bubbles in the sugar syrup subside, then whisk it into the egg whites in a steady stream. Continue whisking until the meringue is cool.

3 Stir the caramel–pecan mixture into the meringue, then fold in the whipped cream. (*Note*: If the meringue is still warm, it will melt the cream.) Spoon the mixture into *parfait* glasses or freezer-resistant bowls, cover and freeze. Parfait can be kept for up to a month in the freezer.

4 An hour before serving, scoop the whipped cream into the pastry bag and star tube. Top each *parfait* with a rosette of cream and a whole pecan. Leave the *parfaits* in the refrigerator to soften for 15 minutes before serving.

Cook's Comment. Strictly speaking not an ice-cream at all, a *parfait* mixture is so rich that it freezes to a smooth texture without churning. This recipe uses Italian meringue which, as it is made with hot sugar syrup to cook the egg whites, holds up for several days in the refrigerator, in contrast to Swiss meringue which deflates within an hour or two. *Pâtissiers* often keep a supply of Italian meringue on hand to ice cakes or to sweeten and lighten pastry cream and Chantilly cream.

Glace aux Pruneaux

PRUNE OR PLUM ICE-CREAM WITH BRANDY

MAKES 2 PINTS (1.25 LITRES) ICE-CREAM TO SERVE 6

6oz (*175g*) prunes or plums in
  brandy (see Cook's Comment
  below)
For the vanilla custard sauce
vanilla pod or a few drops
  vanilla essence

16fl. oz (*500ml*) milk
8fl. oz (*250ml*) double cream
7 egg yolks
5oz (*150g*) sugar

ice-cream maker

1 Make the vanilla custard sauce,* adding the cream with the milk. Strain it and chill.

2 Drain and stone the prunes or plums. (Reserve the brandy to drink after dinner.) Purée the fruit in a food processor or blender, or work it through a sieve. There should be 8fl. oz (*250ml*) of purée.

3 Stir the purée into the cold custard and chill until very cold. Freeze the mixture in an ice-cream maker. The ice-cream can be stored for up to a month in the freezer. Let it soften in the refrigerator for 30 minutes before serving.

Cook's Comment. Eye-catching jars of prunes or plums in cognac or armagnac are not hard to find, but it is also easy to make your own. Pack 6oz (*175g*) prunes or ¾lb (*375g*) plums with stones in a jar and pour over brandy to cover (about 16fl. oz (*500ml*)). Cover tightly and leave to macerate for at least a week at room temperature.

Melon Sorbet

Universities collect personalities, and my tutor at Cambridge, Marjorie Holland, was certainly one of them. Her development seemed to have been arrested in the late 1920s, whence dated her Rolls-Royce and also, it appeared, her tweeds. Her economics (the subject I was studying) was equally antediluvian, stopping with the Victorians. Even Maynard Keynes was beyond her time-frame, which made passing exams a little difficult. Mrs Holland was married to a desiccated professor of history at Trinity College, whom she saw rarely. 'Dear, dear,' she remarked, putting down the phone in the middle of one tutorial, 'Professor Holland has had 'flu for the last three days!' One event for which they did combine was in entertaining their students once a year in the Professor's magnificent set of rooms overlooking the Wren Library in Trinity College. Trinity was as famous for its kitchen as for its architecture, and the food was equally monumental. One memorable year the melon sorbet was frozen in a mould as big as a rugby ball.

MAKES 3¼ PINTS (2 LITRES) SORBET TO SERVE 8

2oz (*60g*) sugar	juice of 2 lemons
2fl. oz (*60ml*) water	2 egg whites, beaten to mix
1 large or 2 medium melons, weighing about 5lb (*2.3kg*)	*ice-cream maker*

1 In a small saucepan, combine the sugar and water and heat until the sugar dissolves. Boil the syrup for 1 minute and let it cool. Cut a thin slice from one end of each melon so that it sits upright. Scoop out the pulp and discard the seeds. Purée the pulp in a blender or food processor, or work it through a sieve. Freeze the melon shells.

2 In a bowl, combine the melon purée with the lemon juice and add sugar syrup to taste. (*Note*: If the melon is sweet, very little syrup will be needed.) Chill the mixture until very cold.

3 Freeze the mixture in an ice-cream maker until slushy. Add the egg whites and continue churning until firm. Pack the sorbet into one shell of each melon, mounding it well, and top with the lid. Wrap the melon and freeze it.

4 Sorbet can be frozen for up to 2 weeks. Let it stand in the refrigerator for 30 minutes to soften before serving.

Cook's Comment. As in all fruit sorbets, the flavour will depend on the ripeness of the fruit. All sorts of tests for choosing a melon have been suggested, but I look for one which smells right – it is as simple as that. Melon-shaped moulds can be found in specialist shops, but it is easier, and just as impressive, to use the melon shells for presentation.

BREADS AND CAKES

More than any other foods, good breads and cakes begin at home. For one thing, they are best baked fresh, in quantities that are too small for even an artisan bakery. Have you ever tasted really good pound cake from a shop? More importantly, bread, and to some extent cakes, depend for individuality on flour, which varies from country to country, or for that matter from mill to mill. Wholewheat Walnut Bread, for instance, tastes quite different when made with high-gluten flour and the rich, oily walnuts of the USA than with the lighter flour and piquant home-grown walnuts we have in Burgundy.

The contrast can be even greater with breads and cakes which use baking powder – look how much a British scone differs from an American baking-powder biscuit, though both contain essentially the same ingredients and are made by the same method. One of the great American treats is a fresh muffin or one of the crumbly New England fruit loaves, and I have yet to find anything comparable in Europe. Equally, English breads like griddle cake do not taste right in the USA.

There is also, of course, the subtle psychological barrier to transposing breads and cakes – those symbols of the hearth – to another background. The delicate French *génoise* seems unimpressive when viewed from Manhattan, while the classic tall American layer cake with its froth of frosting is faintly laughable in France. To a Frenchman my favourite fruit-laden Christmas cake seems leaden and indigestible. So much is in the mind, and personally I enjoy the following cakes and breads almost anywhere.

Irish Soda Bread

Timeless though it may seem, soda bread dates only from the 1850s, when reliable chemical raising agents began to be produced commercially. Soda breads became popular in Ireland because they are particularly suited to Irish wholewheat flour, which is low in gluten, and because they are good baked on a griddle over an open peat fire. As Elizabeth David points out in *English Bread and Yeast Cookery*, the speed and light hand called for in making soda breads are the antithesis of the thorough kneading given to a yeast dough, and the resulting bread is quite different: 'If after all possible care has been taken, your soda bread still seems rather more like cake than bread in texture and in the way it cuts, that is what soda bread is called in most parts of Ireland – cake or "a cake of bread" whereas a loaf of bread is one bought from the bakery.'

MAKES ONE 8in (20cm) ROUND LOAF TO SERVE 6–8

1lb (*500g*) wholewheat flour
1½ teaspoons salt
1½ teaspoons baking soda

16fl. oz (*500ml*) buttermilk, or
more if needed

1 Heat the oven to Gas 6/200°C/400°F and grease a baking sheet.

2 Sift the flour, salt and baking soda into a bowl and make a well in the centre. Add the buttermilk and stir, gradually drawing in the flour to make a smooth dough. While mixing, add more buttermilk, if necessary, so that the dough is soft and slightly sticky. (*Note*: Do not overwork the dough or the bread will be tough.)

3 Working on a heavily floured work surface, shape the dough quickly into a round loaf. Set it on the baking sheet and flatten it to a 2in (*5cm*) thick round. Deeply score it into quarters with a knife and brush off any excess flour.

4 Bake the bread until the loaf sounds hollow when tapped: 30–35 minutes. Eat it while still warm.

Cook's Comment. Don't be tempted to make soda bread ahead; it takes only a few minutes to mix, and it gets very heavy when it stands.

Wholewheat Walnut Bread

'Pain Poilâne . . . need one say more?' exclaims Patricia Wells in her indispensable book, *The Food Lover's Guide to Paris*. 'There is no question that Lionel Poilâne makes the most famous bread in France, perhaps the world. Thousands of Parisians buy his moist sourdough loaf each day.' Scarcely less famous is his walnut bread, served in smart restaurants with the cheese course. This version of mine never tastes quite like the Poilâne original, nor would I expect it to do so. Bread is like vintage wine, endowed with intrinsic characteristics by the flour, the oven, and the person who bakes it.

MAKES 1 LARGE LOAF TO SERVE 6–8

¾lb (*375g*) wholewheat flour,
   or more if needed
4oz (*125g*) plain flour
14fl. oz (*450ml*) lukewarm water
1 tablespoon honey
½oz (*15g*) fresh yeast or
   ¼oz (*7g*) dried yeast

1½ teaspoons salt
5oz (*150g*) walnut pieces
1 egg, beaten to mix with
   ½ teaspoon salt (for glaze)

1 Combine both types of flour in a bowl, make a well in the centre and pour in about a quarter of the water. Add the honey and crumble or sprinkle the yeast on top. Leave for 5 minutes or until dissolved, then stir in the remaining water and salt. Stir with your fingers, gradually drawing in the flour to make a smooth dough. It should be slightly sticky; work in more flour if necessary.

2 Turn the dough on to a floured work surface and knead it until elastic: 8–10 minutes. Add more flour if the dough sticks. Alternatively, knead with the dough hook of an electric mixer. Put the dough in a lightly oiled bowl and turn it over so that the top is oiled. Cover with a damp cloth and leave in a warm place until the dough is doubled in bulk: 1–1½ hours. Lightly grease a baking sheet.

3 Knead the dough lightly, work in the walnut pieces and shape it into a round loaf. Set it on the baking sheet and cover with a damp cloth. Leave again to rise until the dough has doubled in bulk: 30–40 minutes. Heat the oven to Gas 7/220°C/425°F.

4 Brush the loaf with the egg glaze and slash the top in a lattice pattern. Bake the loaf for 15 minutes. Reduce the heat to Gas 5/190°C/375°F and continue baking until the loaf sounds hollow when tapped on the bottom: 30–40 minutes. Transfer from the baking sheet to a rack to cool. Walnut bread is best eaten the day it is baked, or it can be frozen.

Cook's Comment. A round loaf somehow conveys a country air, but it is not very convenient for slicing, so you may prefer to bake the dough in the usual brick shape.

Cheese Brioche

One charm of food people is that they always have something to eat. Take Samuel Chamberlain, author and illustrator of many books on France, including *Clementine in the Kitchen*, which, forty-five years after its first publication, is still one of the most evocative guides to the country cooking of France. Sam would welcome us in mid-afternoon with a bottle of good wine and a bite of cheese before whisking us down to his art studio in Marblehead, an attractive seaside town in Massachusetts. The late Jim Beard could always be relied upon for a substantial snack at any hour, declaring with a belly laugh that his own generous bulk must be properly maintained. I well remember this cheese brioche, which he was testing for *Beard on Bread*. We demolished practically the whole loaf as Jim recounted scurrilous stories about New York foodies, then fixed me with his beady gaze awaiting my contribution.

MAKES 2 MEDIUM LOAVES TO SERVE 6–8

4fl. oz (*125ml*) milk
2oz (*60g*) unsalted butter
1 teaspoon sugar
10oz (*300g*) flour, or more if needed
1 teaspoon salt
1 teaspoon Tabasco
½oz (*15g*) fresh yeast or
  ¼oz (*7g*) dried yeast

2 eggs
2½oz (*75g*) grated Gruyère cheese
1oz (*30g*) grated Parmesan cheese
1 egg, beaten to mix with
  ½ teaspoon salt (for glaze)

two 8 × 4 × 3in (20 × 10 × 7.5cm) loaf tins

1 Heat the milk with the butter and sugar until the butter melts; leave to cool to lukewarm. Sift the flour into a bowl with the salt and make a well in the centre. Add the warm milk and Tabasco to the well and crumble or sprinkle the yeast on top. Leave for 5 minutes or until the yeast is dissolved. Add the eggs and mix the ingredients in the well with your fingers, gradually drawing in the flour to make a smooth dough. It should be soft and slightly sticky; if necessary, work in a little more flour.

2 Turn the dough on to a floured work surface and knead until it is smooth and elastic: 5–7 minutes. Add more flour if it sticks. Alternatively, knead the dough in an electric mixer with a dough hook. Put the dough in an oiled bowl, turning it over so that all the sides are oiled, and cover the bowl with a damp cloth. Leave the dough in a warm place to rise until doubled in bulk: 45–60 minutes.

3 Butter the loaf tins. Knead the dough lightly and work in the grated Gruyère and Parmesan cheeses. Divide the dough in half, shape it into two loaves and set them in the tins. Brush with the egg glaze, cover the loaves with a damp cloth and leave again to rise in a warm place until the dough reaches the top of the tins: 45–60 minutes. Heat the oven to Gas 6/200°C/400°F.

4 Brush the loaves again with the glaze and slash the tops or snip a 'hedgehog' design with scissors. Bake in the oven until brown and the bread sounds hollow when tapped on the bottom: 25–30 minutes. Unmould the loaves and transfer to a rack to cool. Cheese bread is best eaten the day it is baked, or it can be frozen.

Cook's Comment. An excellent bread for toasting.

Focaccia

SAVOURY ITALIAN FLAT BREAD

Some of my favourite food is in Chicago. Among countless ethnic offerings, I've tracked down an authentic French bistro (Les Nomades) and a family-run Italian restaurant, Sogni Dorati, where outstanding food is served amid fake Grecian pillars and tinkling tunes from the pianola. Young Silvio, who does the cooking at Sogni Dorati, has an unerring instinct for updating traditional recipes. With Latin generosity, dish after dish arrives at the table 'just to try'. Mama, upholstered in flowing satin, roams the dining room and often plops down at the table to rest her feet. She works around the clock, and each morning she rises at four to start the dough for the seasoned *focaccia* breads which are just as much a speciality as her son's antipasti.

MAKES TWO 12in (30cm) FOCACCIA TO SERVE 8–10

2lb (*1kg*) flour, or more if needed
2 teaspoons pepper
1¼ pints (*750ml*) lukewarm water

3 tablespoons olive oil
1½oz (*45g*) fresh yeast or ¾oz (*22g*) dried yeast
two flavourings (see opposite)

1 Sift the flour with the pepper on to a work surface and make a well in the centre. Add the water and oil to the well, crumble or sprinkle over the yeast and leave for 5 minutes or until dissolved. With the fingers of one hand, gradually mix the flour into the yeast mixture to make a paste. With a pastry scraper or metal spatula, work in the remaining flour and gather the dough into a ball. It should be soft but not sticky; if necessary, work in more flour.

2 Flour the work surface and knead the dough until smooth and elastic: 5–7 minutes; alternatively, knead it in an electric mixer with a dough hook. Transfer the dough to an oiled bowl and turn it over so that all the sides are oiled. Cover with a damp cloth and leave in a warm place until doubled in bulk: 1–1½ hours. Brush two baking sheets with olive oil.

3 Knead the dough lightly to knock out the air and divide it in half. Flavour and roll each portion of dough as described for each filling below. Cover the dough with a damp cloth and leave to rise in a warm place until almost doubled in bulk: ¾–1 hour. (*Note*: The dough will spread somewhat on the baking sheet.) The bread can be refrigerated for up to 6 hours before baking.

4 Heat the oven to Gas 6/200°C/400°F. Bake the breads one at a time until brown: 20–25 minutes. Serve them warm, as soon as possible after baking.

Cook's Comment. The extra dose of yeast in *focaccia* gives the bread a particularly zesty lightness.

Focaccia alla Salvia

SAGE BREAD

Into one portion of dough knead 2oz (*60g*) coarsely chopped fresh sage. Roll the dough to a 10in (*25cm*) round and brush with olive oil. Sprinkle with 1 tablespoon of coarse salt just before baking.

Focaccia alla Salsiccia

SAUSAGE BREAD

Into one portion of dough knead 5oz (*150g*) coarsely chopped pepperoni sausage and 1 teaspoon salt. Roll to a 10in (*25cm*) round, brush with olive oil, and, if you like, sprinkle with 2 teaspoons Italian dried red pepper flakes.

Focaccia al Scarole

ESCAROLE BREAD WITH GARLIC

Divide 1 small head of escarole into leaves. Blanch the leaves in boiling salted water for 2 minutes; drain, rinse with cold water and drain again thoroughly. Heat 2 tablespoons of olive oil in a pan, add the escarole with 2 crushed garlic cloves, salt and pepper and cook, stirring, until the escarole is thoroughly wilted and all moisture has evaporated. Allow to cool, finely chop and taste – it should be quite peppery.

Knead 1 teaspoon of salt into the dough and divide it in half. Roll one half to a 10in (*25cm*) round and set it on a baking sheet. Spread the escarole mixture almost to the edge of the dough and sprinkle with 1oz (*30g*) grated Parmesan cheese. Roll the remaining dough to a round of equal size, set it on top of the escarole and press the edges together to seal. Brush the top with olive oil.

Focaccia al Noci

WALNUT BREAD

Divide the dough in half and roll to a 10in (*25cm*) round. Transfer to a baking sheet, brush with walnut or olive oil and sprinkle with 3oz (*90g*) walnut pieces and 1 teaspoon coarse salt. Roll out the remaining dough to a round of equal size, set it on top of the walnuts and press the edges together to seal. Brush the top with walnut or olive oil.

[229]

Babas au Rhum

RUM BABAS

I would like to claim that my first trip to France at the age of thirteen was a gastronomic revelation, but this was not the case. The blandishments of freshly gathered mussels and oysters, of turbot and *langouste* (we were staying on the coast near Biarritz) were too much for a sheltered thirteen-year-old. I didn't care for the salads which constituted lunch and found coffee and croissants an inadequate substitute for breakfast bacon and egg. At the end of two weeks, I could not wait to go home. The one bright spot of the stay was a daily visit to the *pâtisserie* after a swimming lesson, where I made a beeline for a large rum baba dripping with syrup.

MAKES 12 MEDIUM BABAS

3oz (*90g*) currants
2 tablespoons rum
7¼oz (*225g*) flour
1 teaspoon salt
1 tablespoon sugar
3 tablespoons lukewarm water
½oz (*15g*) fresh yeast or
  ¼oz (*7g*) dried yeast
4 eggs
4oz (*125g*) unsalted butter,
  creamed

6fl. oz (*175ml*) apricot glaze*
For the sugar syrup
1lb (*500g*) sugar
1⅔ pints (*1 litre*) water
4fl. oz (*125ml*) rum

12 baba, dariole or small brioche
  moulds (6fl. oz (175ml) capacity
  each)

1 Soak the currants in the rum. Sift the flour with the salt into a bowl and stir in the sugar. Make a well in the centre and add the water. Crumble or sprinkle the yeast on top and leave for 5 minutes or until dissolved. Add the eggs and mix with your fingers, gradually drawing in the flour to form a soft dough.

2 Cup your hand and beat the dough vigorously, raising it and letting it fall back into the bowl with a slap. Continue beating until the dough is elastic and looks like chamois leather: 5 minutes. Alternatively, the dough can be kneaded in an electric mixer using the dough hook. Cover the bowl with a damp cloth and leave the dough to rise in a warm place until doubled in bulk: ¾–1 hour. Meanwhile, butter the baba moulds, chill them in the freezer, then butter them again.

3 Beat the dough lightly to knock out the air and then beat in the creamed butter. Mix the currants and any soaking liquid into the dough. Spoon the dough into the moulds, filling them one-third full. Set the moulds on a baking sheet, cover them with a damp cloth and leave to rise in a warm place until the moulds are almost full. Heat the oven to Gas 6/200°C/400°F.

4 Bake the babas until they are browned and begin to shrink from the sides of the mould: 20–25 minutes. Run a knife around the edge and turn the babas out on to a rack to cool. They can be kept for up to 3 weeks in an air-tight container, or frozen. (*Note*: The drier they are when the syrup is added, the lighter they will be.)

5 Not more than 4 hours before serving, make the syrup. Heat the sugar with the water until it dissolves, then simmer for 2–3 minutes. Remove from the heat and add the rum. Soak the babas in the hot syrup, a few at a time, basting them so that they are thoroughly soaked. They will swell and look shiny. Lift them out with a draining spoon, and set them on a serving dish or individual plates. Spoon any remaining syrup over the babas. Melt the apricot glaze and brush it on the babas. Keep them covered at room temperature.

Cook's Comment. Of all the bread and cake doughs, baba dough seems to stick the worst during baking, ruining the chestnut brown surface which is half the cake's appeal. It helps to butter the moulds twice, freezing them between each coating. Like all bread and cake moulds, baba moulds should never be washed. Wipe them out after use while still warm and, if the batter has stuck, rub the mould clean with a damp cloth and salt.

Aunt Louie's Yule Bread

My aunt was a great traditionalist. For supper on Christmas Eve, she cooked frumenty, a medieval porridge made with whole barley spiced with cassia, a strong-flavoured type of cinnamon. With it was served Stilton cheese and Christmas cake, which had been baked months before and left to mellow in muslin soaked in port wine. As the oldest and youngest, she and I would link hands to cut the cake, then light a candle and set it in the hearth, leaving it to burn itself out overnight. If by any chance it blew out, the family's luck was lost for the year.

In early December my aunt baked Yule Bread, a spiced fruit bread raised with yeast. After a week or two in a tin box to moisten and mature, the breads would be distributed to neighbours as part of a pre-Christmas ceremonial round and exchange of presents.

MAKES 1 LARGE LOAF TO SERVE 10

12 fl. oz (*375ml*) water
3¼oz (*100g*) raisins
1¼oz (*100g*) dried currants
1lb (*500g*) flour, or more if
   needed
1 teaspoon salt
½ teaspoon ground cinnamon
½ teaspoon ground cloves
4½oz (*135g*) sugar
½oz (*15g*) fresh yeast or
   ¼oz (*7g*) dried yeast

2 eggs
4oz (*125g*) unsalted butter,
   creamed
1½oz (*45g*) chopped, candied
   orange peel
1 tablespoon sugar dissolved in
   2 tablespoons warm milk (for
   glaze)

9 × 5 × 4in (*22 × 12 × 10cm*)
   loaf tin

1 Bring the water to a boil, pour half over the raisins and currants and leave them to soak. Let the remaining water cool to tepid. Sift the flour into a bowl with the salt, cinnamon and cloves and stir in the sugar. Make a well in the centre and add the tepid water along with the water drained from the dried fruits. Crumble or sprinkle the yeast over the water and leave for 5 minutes or until dissolved. Add the eggs and, with your hand, gradually mix in the flour to form a smooth dough that is soft but not sticky, adding more flour if necessary.

2 Turn the dough on to a floured work surface and knead until it is elastic: 5–7 minutes. Alternatively, knead the dough in an electric mixer with the dough hook. Put the dough in an oiled bowl and turn it over so that all the sides are oiled. Cover the bowl with a damp cloth and leave it in a warm place until doubled in bulk: 2–3 hours. Butter the loaf tin.

3 Work the dough lightly to knock out air and beat in the creamed butter, followed by the dried fruits and candied peel. Shape the dough into a loaf and put it in the prepared tin. Cover with a damp cloth and leave to rise until the tin is full: 1–1½ hours. Heat the oven to Gas 6/200°C/400°F.

4 Brush the loaf with the glaze and bake for 20 minutes. Brush the loaf again with the glaze. Lower the oven to Gas 4/175°C/350°F and continue baking until the loaf sounds hollow when tapped on the bottom: 20–30 minutes. Unmould the loaf and transfer to a rack to cool. The bread can be stored in an air-tight container for up to 1 month, and the flavour improves on standing. It can also be frozen.

Cook's Comment. I like Yule Bread best for breakfast, toasted or plain and spread with butter, though in its native Yorkshire it is served for afternoon tea.

Pain d'Epices

HONEY SPICE BREAD

When I first began my career in cooking, one of my great advantages was a university education. Few food writers were trained in cooking and even fewer professional cooks could write a recipe, let alone a book. Pushed to the limit, Paul Bocuse bought the rights to a defunct work published a generation earlier and repackaged it under his own name as *La Cuisine du Marché*.

Now the scene has changed. More and more food journalists have worked in a professional kitchen (high time!) and I can think of many university graduates who surprised their professors by going into cooking. For example, Jeremiah Tower, alumnus of King's College, Cambridge, is now chef-owner of one of America's most famous restaurants, *Stars* in San Francisco. At La Varenne, many of our best students have moved on to combine cooking with writing. I was particularly fortunate to have an excellent team in place to help write *French Regional Cooking*, a book which called for two years of research and recipe experiment.

The Pain d'Epices recipe was particularly troublesome, necessitating more than a dozen tries. We researched old recipes, but none of them seemed to taste as good as the pastry-shop version, beloved of every French schoolchild. We finally printed an 'authentic' recipe made with rye flour and raised with yeast – an obstinately solid combination. I've never been happy with it and now, ten years later, have settled for the following moist, honey-laden version raised with baking powder. It just shows, no recipe is ever final – it can always be improved!

MAKES 2 LOAVES TO SERVE 10–12

½ pint (*300ml*) water
6½oz (*200g*) sugar
13oz (*400g*) honey
12oz (*375g*) rye flour
6½oz (*200g*) plain flour
2 egg yolks
1oz (*30g*) chopped, candied
   orange peel
2 teaspoons baking soda

½ teaspoon ground anise
½ teaspoon ground cinnamon
½ teaspoon ground cloves
For the icing
2 egg whites
6oz (*375g*) icing sugar

*two 8 × 4 × 3in (20 × 10 × 7.5cm)
loaf tins*

1 Heat the oven to Gas 4/175°C/350°F. Butter the loaf tins, line them with greaseproof paper and butter the paper. Heat the water, sugar and honey in a saucepan, stirring until the sugar dissolves. Bring just to a boil, then remove from the heat and cool to tepid.

2 Stir the two flours together in a bowl, make a well in the centre and add three-quarters of the cooled honey mixture and the egg yolks. Stir with a wooden spoon, gradually drawing in the flour to make a smooth batter. In a small bowl, mix the candied peel, baking soda and spices. Stir in the remaining honey mixture and stir this mixture into the flour batter.

3 Spoon the batter into the tins and bake in the oven until the breads test done:* ¾–1 hour. If the bread browns too quickly during cooking, cover the top loosely with foil. Run a knife around the edges and turn the breads out on to a rack. Remove the paper.

4 While the loaves are still warm, make the icing. Whisk the egg whites until frothy. Gradually whisk in the icing sugar to make an icing which pours easily. Pour it over the warm breads so that it thinly coats the top and drips down the sides.

5 Spice bread can be stored for up to 2 weeks in an air-tight container, and the flavour will mellow. It can also be frozen.

Cook's Comment. Fantasy moulds are *de rigueur* for spice bread. In Burgundy, where it is a great speciality, I've seen beehives, rabbits, and even a spice-bread snail.

Yorkshire Gingerbread

English gingerbread and French spice bread are basically the same thing – a spiced cake raised with baking powder or soda. But how different they turn out in practice! With my Yorkshire prejudices, I have always felt that good gingerbread should be dark and crumbly, flavoured with black treacle, baked in a shallow pan and cut into squares. Just as delectable, French *pain d'épices* (see page 234) is more like a bread, baked in a loaf shape and firm enough to be sliced and buttered. The bread is golden and perfumed with anise and candied orange peel. Note also the contrast in mixing methods for the two recipes.

MAKES ONE 8in (20cm) SQUARE GINGERBREAD TO SERVE 8

½lb (250g) flour
2 tablespoons ground ginger
1 tablespoon ground allspice
½ teaspoon salt
1 teaspoon baking soda
4oz (125g) unsalted butter, softened

4½oz (135g) dark brown sugar
3 eggs, beaten to mix
½lb (250g) black treacle

8in (20cm) square cake tin

1 Heat the oven to Gas 3/160°C/325°F. Butter the cake tin, line it with greaseproof paper and butter the paper. Sift the flour with the ginger, allspice, salt and baking soda.

2 Cream the butter, beat in the brown sugar and continue beating until very soft. Beat in the eggs, one by one, followed by the treacle. Gently stir in the flour in two or three batches.

3 Spoon the batter into the cake tin and bake in the oven until the cake tests done:* 50–60 minutes. Run a knife around the edge and turn the gingerbread on to a rack to cool, then remove the paper. It can be kept for up to 2 weeks in an air-tight container, or frozen.

Cook's Comment. For a good upside-down cake, pour the gingerbread batter over halved poached pears, set cut side down in the tin.

Apple Dapple Coffee Cake

Madeira cakes, ratafia biscuits and coffee cakes are all designed to be served with the drinks for which they are named. I think of this recipe as the archetypal coffee cake in the Central European tradition – impressively large and crusty and so lusciously sticky that a fork is needed to eat it. The name comes from the dappled effect given by sliced apples.

SERVES 8–10

¾lb (375g) flour
1 teaspoon baking soda
1 teaspoon salt
½ pint (300ml) vegetable oil
13oz (400g) sugar
3 eggs
3 medium, tart apples, peeled, cored and thinly sliced

a few drops vanilla essence
For the topping
6½oz (200g) dark brown sugar
2fl. oz (60ml) milk
4oz (125g) unsalted butter
a few drops vanilla essence

10in (25cm) bundt tin or 6½-pint (4-litre) ring mould

1 Heat the oven to Gas 4/175°C/350°F and butter the tin. Sift the flour with the baking soda and salt.

2 Cream the oil with the sugar until light and smooth. Beat in the eggs one by one, beating well after each addition. Fold in the flour mixture in three batches. As lightly as possible, stir in the apples and vanilla.

3 Spoon the batter into the tin and bake until the cake tests done:* 1¼–1½ hours. Turn the cake out on to a rack to cool.

4 *Prepare the topping.* Combine the brown sugar, milk, butter and vanilla in a pan and melt over a low heat, stirring constantly until smooth. Boil for 2 minutes, then allow to cool, stirring occasionally. Stir the topping over ice until it starts to stiffen, then pour it over the cake, allowing it to drip down the sides.

Cook's Comment. Like all cakes containing fresh fruit, the longer Apple Dapple Coffee Cake is kept, the moister it becomes.

Christmas Cake

One treat we had throughout the Second World War was Christmas Cake. Prunes and dates had to be substituted for currants and raisins, walnuts took the place of almonds and we had to forget about candied peel. However, my mother kept a hoard of tinned butter and the cake she made was astonishingly good. The baking was quite a ritual, always at the tail end of the day so that the temperature of the coal-fired oven had abated to the steady warmth needed for a rich fruit cake. The battered old tins were thickly lined with newspaper to diffuse the heat. The fruits were picked over and washed – quite a job in those days – and carefully rubbed with flour so that they clung to the dough. Finally Emily, the cook, sat down with the big brown bowl in her lap and began beating with her hand, for the warmth made creaming easier and helped prevent the eggs from curdling.

The batter completed, the kitchen went under siege. All doors and windows were shut lest a draught cause a surge of heat in the oven. Even I, normally a privileged spectator, was sent upstairs. After a couple of hours or more, the results would be announced. Had the cake cracked, betraying dryness and too high a heat? Had it risen unevenly, or was it charred on top? Worst of all, had it sunk in the middle, leaving the fruit at the bottom of the cake and a layer of white batter on top? A divided cake was more than a culinary disaster; it meant a death in the family during the coming year. To this day I swear the cake divided in 1943, the year my great-grandmother, born in 1846, died.

MAKES ONE 10in (25cm) CAKE TO SERVE 12–16

¾lb (*375g*) flour
1lb (*500g*) raisins
1lb (*500g*) dried currants
4oz (*125g*) chopped, candied
    orange peel
4oz (*125g*) chopped, candied
    citrus peel
½ teaspoon salt
½ teaspoon grated nutmeg
½ teaspoon ground allspice

¾lb (*375g*) unsalted butter,
    softened
¾lb (*375g*) sugar
6 eggs, at room temperature
4oz (*125g*) slivered almonds
3 tablespoons brandy
6–8 tablespoons sweet sherry or
    Madeira (for basting)

10in (25cm) springform tin

1 Heat the oven to Gas 2/150°C/300°F and set the shelf low. Butter the tin, line the base and sides with a double layer of greaseproof paper and butter the paper. Mix a few teaspoons of flour with the raisins, currants and candied peel and mix until the fruit is well coated. Sift the remaining flour with the salt, nutmeg and allspice.

2 Cream the butter, beat in the sugar and continue beating until soft and light: 5 minutes. Add the eggs one by one, beating thoroughly after each addition. Stir in the flour in two or three batches, then stir in the dried fruit and almonds. Finally, stir in the brandy.

3 Spoon the batter into the prepared tin and smooth the top, leaving the centre slightly hollow. Bake in the oven until the cake tests done:* 1¾–2¼ hours. If it browns too much during cooking, cover the top loosely with foil.

4 Leave the cake to cool in the tin, then unmould it and peel off the paper. Baste the top with 2–3 tablespoons of sherry, wrap it in muslin or cheesecloth soaked in sherry and store in an air-tight container for at least one month, and up to a year or more if you wish.

Cook's Comment. Christmas cake has followed us around the world. I like to make it at least a year ahead, basting it every month or two with whatever liqueurs, sweet wine or brandy we happen to have on hand. Often we don't even eat it at Christmas, for Christmas Cake has become traditional to sustain us when we move house, an activity that seems to be biennial.

Simnel Cake

The forerunner of Mother's Day, English Mothering Sunday fell much earlier in the year, towards the end of Lent. Mothering Sunday was the day that children went home to visit mother, though some say mother was originally the church rather than the family. With them they took gifts such as fig pie (an acquired taste, given all the seeds in dried figs) or Simnel Cake, a rich fruit cake with a layer of marzipan. (The name comes from the Latin *simila*, meaning fine flour.) Today Simnel Cake is served at Easter and is often topped with marzipan eggs.

MAKES ONE 10in (25cm) CAKE TO SERVE 12–16

Christmas Cake batter (see
  page 238)
8 tablespoons apricot glaze,*
  melted
1 egg, beaten to mix with
  ½ teaspoon salt (for glaze)
For the marzipan
½lb (*250g*) icing sugar
13oz (*400g*) caster sugar

1lb (*500g*) ground almonds
1 egg
2 egg yolks
juice of 1 lemon
3 tablespoons orange-flower
  water or orange juice
a few drops vanilla essence

10in (25cm) springform tin

1 *To make the marzipan.* Sift the icing sugar into a bowl, stir in the caster sugar and the ground almonds and make a well in the centre. Beat the egg, egg yolks, lemon juice, orange-flower water or orange juice and vanilla essence until mixed. Add to the almond mixture, stir until mixed, then knead to form a paste. It will be dry at first, but continue kneading until the paste is smooth and quite soft.

2 Heat the oven to Gas 2/150°C/300°F. Prepare the Christmas Cake batter. Spread half the batter in the tin. Sprinkle a work surface with sugar and roll one-third of the marzipan to a 9in (*22cm*) round. Set the round on the batter, cover with the remaining batter and bake, following the procedure for Christmas Cake. Keep the remaining marzipan at room temperature, tightly wrapped.

3 When the cake is cool, peel off the paper and brush the top of the cake with melted apricot glaze. Heat the oven to Gas 4/175°C/350°F. Roll out half of the remaining marzipan to a 10in (*25cm*) round and cover the top of the cake, fluting the edges with your fingers. Brush the marzipan with the egg glaze. Roll the remaining marzipan into small ovals, set them around the rim of the cake and brush them with egg glaze. Put the cake back into the cake tin and bake until the marzipan eggs are browned: 25–35 minutes. The cake can be stored for up to 2 months in an air-tight container.

Cook's Comment. Commercial almond paste can be used, provided it has a high proportion of almonds. Decorative eggs and chicks can be added to the top of the cake, but I rather like the simple finish of browned marzipan eggs.

Blueberry Orange Muffins

Recipes on the backs of commercial packets are not always to be despised. On the whole they are simple, clearly described and you can be sure they are reliable, for what company can afford to give misleading instructions for using their product? Here is one American favourite from a bag of flour.

MAKES 12 MEDIUM MUFFINS

10oz (*300g*) fresh or frozen
  blueberries
¾lb (*375g*) wholewheat flour
2 teaspoons baking powder
1 teaspoon baking soda
¾ teaspoon salt
5oz (*150g*) sugar

1 tablespoon wheatgerm
2 eggs
grated rind and juice of 1 large
  orange
1½oz (*45g*) melted butter

12 medium muffin tins

1 Heat the oven to Gas 6/200°C/400°F and butter the muffin tins. Pick over fresh blueberries; do not defrost frozen ones.

2 Sift the flour into a bowl with the baking powder, baking soda and salt. Stir in the sugar and wheatgerm. In a separate bowl, beat the eggs until frothy. Stir in the orange rind and juice and the melted butter. Make a well in the flour, add the orange mixture and blueberries and stir together as lightly as possible. (*Note*: Do not over-mix; leave the batter slightly lumpy.)

3 Spoon the batter into the prepared tins and bake until the muffins test done:* 20–25 minutes. Serve them warm, fresh from the oven. If they must be stored, muffins are best frozen at once rather than kept for even a few hours at room temperature.

Cook's Comment. A home-baked muffin can vie with croissants as the world's best breakfast!

Torta di Nocciole con Cioccolato

CHOCOLATE HAZELNUT TORTE

Behind every good book there lies a skilled editor. I learned this very rapidly when I worked on the American edition of the *Cordon Bleu Cookery Course*, masterminded in London by M.J. Lancaster, whose editorial expertise was as crucial to the success of the series as any cookery skill. Since then, the popularity of the cookery part-work – an encyclopedia of twenty or more volumes produced in sequence as a collection – has made the fortunes of more than one publisher, particularly in Italy. A part-work's great strength is attractive, low-cost colour photography, and many a serial magazine and cookbook you now see on the shelves in English began its life south of the Alps. Just recently I was asked to assess the possibility for translating an entire sixty-two-part Italian pastry series into English. My head spun as I gazed at scores of recipes and pictures of *biscotti*, *gelati* and *torte*. Here is just one of them.

SERVES 8

8oz (*250g*) hazelnuts, toasted*
7oz (*220g*) unsweetened
  chocolate
8oz (*250g*) unsalted butter
6½oz (*200g*) sugar

4 eggs, separated
icing sugar (for sprinkling)
Chantilly cream* or vanilla ice-
  cream (for serving)

8in (20cm) springform tin

1 Butter the tin, line the bottom with greaseproof paper and butter the paper. Heat the oven to Gas 3/150°C/300°F.

2 Grind the hazelnuts with the chocolate in two batches in a food processor, or a little at a time in a blender. Alternatively, grind the nuts and chocolate separately with a rotary cheese-grater, then mix them.

3 Cream the butter, add three-quarters of the sugar, and beat until fluffy and light. Beat in the egg yolks, then stir in the chocolate mixture. Stiffly whip the egg whites, add the reserved sugar and continue whipping for about 30 seconds to make a meringue. Fold the meringue into the hazelnut mixture in three batches.

4 Spoon the batter into the prepared tin and smooth the top. Bake until the *torta* tests done:* 40–50 minutes. Let it cool in the tin, then run a knife around the edge and remove the sides. (*Note*: The *torta* is very delicate and must be handled gently. You may prefer to serve it from the base of the tin.) It can be stored in an air-tight container for up to a week, or frozen.

5 Just before serving, sprinkle the *torta* with icing sugar. Serve the Chantilly cream or ice-cream separately.

Cook's Comment. Nuts are tricky to reduce to a powder, particularly when they have been roasted; their oil is easily extracted, making them heavy and coarse. If using an electric machine, they are best mixed with some other dry ingredient – in this case chocolate. A rotary cheese-grater produces a much finer powder, which will be reflected in the texture of whatever cake or pastry you are making. For this recipe, either method is acceptable.

Gâteau Breton

BRITTANY BUTTER CAKE

Gâteau Breton is quite the best butter cake you have ever tasted, a cross between very rich shortbread and pound cake. For some inexplicable reason it has remained a speciality of Brittany, whereas trickier, more expensive recipes, such as the almond-based *pain de gênes*, are commonplace throughout France. The method of mixing can only be described as the cook's equivalent of mud pies. Even our finicky *pâtissier*, Chef Jorant, plasters himself well above the wrist when he makes it at La Varenne.

MAKES 20 SMALL GÂTEAUX OR 1 LARGE ONE TO SERVE 8

6 egg yolks
7½oz (225g) flour
½lb (250g) unsalted butter, cut
    into pieces

½lb (250g) sugar

one 10in (25cm) cake tin or twenty
3in (7.5cm) tartlet tins

1 Heat the oven to Gas 5/190°C/375°F and butter the tins. Mix a teaspoon of egg yolk with a tablespoon of water for the glaze.

2 Sift the flour on to a work surface and make a large well in the centre. Put the sugar, butter and the remaining egg yolks into the well and work with your fingertips until smooth. Gradually draw in the flour using a pastry scraper or metal spatula, then mix with your fingers and the heel of your hand, working the dough gently until smooth. (*Note*: It will be quite sticky.)

3 Scoop the dough into the tins and smooth the tops, flouring the back of your hand to prevent sticking. Brush the gâteaux with the glaze and mark a lattice design on top with the prongs of a fork.

4 Bake the gâteaux in the oven for 15 minutes. Lower the heat to Gas 4/175°C/350°F and continue baking until the cakes are golden and firm to the touch: 5–10 minutes longer for small gâteaux; 30–35 minutes longer for the large one. Leave to cool in the tins, then unmould carefully. The gâteaux can be stored for up to 2 weeks in an air-tight container, or frozen.

Cook's Comment. Until I lived in France I never realised what the expression 'the best butter' could mean. The finest unsalted butter has a fresh sweetness quite unlike the faintly rancid taste of cheaper varieties containing too much whey. In Gâteau Breton, not even vanilla interferes with the flavour.

Génoise au Citron

LEMON SPONGE CAKE

The sloping sides, thin icing and julienned strips of lemon make Génoise au Citron unmistakably French. In England, the cake would be straight-sided, with a thick white icing and perhaps a filling of lemon curd. American bakers would tend to make the cake taller still, adding multiple layers and a whipped frosting.

MAKES A 9in (22cm) CAKE TO SERVE 6–8

3oz (*90g*) flour
a pinch of salt
1½oz (*45g*) unsalted butter
3 eggs
3oz (*90g*) sugar
grated rind of 1 lemon

For the icing
1 lemon
4oz (*125g*) icing sugar, or more
  if needed
1 egg white, beaten until frothy

9in (22cm) sloping-sided cake tin

1 Butter the cake tin, line the bottom with greaseproof paper and butter the paper. Sprinkle the tin with flour, discarding the excess. Sift the flour with the salt. Warm the butter in a bowl over a pan of hot water until it is soft enough to pour. (*Note*: Do not melt it until it becomes oily.) Heat the oven to Gas 4/175°C/350°F.

2 Put the eggs, sugar and lemon rind in a bowl set over a pan of hot but not boiling water. Beat until the mixture is light and thick enough to leave a ribbon trail for 10 seconds after the whisk is lifted: 5–7 minutes. Remove from the heat and continue beating until cool. If using an electric mixer, no heat is necessary.

3 Sift the flour over the egg mixture in two or three batches and fold together as lightly as possible. When almost mixed, gently fold in the butter. (*Note*: Once the butter is added, the batter loses volume quickly.)

4 Pour the batter into the tin and bake until the cake shrinks slightly and the top springs back when lightly pressed with a fingertip: 25–30 minutes. Run a knife around the sides of the cake and turn it out on to a rack to cool. It can be kept for 2–3 days in an air-tight container, or frozen.

5 Not more than 3 hours before serving, make the icing. Pare the rind from the lemon and cut it into the thinnest possible julienne strips. Blanch the strips by boiling them in water for 2 minutes, then draining. Juice the lemon. Sift the icing sugar into a bowl and stir in the egg white, lemon juice and julienne strips. Set the bowl in a pan of hot water and heat, stirring, until the icing thickens enough to coat the back of the spoon. Pour the icing over the cake, spreading it with a metal spatula so that it drips down the sides.

Cook's Comment. Such a simple little cake, I'm surprised it isn't better known.

[245]

PASTRIES AND BISCUITS

When I was a child, our household followed the traditional pattern of Monday washday and Tuesday ironing day with market day on Wednesday and baking day on Thursday. Packed with action, and plenty to eat at the end of it, Thursday was just about a child's heaven. Already at breakfast the tension was palpable as the coal-fired oven was stoked up. Was the wind in the right quarter for the chimney to draw? All being well, by mid-morning the little pastries which needed a high heat were emerging – Eccles cakes stuffed with currants, buttermilk scones, maids of honour. After lunch came larger cakes like ribbon or cornflour cake, ginger biscuits and Anzac biscuits made with oatmeal. Finally, as the fire died down, the oven produced a batch of custard tarts, or curd tarts if the farm had obliged with some fresh cheese. In principle, Emily, the cook, kept me in a corner away from 'under her feet', but I was allowed to stamp dough rounds, lick bowls and eat up biscuit trimmings (better, it seemed to me, than the finished product). Not everyone was so lucky. Emily made the rest of the household wait until the following day, for freshly baked pastries, she said, were cruel hard on the digestion.

Tarte aux Poires Normande

NORMANDY PEAR TART

When I demonstrate this tart in cooking class, it never fails to draw a gasp of pleasure, even in France where the arrangement of thinly sliced pears in almond cream is familiar in pastry-shop windows. One reason is the technical legerdemain of slicing the pears crosswise so that they can be fanned out with a quick pressure of the fingertip. The other is the transformation of the tart in the oven from a nondescript beige to a brilliantly shining white-and-golden flower.

SERVES 8

3 or 4 ripe pears
sugar (for sprinkling)
6oz (180g) apricot glaze*
For the pâte brisée
6½oz (200g) flour
3¼oz (100g) unsalted butter
1 egg yolk
½ teaspoon salt
3 tablespoons cold water, or
 more if needed

For the almond cream
3oz (90g) unsalted butter,
 softened
3oz (90g) sugar
1 egg, beaten to mix
1 egg yolk
1 tablespoon kirsch (optional)
3oz (90g) ground almonds
2 tablespoons flour

*10in (25cm) tart tin with
 removable base*

1 Make the *pâte brisée** dough and chill for 30 minutes. Butter the tart tin. Roll out the dough, line the tart tin and flute the edges. Chill for 15 minutes or until firm. Heat the oven to Gas 6/200°C/400°F and set a baking sheet in the oven to heat.

2 *For the almond cream.* Cream the butter, gradually beat in the sugar and continue beating until the mixture is light and fluffy. Gradually add the egg and egg yolk, beating well after each addition. Add the kirsch, if using, then stir in the ground almonds and flour. Spread two-thirds of the almond cream in the pastry.

3 Peel the pears, halve them and scoop out the cores and any stem fibres. Keeping the slices of each pear half together, cut the halves crosswise into very thin slices and set them on the almond cream, stem end inwards. Press the slices gently towards the rim of the pie to flatten and fan them so that they resemble the petals of a flower. Spoon the remaining almond cream into the spaces between the pears.

4 Set the tart on the hot baking sheet and bake until the pastry edges start to brown: 10–15 minutes. Lower the heat to Gas 4/175°C/350°F and continue baking until the almond cream is almost set: 5–10 minutes. Sprinkle the tart with sugar and continue baking until the pastry and almond cream are well browned: another 20–25 minutes. Let the tart cool slightly before unmoulding.

5 An hour or two before serving, melt the apricot glaze and brush it over the tart and pastry. Serve the tart at room temperature. Normandy Pear Tart is best eaten the day it is made, but can be kept for a day in an air-tight container.

Cook's Comment. The key to this tart is really thorough baking so that the pastry emerges brown and crisp.

Tarte des Demoiselles Tatin

UPSIDE DOWN CARAMELISED APPLE TART

Tarte Tatin is an offspring of the motor revolution which launched Michelin to such success, selling not just tyres but places at table as well. The *demoiselles* Tatin, the story goes, lived in an obscure railway hotel in the popular wild-game district of the Sologne, near Orléans. Left penniless when their father died, they took to baking his favourite tart and selling it. Apocryphal or not, there is still an Hôtel Tatin at Lamotte-Beuvron which offers a remarkable crusty tart, the apples dark with caramel and just a trifle charred on top. In my version, the apples are cooked with butter and sugar until the juice caramelises deep inside the fruit. Then the pastry is added and the tart is baked in the oven. You'll need a large, deep frying pan, preferably with a non-stick finish, or a cast-iron skillet. The French even make a special tin-lined copper pan just for Tarte Tatin.

SERVES 8–10

6oz (*175g*) unsalted butter
13oz (*400g*) sugar
6lb (*2.8kg*) firm apples, such as
   Golden Delicious
crème fraîche or Chantilly cream*
   (for serving)
For the pâte brisée
6½oz (*200g*) flour

3¼oz (*100g*) unsalted butter
1 egg yolk
2 tablespoons sugar
½ teaspoon salt
3 tablespoons cold water, or
   more if needed

12–14in heavy non-stick frying pan
   or skillet

1 Melt the butter in the pan and sprinkle with the sugar. Peel, halve and core the apples. Arrange the halves, cored side up, in concentric circles on top of the sugar; they should fill the pan completely and be snugly packed. Cook the apples on top of the stove until a deep golden caramel is formed: 15–20 minutes. (*Note*: The apples will make juice, which must evaporate before it will caramelise.)

2 Meanwhile, heat the oven to Gas 7/220°C/425°F. Make the *pâte brisée** dough and chill. When the apples are cooked, let them cool slightly. Roll out the dough to a circle slightly larger than the diameter of the pan. Set the dough on the apples so that they are completely covered, tucking the pastry in at the edges. (*Note*: Work fast so that the dough does not soften from the heat of the apples.) Bake until the pastry is crisp and brown: 20–25 minutes. Let the tart cool in the pan. Tarte Tatin can be prepared up to 8 hours ahead and refrigerated.

3 Not more than half an hour before serving, if necessary, warm the tart on top of the stove. Turn it out on to a tray or large plate. (*Note*: If any juice is left, it may splash.) If any apple sticks to the bottom of the pan, transfer it to the top of the tart with a spatula. Serve the tart warm, with *crème fraîche* or Chantilly cream separately.

Cook's Comment. Tarte Tatin is another of my demonstration regulars, but I wish it were such a sure-fire success as Tarte aux Poires Normande (see page 248). When Tarte Tatin is good it is very, very good, but when the apples fall apart before they caramelise, it is a disaster. Much depends on the type of apple: Golden Delicious is the standard recommendation, but any apple that will hold its shape during the caramelisation will do. To add an acid contrast to the caramel, sprinkle a tablespoon of fresh lemon juice over the apples before you caramelise them.

An International Trio

When first I moved to the USA, one of my first assignments as a freelance caterer was peach pie. Never having met the American version, I baked an English pie with only a top and no bottom crust. My clients were mystified, though not unhappy. An American peach pie, they explained, has two crusts enclosing a filling of sliced peaches flavoured with cinnamon and thickened with cornflour. (I had made what Americans call a deep dish pie, flavoured with honey.) Contrast that with yet a third idea – French open peach tart, filled with poached peaches, decorated with raspberries and glazed with syrup.

This tart made history by being served by La Varenne students to Mrs Reagan during an official visit to Paris. The school was asked to cook and serve a dish or two at a mid-afternoon reception and Mrs Reagan so enjoyed the tart that she asked for another slice. She was about to dig in with a fork, when a secret service man from the poisons division whisked away the plate for testing. We could only suppose that the days of the Borgias were not yet over!

Tarte aux Pêches

FRENCH PEACH TART

SERVES 8

2lb (1kg) ripe peaches
5–6 tablespoons apricot jam
4oz (125g) raspberries (optional)
For poaching the peaches
16fl. oz (500ml) water, or more
   if needed
13oz (400g) sugar
vanilla pod, split
pared rind and juice of 1 lemon

For the walnut pastry
1½oz (45g) walnuts
6oz (175g) flour
3½oz (115g) unsalted butter
1 egg yolk
3¼oz (100g) sugar
½ teaspoon salt
2 tablespoons water, or more if
   needed

*10in (25cm) tart tin with
   removable base*

1 *For the tart shell.* Grind the walnuts with the flour in a food processor or work the mixture, a little at a time, in a blender. Make the walnut pastry dough as for *pâte sucrée** and chill for 30 minutes. Butter the tart tin. Roll out the dough on a floured surface, line the tin and flute the edges. Chill thoroughly, then bake blind,* cooking the shell completely.

2 Meanwhile, poach the peaches. In a deep saucepan, heat the water with the sugar, vanilla pod, lemon juice and rind until the sugar dissolves. Simmer the syrup for 5 minutes. Halve the peaches, discard the stones, and poach them in the syrup until they are tender and transparent: 8–15 minutes, depending on their ripeness. (*Note*: Put the peaches in the syrup cut side up and poach in two batches so that they are completely covered with syrup.) Lift them out with a draining spoon and peel them.

3 *For the glaze*. Boil the poaching liquid until reduced to 5–6 tablespoons. Remove the vanilla pod – it can be used again. Add the apricot jam to the sugar syrup and stir until melted, then work the glaze through a strainer.

4 The poached peaches, glaze, and tart shell can all be prepared 24 hours ahead; keep the peaches in the refrigerator and the pastry shell in an air-tight container.

5 Not more than 2 hours before serving, melt the glaze and brush it over the base of the tart shell. Arrange the peach halves inside, cut side down, and add the raspberries, if using, in the gaps. Brush the fruit and pastry generously with glaze.

Cook's Comment. Peaches poached like this in their skins acquire a maidenly blush on the cheek.

English Peach Pie

SERVES 8

walnut pastry dough (see opposite)
3lb (*1.4kg*) ripe peaches, halved and peeled*
juice of 1 lemon
2–3 tablespoons honey

Chantilly cream* (for serving)
For the topping
1 egg white, whipped until frothy
1 tablespoon sugar

10in (25cm) deep pie dish

1 Make the walnut pastry dough as for French Peach Tart (see opposite) and chill for 30 minutes. Arrange the peeled peach halves in the pie dish, overlapping them and packing them tightly. Sprinkle with the lemon juice and spoon over the honey.

2 Roll out the pastry dough on a floured surface to a 12in (*30cm*) round. Trim the edge with a knife, using a plate or pan lid as a guide. Cut a 1in (*2.5cm*) ring from the edge of the round. If the pie-dish edge has a flat lip, brush it with water and set the pastry ring on top. If the edge is narrow, drape the dough over the edge. Lift the remaining 10in (*25cm*) dough round on to the peaches and flute the edge to seal to the dough underneath. Poke two or three holes in the centre of the pie for steam to escape and chill for 20 minutes or until firm. Heat the oven to Gas 7/220°C/425°F.

3 Brush the pie with the beaten egg white and sprinkle with the sugar. Bake the pie until the dough edges start to brown: 15–20 minutes. Reduce the heat to Gas 4/175°C/350°F and continue baking until the pastry is crisp and the peaches are tender when pierced with a skewer: 20–25 minutes. Peach pie is best eaten the day of baking, though it can be kept for 24 hours in an air-tight container. Serve it warm, with Chantilly cream passed separately.

Cook's Comment. As peaches cook, they produce a good deal of luscious juice which soaks quickly into any pie crust underneath it. In American Peach Pie the juice is thickened so that it penetrates the crust less quickly (see below). The French prefer to cook the crust separately, and in this British version, the pastry is baked on top instead of under the fruit.

American Peach Pie

SERVES 8

1½lb (*750g*) ripe peaches,
   peeled and sliced*
1 tablespoon lemon juice
3¼oz (*100g*) sugar
3 tablespoons cornflour
1 teaspoon ground cinnamon
1 egg, beaten to mix with
   ½ teaspoon salt (for glaze)
vanilla ice-cream (for serving)

For the walnut pastry
2oz (*60g*) walnuts
7oz (*225g*) flour
5oz (*150g*) unsalted butter
1 egg yolk
4½oz (*135g*) sugar
1 teaspoon salt
1 tablespoon water, or more

10in (25cm) pie tin

1 *For the walnut pastry.* Grind the walnuts with the flour in a food processor or work the mixture a little at a time in a blender. Make the walnut pastry dough as for *pâte sucrée** and chill for 30 minutes. Butter the pie tin. Roll out two-thirds of the pastry on a floured work surface. Line the pie tin with the pastry and trim the edges; chill.

2 In a bowl, toss the peaches with the lemon juice. Add the sugar, cornflour and cinnamon, and stir to mix. Spread the peaches in the pie shell.

3 Roll out the remaining pastry and trimmings to a 10in (*25cm*) round. Lift the dough on to the peaches and flute the edges to seal it to the bottom layer of dough. Poke 2–3 steam holes with a knife and chill the pie for at least 30 minutes. It can be refrigerated for up to 8 hours before baking.

4 Heat the oven to Gas 5/190°C/375°F and set the oven shelf down low. Brush the pie with the egg glaze and bake until the pastry is golden brown and starts to shrink: 35–40 minutes. Let the pie cool slightly.

5 Peach pie is best eaten the day it is baked, though it can be kept for a day or two in an air-tight container. Serve it warm or cold with vanilla ice-cream *à la mode*.

Cook's Comment. Follow this same recipe, using stoned cherries, for cherry pie, which achieved notoriety in the late 1960s when the radical black leader Rap Brown declared 'violence is as American as cherry pie.'

Tarte au Citron

LEMON TART

Some recipes, by seemingly happy chance, have just the right combination of ingredients and this is one of them. It was brought to La Varenne by Michel Marolleau, our first chef, who was not just a good cook but also a great one for women. Before a cooking demonstration, Michel could be seen tipping his *toque* to just the right angle in the overhead mirror. Despite his inability to speak English, he had no trouble at all in communicating with the prettier of our female students.

SERVES 8

For the filling
2 eggs
3¼oz (*100g*) sugar
grated rind and juice of
    1½ lemons
1 lemon, cut into 6–8 very thin
    slices, including the peel
3¼oz (*100g*) unsalted butter,
    melted
3¼oz (*100g*) ground almonds
icing sugar (for sprinkling)

For the pâte sucrée
6½oz (*200g*) flour
pinch of salt
3¼oz (*100g*) unsalted butter
3¼oz (*100g*) sugar
4 egg yolks
a few drops vanilla essence
1–2 tablespoons water, if
    needed

*10in (25cm) tart tin with
    removable base*

1 Make the *pâte sucrée** dough and chill for 30 minutes. Butter the tart tin. Roll out the dough, line the tin and bake blind* for 15 minutes.

2 Lower the oven to Gas 3/160°C/325°F and put a baking sheet low down in the oven. Beat the eggs and sugar until light and thick enough to leave a ribbon trail when the whisk is lifted. Stir in the lemon rind and juice, followed by the melted butter and ground almonds. Pour the filling into the tart shell.

3 Set the tart on the baking sheet and bake until the filling is set on top: 10–15 minutes. Arrange the lemon slices on top and continue baking until the filling is golden brown and set: 15–20 minutes. Let the tart cool slightly before unmoulding. (*Note*: The filling will shrink as it cools.) The tart can be kept for 2–3 days in an air-tight container. Sprinkle it with icing sugar just before serving.

Cook's Comment. Choosing lemons is a gamble. I look for smooth skins, no knobs at the end, and a juicy feel when you squash the lemon, but there's really no telling how thick the skin is until you cut it open. One tip I can pass on is to roll the lemon on the table with your palm before cutting it open. The juice will be easier to extract.

Pecan Pie

I first tasted Pecan Pie in Charleston, South Carolina, of all Southern cities the most evocative of pre-Civil War elegance and plantation living. The local cooking is a lavish mix: oyster stew, pork barbecue, fried chicken, peach-fed ham with red-eye gravy (made with black coffee), corn bread and hominy grits, which resemble *polenta*. A bewildering variety of local pies includes persimmon, black bottom (chocolate topped with rum custard), coconut cream pie and the pecan which I instantly adored. Pecan Pie resembles my grandmother's treacle tart, but with adult embellishments. So popular has it become in the family that we tote the pecans to France and serve it for Christmas dinner with *foie gras* and roast goose Yorkshire style.

SERVES 8

For the pie pastry
6oz (*175g*) flour
½ teaspoon salt
3oz (*90g*) lard
2 tablespoons water, or more if
    needed

For the filling
4 eggs
7oz (*225g*) light brown sugar
¼lb (*125g*) black treacle
a few drops vanilla essence
2oz (*60g*) melted butter
8oz (*250g*) pecan halves

10in (25cm) pie tin

1 Make the pie pastry dough as for shortcrust pastry* and chill for 30 minutes. Grease the pie tin, line it with the dough and chill. Heat the oven to Gas 7/220°C/425°F and set a baking sheet on a low shelf to heat.

2 *For the filling.* Whisk together eggs, brown sugar and black treacle until smooth and light: about 5 minutes. Stir in vanilla and melted butter. Sprinkle half the pecans in the pie shell. Pour the filling into the pie shell and arrange the pecan halves in concentric circles on top.

3 Set the pie on the hot baking sheet and bake for 5 minutes. Lower the oven heat to Gas 4/175°C/350°F and continue baking until the pastry is browned and the filling is firm: 40–50 minutes. Pecan Pie is best eaten the day it is made, though it can be stored for 2–3 days in an air-tight container.

Cook's Comment. Corn syrup and pecans make the classic pecan pie, though an interesting European version results if you substitute honey and walnuts. (Pecans resemble a rich walnut, and they are distantly related.)

Sablés Normande

NORMAN BUTTER BISCUITS

I hold an iconoclastic view of Norman cooking, though possibly it can be justified by history and geography. It is not so very different from British. Tempting though the restaurant pickings may seem when you step off the boat in Dieppe or Le Havre, I would argue that Norman cooking consists of few variations and even fewer themes. After living there for five years, we despaired of finding a sauce that was not based on cream, usually with Calvados. Looking at the lush pastures and plump black-and-white cattle, I kept hoping there must be something more to Norman cooking than veal chop with apples and *tripes à la mode de Caen*. In the local markets, the famous Camembert and Pont l'Evêque cheeses were chalky and dry, victims of pasteurisation; all farmhouse produce was shipped directly to Paris. The same could be said of most of the fish, whisked by early-morning train from the coast to Rungis, the wholesale market in Paris. Local cooking seemed limited to noteworthy platters of raw shellfish, king-size scallops baked in butter, mussels served *marinière*, and Dover sole meunière, thinner and thinner each year so that by now they must be almost transparent. Even the Bretons seemed to beat the Normans at making the finest cakes with their butter, though croissants and biscuits like these were another matter.

MAKES 15 LARGE BISCUITS

6½oz (200g) flour
4 egg yolks
½ teaspoon salt
3¼oz (100g) icing sugar
grated rind and juice of 1 lemon

4oz (125g) unsalted butter
1 egg, beaten with ½ teaspoon
  salt (for glaze)

4in (10cm) fluted pastry-cutter

1 Make the dough as for *pâte sucrée*,* adding the grated rind instead of vanilla essence. Chill the dough for 30 minutes. Butter two baking sheets.

2 On a floured work surface, roll out the dough to ¼in (6mm) thickness and stamp out rounds with a pastry-cutter. Transfer them to baking sheets, brush with the egg glaze and mark a triangle on each *sablé* with the tines of a fork. Roll and shape more *sablés* with dough trimmings. Chill the *sablés* for 15 minutes or until firm. Heat the oven to Gas 5/190°C/375°F.

3 Bake the *sablés* until lightly browned: 10–15 minutes. Transfer them to a rack to cool. They can be stored for up to a week in an air-tight container, or frozen.

Cook's Comment. *Sablés* should be baked only until light golden. They burn easily because of the high sugar content and become bitter if overcooked.

Speculaas

FLEMISH SPICED WAFERS

Bruges, the home of lace, is a city after my own heart. Immured in the depths of the countryside, as a child I learned to knit, tat, smock, make gloves and to crochet, quilt, make Limerick lace embroidered on net, to fashion needlepoint lace in Alençon style, and bobbin lace in the style of Brussels. Half a mile from the nearest farm, what else was there to do for someone with a rooted dislike of the outdoors? So when I visited Bruges thirty years later and found lacemakers seated on the bridges over the canals, tossing their bobbins in the sun, I felt a personal welcome. All the more, when I repaired to a café and was served a large brass pot of coffee instead of the standard cup, accompanied by delicious little spiced wafers, known as *speculaas*.

MAKES 40–50 WAFERS

5oz (*150g*) flour	4oz (*125g*) unsalted butter
½ teaspoon ground ginger	3½oz (*110g*) light brown sugar
½ teaspoon ground allspice	½ teaspoon baking powder
pinch of ground cinnamon	¾oz (*22g*) sliced almonds

1 Sift the flour and spices on to a work surface and make a well in the centre. Add the butter, brown sugar and baking powder and work to a paste with your fingertips. Using a pastry scraper or a metal spatula, gradually work in the flour to form large crumbs. If the dough seems dry, add a tablespoon of water; if it is sticky, work in a little more flour.

2 Press the dough into a ball and knead it for 1–2 minutes, pushing it away with the heel of your hand and gathering it up with the scraper until it peels away easily in one piece. Press the dough into a block about 6 × 3 × 1in (*15 × 7.5 × 2.5cm*). Wrap it and chill it until firm enough to slice: about 2 hours.

3 Heat the oven to Gas 6/200°C/400°F and line two baking sheets with foil. With a sharp knife, cut the thinnest possible shaved slices of dough and set them on the foil. Sprinkle each wafer with a few sliced almonds, pressing them down lightly, and bake until golden: 5–7 minutes. Remove them from the foil and transfer them to a rack to cool. (*Note*: If left on the foil, they will stick.) *Speculaas* can be stored for a week or more in an air-tight container, or frozen.

Cook's Comment. These wafers are more closely related to Scandinavian and German biscuits than to anything British or French.

Strawberry Chantilly Swans

We were in Texas and the day was hot. Some four hundred members of the Garden Club of America, an organisation designed for grand people with even grander gardens, were expected for a lunch masterminded by yours truly. This was 1980, Texan oil was liquid gold and the natives were running true to form in an amazing display of *grand luxe*. (I'm sufficiently *nouveau* to rather like it, and the gracious hospitality of the Lone Star State is hard to beat.) Back in the kitchen, a volunteer helper who was almost as rich as the hostess fussed over her buttermilk yeast rolls, which persisted in popping out of their pans in the moist heat. I was presiding over an equally delicate item – choux pastry swans filled with whipped cream, to be served on a collection of Chinese Export plates as rare as they were colourful. Impossible to fit the swans in the refrigerator; too late to wait and fill all four hundred at the last minute. The servers watched in sympathy as one of them, a minister with a Cadillac and matching blazer (both mint green), raised his voice to call upon the Lord. As his invocations eddied around the kitchen, the swans' heads flopped one by one. By the time the guests finally arrived, we were all too high on rhetoric to mind the meal's shortcomings.

SERVES 10–12 SWANS

1 egg, beaten with ½ teaspoon
   salt (for glaze)
about 12 large ripe
   strawberries, hulled
icing sugar (for sprinkling)
Strawberry Sauce (see opposite)
   (for serving)
For the choux pastry
5oz (*150g*) flour
8fl. oz (*250ml*) water

¾ teaspoon salt
3¼oz (*100g*) unsalted butter
4–5 eggs
For the Chantilly cream
½ pint (*300ml*) double cream
1–2 tablespoons icing sugar
a few drops vanilla essence

pastry bags; ¼in (6mm) and ⅜in
   (1cm) plain tubes and medium
   star tube

1 Make the choux pastry* dough. Heat the oven to Gas 6/200°C/400°F and lightly butter two baking sheets. Scoop the choux pastry into a pastry bag fitted with the larger plain tube and pipe out 10–12 ovals 3 ×1½in (7.5 × 4cm) to make the swan bodies. Hold the small plain tube firmly over the larger one and pipe out 12–15 large 'S' shapes on the other baking sheet to form the swan necks. (*Note*: Make extra necks because they tend to break.)

2 Brush the bodies and necks lightly with the egg glaze. Bake the necks until crisp and browned: 12–15 minutes. Remove them and bake the bodies until they are puffed and very crisp: 20–25 minutes. Test by removing one choux puff and letting it cool; if it remains crisp, remove the rest and transfer to a rack to cool. Choux pastry can be stored for 2–3 days in an air-tight container.

3 Not more than 3 hours before serving, cut the strawberries into large pieces. Make the Chantilly cream* and scoop it into a pastry bag fitted with a star tube.

4 Cut the choux pastry bodies in half horizontally; cut the tops in half to form wings. Pipe a little cream into each body, top with strawberry pieces and cover with the remaining cream. Set a swan neck at the front of each body, and set the wings at an angle on the sides. Sprinkle with icing sugar and refrigerate.

5 Just before serving, spoon the Strawberry Sauce on to individual plates or one large serving dish and set the swans 'floating' on top.

Cook's Comment. This is a twentieth-century version of the *pièces montées* which graced every medieval feast.

Strawberry Sauce

A happy end for any squashed berries.

MAKES 16fl. oz (500ml) SAUCE

1lb (*500g*) strawberries, hulled
3–4 tablespoons sugar, or more
 if needed

1 tablespoon kirsch, or juice of
½ lemon

Purée the strawberries in a food processor or blender with the sugar and kirsch or lemon juice. Strain the sauce to remove the seeds and taste, adding more sugar if needed. Chill before serving. The sauce can be refrigerated for up to 3 days, or frozen.

Strawberry Hazelnut Galette

The life of the freelance caterer is never dull. I have a most vivid memory of carrying two of these galettes, strung in packages but still on their baking sheets, at a brisk trot down New York's Park Avenue, trying to beat the heat of July. I lacked only a yoke to complete the profile of a Chinese coolie.

SERVES 8

2lb (1kg) strawberries, hulled
For the Chantilly cream
½ pint (300ml) double cream
1–2 tablespoons icing sugar
2 tablespoons brandy or kirsch
For the hazelnut pastry
½lb (250g) hazelnuts, toasted
   and ground*

6½oz (200g) flour
½ teaspoon salt
4oz (125g) unsalted butter
4oz (125g) caster sugar
1 egg yolk
2 tablespoons water (optional)

pastry bag and medium star tube

1 For the hazelnut pastry. Grind the hazelnuts with the flour in a food processor or work the mixture, a little at a time, in a blender. Make the hazelnut pastry dough as for pâte sucrée* and chill for 30 minutes. Divide the dough into thirds and pat each piece out on a baking sheet with the heel of your hand to 8in (22cm) rounds. Chill for 15 minutes and heat the oven to Gas 5/190°C/375°F.

2 Bake the rounds in the oven until the pastry is firm and the edges are quite dark: 10–12 minutes. (Note: Hazelnut pastry burns easily.) Take from the oven and, while still warm, trim the rounds neatly using a pan lid or flan ring as a guide. Cut one round into 8 wedges. Transfer the rounds and wedges to a rack to cool. The pastry can be kept for 2–3 days in an air-tight container.

3 Not more than 3 hours before serving, make the Chantilly cream.* Set a pastry round on a serving dish and spread it with a little cream. Reserve 9 strawberries for garnish, cut the rest into pieces and arrange half on the cream. Fill the pastry bag fitted with a star tube with the remaining cream and pipe rosettes at the edge of the pastry round. Top with the second round, spread it with a little cream and pipe 8 lines of cream from the centre to the edge, in spoke fashion. Arrange the cut strawberries between the lines of cream. Pipe 8 cream rosettes at the edge of the pastry, on top of the cut strawberries, and top each rosette with a whole strawberry. Set the long side of the pastry wedges on the lines of cream, propping them at an angle over the whole strawberries. Pipe a single rosette in the centre of the galette and top with a strawberry. Chill until ready to serve.

Cook's Comment. This same hazelnut dough makes a classic French pastry called a 'tommie' (no connection with the nickname 'Tommy Atkins' or 'Tommies' given to British soldiers). Pastry tommies are delicious little squares, sandwiched with honey and topped with chocolate icing.

Glossary

Apricot glaze For 8fl. oz *(250ml)* apricot glaze, combine 8oz *(250g)* apricot jam in a saucepan with the juice of 1 lemon and 3–4 tablespoons of water. Heat until melted, then strain the glaze through a sieve. Melt it again when ready to use.

Arrowroot Arrowroot (or potato starch) is used to thicken sauces lightly at the end of cooking. Mix the arrowroot in a cup with water, allowing about 1 tablespoon of water per teaspoon of arrowroot. It will make a thin, opaque mixture, which separates on standing but can easily be recombined. Whisk this mixture into a boiling liquid, adding just enough to thicken the sauce to the desired consistency. Do not boil the sauce for more than 2–3 minutes or it will become thin.

Bacon Bacon may be salted, or both salted and smoked; for most recipes either type is suitable. For lardons, bacon should be quite lean and streaked with fat. To cut lardons, trim off the bacon rind. Slice the bacon ¼in *(6mm)* thick, then cut across the slices into short strips. If the bacon is salty it should be blanched. Put the lardons into a pan of cold water, bring to a boil and simmer for 2–3 minutes. Drain, rinse with cold water and drain again thoroughly.

Bain marie (water bath) A *bain marie* or water bath is used for cooking foods which need a consistently low heat so that they cook in the centre without overcooking on the outside. Set the foods (in their dishes) in a large shallow pan, such as a roasting pan, and fill with hot water to within 1in *(2.5cm)* of the rim of the dish. Bring the water to a boil on top of the stove, then transfer the *bain marie* to the oven. Start counting cooking time from the moment the bath is put in the oven.

Baking blind see Pastry.

Boning birds see Poultry and game birds.

Bouquet garni A bunch of herbs used to add flavour to soups and stews. It should include a sprig of thyme, a bay leaf and several sprigs of parsley, tied together with string.

Butter, clarified Melt butter over a low heat, skim the froth from the surface and allow to cool to tepid. Pour the clarified butter into a bowl, leaving the milky sediment at the bottom of the pan.

Butter, kneaded Kneaded butter is a paste made with butter and flour that is used to thicken a liquid at the end of cooking. It makes a richer, more traditional sauce than arrowroot does. To make it, mash equal amounts of butter and flour together with a fork until smooth. Add the kneaded butter to boiling liquid, whisking constantly so that the butter melts and distributes the flour, thus thickening the sauce evenly. Add the butter piece by piece until the sauce has thickened to the desired consistency. Kneaded butter can be made in large quantities and kept for several weeks in the refrigerator, or frozen.

Cakes To test if done: In general, cakes are done when they start to shrink from the sides of the tin. With light mixtures such as sponges, the cake will spring back when lightly pressed in the centre with your fingertip. For richer mixtures such as fruit cake, a skewer inserted in the centre should be clean, not sticky, when withdrawn.

Caramel For measurements, see individual recipes. In a heavy pan, over a high heat, melt the sugar in the water, stirring until dissolved. Boil the syrup without stirring until it starts to turn golden around the edge. Lower the heat (caramel cooks quickly once it starts) and continue boiling until the caramel is deep golden and just starting to smoke. Remove at once from the heat, as it burns easily. Let the bubbles subside and use as directed. (*Note*: Take care with caramel, as it is extremely hot.)

Chantilly cream Put chilled cream in a bowl over ice and water and whisk until stiff. (*Note*: If the cream is not cold it may curdle before it stiffens.) Add sugar to taste, with vanilla or other flavouring, and continue whisking until the cream stiffens again. (*Note*: Do not over-beat or the cream will curdle.) Chantilly cream can be stored in the refrigerator for up to 12 hours. It will separate slightly on standing, but will recombine if briskly stirred.

Chicken see Poultry and game birds.

Chicken stock see Stock.

Choux pastry see p. 264.

Clams see Mussels.

Clarified butter see Butter.

Crème fraîche This French cream has a slightly

tart flavour which is particularly good in sauces. To make 1¼ pints *(750ml) crème fraîche*, stir together in a saucepan 16fl. oz *(500ml)* double cream and 8fl. oz *(250ml)* buttermilk or sour cream. Heat gently until just below body temperature (25°C/75°F). Pour the cream into a container and partly cover it. Keep it at this temperature for 6–8 hours or until it has thickened and tastes slightly acid. The cream will thicken faster on a hot day. Stir it and store it in the refrigerator; it will keep for up to 2 weeks.

Croûtes Croûtes are fried slices of bread used to add texture as well as to garnish dishes. If using French bread, cut the loaf into thin diagonal slices; if using sliced white bread, cut the bread into triangles, rounds, hearts or teardrop shapes, discarding the crusts. To fry *croûtes*, heat enough vegetable oil or butter, or a mixture of the two, in a frying pan to coat the bottom generously. Add *croûtes* in a single layer, brown them on both sides over a brisk heat and drain them on paper towels. *Croûtes* can be made ahead and reheated in a low oven.

Croûtons *Croûtons* are small *croûtes* made of diced, crustless, sliced white bread. To fry *croûtons*, heat enough vegetable oil or butter, or a mixture of the two, for the *croûtons* to float. When the fat is very hot, add the diced bread and fry briskly, tossing constantly so that the *croûtons* brown evenly. Lift them out with a draining spoon and drain them on paper towels. *Croûtons* can be made ahead and re-heated in a low oven.

Duck see Poultry and game birds.

Fish stock see Stock.

Glaze When the cooking juices of meat or poultry are boiled down, they darken and caramelise to a shiny glaze which gives rich flavour to sauces and gravies. Glaze should be deep golden and of a sticky consistency. If cooked too far, it will burn.

To deglaze a pan: Boil the juices to a glaze which sticks to the bottom of the pan (this may happen naturally during cooking). Pour off any fat, add liquid and boil, stirring to dissolve the glaze. Continue boiling until the liquid is reduced and has plenty of flavour.

Hazelnuts To toast and peel: If hazelnuts are not already peeled, they must be toasted to loosen their skins; toasting also adds flavour. Bake them in a Gas 5/190°C/375°F oven until browned: 10–15 minutes. To peel them, put them in a rough towel and rub vigorously while still very hot.

Herbs When fresh herbs are called for in a recipe, do not substitute dried ones, unless specifically suggested. Instead, use whatever fresh herbs are available, even if only parsley. Note that in these recipes the parsley quantities assume that the herb is fresh.

Kneaded butter see Butter.

Mussels and clams Wash mussels or clams under cold running water, scraping the shells clean with a knife and removing any weeds. Discard any shells which do not close when tapped, because this indicates that the mussel or clam may be dead. Put them into a large pan, cover and cook over a high heat, shaking the pan occasionally so that they cook evenly, for about 5 minutes or just until the shells open. Discard any shells that do not open.

Pastry, choux For measurements, see individual recipes. In a small saucepan, gently heat the water, salt and butter until the butter is melted. Meanwhile, sift the flour on to a piece of paper. Bring the butter mixture just to a boil (prolonged boiling evaporates the water and changes the proportions of the dough). Remove from the heat and immediately add all the flour. Beat vigorously with a wooden spoon for a few moments until the mixture pulls away from the sides of the pan to form a ball. Beat ½–1 minute over a low heat to dry the dough. Beat one egg until mixed and set it aside. Beat the remaining eggs into the dough, one at a time, and beat thoroughly after each addition. Beat in enough of the reserved egg so that the dough is shiny and just falls from the spoon. If too much egg is added, the dough will be too soft to hold its shape.

Pastry, pâte brisée For measurements, see individual recipes. Sift flour on to a work surface and make a large well in the centre. Pound the butter with a rolling pin to soften it. Put the butter, eggs or egg yolks, salt and water in the well with flavourings such as sugar. (*Note*: In sour-cream pastry, sour cream replaces the water.) Work together with your fingertips until partly mixed. Gradually draw in the flour with a pastry scraper or metal spatula, pulling the dough into large crumbs using the fingertips of both hands. If the crumbs are dry, sprinkle with another tablespoon of water. Press the dough together: it should be soft but not sticky. Work small portions of dough, pushing away from you on the work surface with the heel of your hand, then gathering it up with a scraper. Continue until the dough is smooth and pliable. Press the dough into a ball, wrap it and chill it for 30 minutes or until firm. *Pâte brisée* can be refrigerated overnight, or frozen.

Pastry, pâte sucrée For measurements, see individual recipes. Sift the flour on to a work surface and make a large well in the centre.

[264]

(*Note*: In nut pastries, ground walnuts or hazelnuts may replace some of the flour.) Pound the butter with a rolling pin to soften. Put the butter, egg yolks, salt, sugar and vanilla into the well and work with your fingertips until they are well mixed and the sugar is partly dissolved. Draw in the flour, then work the dough and chill as when making *pâte brisée*.

Pastry, shortcrust For measurements, see individual recipes. Sift the flour with salt into a bowl. Add the fat and butter and cut them into the flour in small pieces, using two knives. Rub the fat and flour with your fingertips until it resembles crumbs. Add the water and eggs and mix in lightly with your fingers so that the crumbs stick together; if they seem dry, add more water. Press the crumbs together to form a ball, wrap and chill for 30 minutes or until firm. Shortcrust pastry can be refrigerated overnight, or frozen.

Pastry shell, to shape If possible, use a tart tin with a removable base so that the shell can be removed easily. Grease the tin and roll out the dough ¼in (6mm) thick. Wrap the dough around the rolling pin, lift it over the tin and unroll it. Let dough rest loosely over the edge of the tin, overlapping it slightly inside. Gently lift the edges of the dough with one hand and press it well into the bottom corners of the tin with the other. Pass the rolling pin over the top of the tin to cut off excess dough. With your forefinger and thumb, press dough evenly up the sides from the bottom to increase height of the edge. Neaten the edge with your finger and thumb, and flute it if you are making a sweet tart. Prick the base of the shell so that the dough cooks evenly. Chill before baking.

Pastry shell, to bake blind Cut a round of greaseproof paper 2in (5cm) larger than the tin. Crumple the paper, then use it to line the shell, pressing it well into edges. Fill the shell three-quarters full with uncooked dried beans or rice to hold the dough in shape. Bake in a Gas 5/190°C/375°F oven for 15 minutes or until the dough is set and the edges are brown. Remove the paper and beans. If a fully baked shell is called for, continue baking for 10–15 minutes until the pastry is crisp and browned.

Peaches To peel: Plunge whole fresh peaches into boiling water and leave them for ½–1 minute, depending on their ripeness. Drain them. Cut the peaches in half vertically, then give them a quick twist to loosen the halves from the stone. Discard the stone. Peel the peach halves and use them at once, as they discolour rapidly.

Pheasant see Poultry and game birds.

Poultry and game birds

To bone: Cut off the wing tips and middle section, leaving the largest wing bone attached. With the bird breast side down, slit the skin along the backbone from the neck to the tail. Cut and scrape the flesh and skin away from the carcass on one side of the bird, working evenly with short, sharp strokes of the knife. Cut the flesh from the sabre-shaped bone near the wing. Cut the rough joint and remove. When you reach the ball-and-socket joints connecting the wing and thigh bones to the carcass, sever them. Continue cutting the breast meat from the bone until the ridge of the breastbone is reached, where the skin is closely attached. Turn the bird around and repeat on the other side. The skin and meat will remain attached to the carcass only at the breastbone. Cut along the ridge of the breastbone to separate the skin and meat from the carcass, taking care as the skin here is easily torn. To remove the leg and wing bones: Hold the end of the bone in one hand, cut through the tendons and scrape the meat from the bone. Pull out the bone, using a knife to free it. Repeat with the remaining leg and wing bones.

To cut in half: Set the bird, back side down, on a board. Slit closely along the breastbone with a knife to loosen the meat. With scissors, split the breastbone. Turn the bird over, cut along each side of the backbone and discard it. Trim the leg bones and wing pinions with scissors or a knife.

To cut into pieces: With a heavy knife, cut off the wing tips. Cut between the leg and body of the bird, following the outline of the thigh, until the leg joint is visible. Locate the oyster meat lying against the backbone, and cut around it so that it remains attached to the thigh. Twist the leg sharply outwards to break the thigh joint. Cut each leg from the body, including the oyster meat. With a knife or poultry shears, cut away the backbone and cut along the breastbone to halve the carcass. The bird is now in four pieces. To cut into six pieces, cut the legs in half through the joint, using the white line of fat on the underside as guide. To cut into eight pieces, divide each breast in half, cutting diagonally through the meat, then through the breast and rib bones so that a portion of breast meat is cut off with the wing. Cut the legs in half through the joint, using the white line of fat on the underside as a guide. When cooking, add the backbone and wing tips with other pieces to help flavour the sauce.

To truss: Set the bird on its back, pushing the

legs down so that the ends stick up in the air. Stick a trussing needle into one leg joint, push the needle through the bird and out through the other leg joint. Turn the bird over on to its breast and push the needle through both sections of one wing and then into the neck skin, under the backbone of the bird and out the other side. Now catch the second wing in the same way as the first. Pull the ends of the string from the leg and wing firmly together and tie securely. Re-thread the trussing needle and turn the bird breast side up. Tuck the tail into the cavity. Insert the needle into the end of the drumstick, make a stitch through the skin (which should be overlapped to cover the cavity), and insert the needle through the end of the other drumstick. Turn the bird over and push the needle through the tail. Tie the string ends together.

Shortcrust pastry see Pastry.

Spinach Tear off the stems and discard. Wash the leaves thoroughly in several changes of water. Pack the spinach into a large pan with half an inch (1.25cm) of water and cover tightly. Cook over a high heat, stirring occasionally, for about 5 minutes or until the leaves are wilted. Drain and allow to cool slightly. Press the spinach in your fists to extract all the water.

Stock, chicken For about 4 pints (2.5 litres) stock, in a large pan combine 3lb (1.4kg) chicken backs and necks; 1 onion, quartered; 1 carrot, quartered; 1 stalk celery, cut into pieces; a bouquet garni;* 1 teaspoon peppercorns and about 6½ pints (4 litres) water. Bring slowly to a boil, skimming often. Simmer uncovered, skimming occasionally, for 2–3 hours. Strain, taste and, if the stock is not concentrated, boil it until well reduced. Refrigerate it and, before using, skim any solidified fat from the surface. Stock can be kept for up to 3 days in the refrigerator, or frozen.

Stock, fish For about 1⅔ pints (1 litre) stock. Break 1½lb (750g) fish bones into pieces and wash them thoroughly. In a pan cook 1 sliced onion in 1 tablespoon butter until soft but not brown. Add the fish bones, 1⅔ pints (1 litre) water, bouquet garni,* 10 peppercorns and 8fl. oz (250ml) dry white wine. Bring to a boil and simmer uncovered for 20 minutes, skimming often. Strain and cool.

Stock, brown veal For about 4 pints (2.5 litres) stock. Roast 5lb (2.3kg) veal bones in a very hot oven for 20 minutes. Add 2 quartered carrots and 2 quartered onions and continue roasting for 30 minutes or until very brown. Transfer the bones and vegetables to a stock pot, discarding any fat. Add a bouquet garni,* 1 teaspoon whole peppercorns, 1 tablespoon tomato paste and about 8 pints (5 litres) water. Bring slowly to a boil, then simmer uncovered for 4–5 hours, skimming occasionally. Strain the stock, taste and, if the flavour is not concentrated, boil it until well reduced. Chill the stock and skim off any fat before using. Stock can be refrigerated for up to 3 days, or frozen.

Stock, white veal Proceed as for brown veal stock, but do not brown the bones and vegetables, and omit the tomato paste. Blanch the bones by bringing them to a boil in water to cover, simmering for 5 minutes, draining, then rinsing in cold water. Then continue as for brown veal stock.

Tomatoes To peel, seed and chop: Core the tomatoes and mark a small cross at the opposite end with the tip of a knife. Pour boiling water over the tomatoes and leave for 10 seconds or until the skin starts to peel at the cross. Drain the tomatoes and peel them. Halve them crosswise, squeeze them to remove the seeds, then chop them. The seeds can be sieved to extract the juice.

Vanilla custard sauce For measurements, see individual recipes. Scald the milk with the vanilla pod, cover and leave to infuse for 10–15 minutes. Beat the egg yolks with the sugar until thick and pale. Stir in the hot milk and return the mixture to the pan. Heat gently, stirring with a wooden spoon, until the custard thickens enough to leave a clear trail when you draw your finger across the back of a spoon. (*Note*: Do not boil or overcook the custard or it will curdle.) At once remove from the heat and strain the custard into a bowl. The vanilla pod can be rinsed and used again.

Veal stock see Stock.

Vinaigrette dressing Vinaigrette dressing can be made with neutral vegetable oil, olive oil or a nut oil. Red or white wine vinegar is most common, but sherry, balsamic and fruit vinegars can be used. About half the quantity of lemon juice can be substituted for the vinegar. For 4fl.oz (125ml) dressing, in a small bowl whisk 1 teaspoon Dijon mustard with salt, pepper and 2 tablespoons vinegar until the salt dissolves. Gradually add 6 tablespoons oil, whisking constantly so that the dressing emulsifies and thickens slightly. Vinaigrette can be made ahead and kept for several days at room temperature; it will separate but will re-emulsify when whisked. Flavourings such as chopped shallot or herbs should be added just before using.

Index